The Politics of Conjugal Love

The Politics of Conjugal Love

A Baptismal and Trinitarian Approach to Headship and Submission

BY
Conor Sweeney
AND
Brian T. Trainor

FOREWORD BY
Margaret Pargeter

☙PICKWICK *Publications* • Eugene, Oregon

THE POLITICS OF CONJUGAL LOVE
A Baptismal and Trinitarian Approach to Headship and Submission

Copyright © 2019 Conor Sweeney and Margaret Pargeter. All rights reserved. Except for brief quotations in critical publications or reviews, no part of this book may be reproduced in any manner without prior written permission from the publisher. Write: Permissions, Wipf and Stock Publishers, 199 W. 8th Ave., Suite 3, Eugene, OR 97401.

Pickwick Publications
An Imprint of Wipf and Stock Publishers
199 W. 8th Ave., Suite 3
Eugene, OR 97401

www.wipfandstock.com

PAPERBACK ISBN: 978-1-5326-6367-3
HARDCOVER ISBN: 978-1-5326-6368-0
EBOOK ISBN: 978-1-5326-6369-7

Cataloguing-in-Publication data:

Names: Sweeney, Conor, author. | Trainor, Brian T., author. | Pargeter, Margaret, foreword.

Title: The politics of conjugal love : a baptismal and trinitarian approach to headship and submission / by Conor Sweeney and Brian T. Trainor ; foreword by Margaret Pargeter.

Description: Eugene, OR : Pickwick Publications, 2019 | Includes bibliographical references and index.

Identifiers: ISBN 978-1-5326-6367-3 (paperback) | ISBN 978-1-5326-6368-0 (hardcover) | ISBN 978-1-5326-6369-7 (ebook)

Subjects: LCSH: Sex—Religious aspects—Catholic Church. | Marriage—Religious aspects—Catholic Church. | Human body—Religious aspects—Catholic Church. | John Paul—II,—Pope,—1920–2005.—Theology of the body. | Theology of the body (John Paul II, Pope).

Classification: BX1795.S48 S93 2019 (print) | BX1795.S48 S93 (ebook)

Manufactured in the U.S.A.   06/25/19

For the Trainor Family

Contents

Foreword by Margaret Pargeter | ix
Preface | xi
Acknowledgments | xv

Introduction: Reframing the Question | 1

1   Conjugal Politics: Taking Stock | 11
    Complementarians and Egalitarians, Maximalists and Minimalists | 12
    Patristic and Scholastic Hermeneutics and Exegesis | 17
    An Historical-Critical Exegetical Test Case | 36
    New Interpretive Horizons | 40

2   The Trinity and Male Headship of the Family | 45
    Ontological and Immanent Language | 47
    Homogenization and Differentiation | 51
    The Trinity: Single Sovereignty or Triple Sovereignty | 56
    The Trinity and the Family | 59
    The Courage to be Counter-Cultural | 64

3   A Baptismal Anthropology of the Acting Person | 67
    From Imitation to Incorporation | 70
    Ratzinger on Person | 72
    Balthasar on Person | 74
    John Paul II on Person | 76
    Becoming a Person in Christ | 80
    Sacramental Incorporation and Participation | 89

The Nuptial Trilogy | 90
The Eucharist and Baptism as Nuptial Mysteries | 94
Trinitarian Incorporation and Participation | 101

4 Sexual Difference in the Baptismal Relation | 109
Becoming a Man and Woman in Christ | 113
The End of Sexual Difference in Light of the Eschaton? | 117
Sexual Difference According to the Primordial Beginning | 121
Sexual Difference Within the Baptismal Relation | 124
Reconsidering the Textual Foundation of Difference | 130

5 Conjugal Politics in the Baptismal Relation | 140
A Spirit-Filled State | 143
Discovering Conjugal Politics in the Action of the Spirit | 147
"For the Husband is Head of his Wife, just as Christ is the Head of the Church . . ." | 151
"Wives Should be Subject to their Husbands as to the Lord" | 165
Headship and Submission in the Ontological Difference | 174

Conclusion | 183

Bibliography | 189
Author Index | 197
Subject Index | 199

Foreword

By Margaret Pargeter

This book has certainly been a "marriage of minds" between two independent academics who migrated to Australia from far-flung corners of the globe. Dr. Conor Sweeney hails from Canada, and Dr. Brian Trainor, from Northern Ireland. The pair collaborated in their adopted home to present a shared vision for an ideal marriage, which is intensely rich, dynamic, and fulfilling. *The Politics of Conjugal Love* offers an invitation to appreciate the covenant of marriage, the sacrament of baptism, and the existence of the Trinity in a profoundly new way. Dr. Conor Sweeney and Dr. Brian Trainor take their readers on an intrepid journey of the heart, mind, and soul which boldly challenges the crux of life and marital happiness and reveals an exquisitely fresh Trinitarian vista, more good, true, and beautiful than previously imagined. By focusing squarely on the blazing love of the Trinity and the transformative grace of baptism, it calls each of us to return to the humble basics of losing one's self in a deep, Trinitarian-like love for our beloved, our kin, and our neighbour to achieve a truly happy life.

Thank you to Dr. Conor Sweeney for your support, guidance, and loyalty to my father, Dr. Brian Trainor. Without you, this book would not have come to fruition. You have honoured Brian's vision to the best of your ability, and the Trainor family is eternally grateful for your assistance with this publishing initiative.

Brian was an incredible husband, father, and man, who is remembered by all as a cheerful giver, a wise soul, and a brave voice for truth. His strength was particularly evident in the dignified deportment he maintained throughout his three-year battle with cancer. On 12 July 2013 at 65 years of age he reposed with the Lord. This man truly embraced his baptismal call to serve others through the grace of God. His legacy lives on through the people he touched and the words he left us.

Brian grew up in a Belfast where the sectarian conflict was in full flight between the Irish Catholics and Protestants. Brian made a conscious decision to leave the Troubles of Belfast in the early 1970s after marrying his sweetheart, Marie, and starting a family. The couple travelled to Australia under the "Ten Pound Pom" scheme, seeking a safer abode for themselves and their children. In 1973 the young Trainor clan settled in Adelaide, South Australia, where there was work aplenty, opportunity and other family already settled. Australia became Brian's home for the next forty years.

Keeping their faith at the heart of the home was important to Brian and Marie. Childhood memories are filled with praying grace at meal times, saying the rosary together in the evening, and attending mass together on Sunday mornings. The faith which my parents espoused inspired social justice action. As an example, they committed themselves to welcoming newly arrived migrants to Australia. Together they supported Vietnamese and African families who made a home in South Australia. They ensured refugee families were connected with the necessary social support and community services. In turn, they received much hospitality and kindness as a gesture of gratitude. Men in the Australian African community often called Brian by the name "father."

Being young at heart, Brian had a great affinity with young people and would seize any opportunity to sign up young people to university studies if they were looking for work or career opportunities. He encouraged youth to plant themselves in a loving, committed, and faithful relationship centred on God. He assured young people that if they invited the good Lord to shine his light and wisdom in their marriage, they would surely flourish in their vocation.

Brian was a champion for Christian marriage because marrying his beloved Irish lass Marie gifted him with a lifetime of happiness and fulfilment. They were a formidable team and created a simple life which they relished and preciously guarded. Brian was the breadwinner, Marie the homemaker, and the complementarity of their individual gifts and talents worked a treat. As a tight unit, the pair enjoyed sharing deep conversation and prayer, as well as long walks, usually in the park next to their home.

Brian's raison d'être was faith, marriage, and family. His major publications are infused with these themes so it comes as no surprise that this final work affirms the beauty, dignity, and integrity of marriage.

Preface

I met Brian T. Trainor, then Senior Lecturer at Tabor College in Adelaide, South Australia, in late 2012. Over several ensuing email conversations, we discovered a common interest in a somewhat unlikely topic: the New Testament teaching of headship and submission in marriage, or what could more generally be described as the "conjugal politics" of the relationship of man and woman in marriage. More to the point, we had both done work in the broad territory of Pauline anthropology as it bears on the question of what it means to be a man and what it means to be a woman in the context of spousal and familial life. On the basis of certain shared convictions in this field, we embarked on a book project together.

Sadly, after only several months of collaborative work on the book, Brian went to the Lord in July 2013. Up to that point, with his health declining, I had taken on the lion's share of writing new material and incorporating existing material, and we had more or less hammered out a structure and narrative. At the time, it had been my intention to bring it all together by the end of that year.

Fast-forward several years, and the project had well and truly stalled. Other academic demands had taken over for me, and our project had become one of those things that always take a backseat to more pressing immediate imperatives. And during this time, my own thought had continued to develop, such that when I finally returned to our manuscript it became necessary to somewhat modify and nuance the scope and contents of the project.

To put it briefly, what had begun as a quite ambitious systematic project that aimed to explore the broad historical backdrop of and establish the present systematic conditions for a trinitarian reimagining of conjugal politics, I now decided should be somewhat trimmed back. We had initially planned to combine the work that each of us had already done on the topic and present it as an integrated single vision written in one voice. This soon morphed into a more expansive vision which precipitated my writing of a large amount of supplementary material. But in returning to the project years later, I now found myself constrained by the fact that both my own original contribution and the supplementary material that I had added no longer completely satisfied me. As a consequence, I determined to scale back and refocus the project in such a way that I could be faithful, both to Brian's original contribution and to my own updated convictions.

None of this is to say that my present sensibilities were such that they invalidated the original vision of the project as a whole. I stand by the original vision that generated the project, even as I today add certain qualifications and nuances. But given these qualifications and nuances, and the fact that Brian is no longer with us, I now think it best to present our shared vision in such a way that both the main of Brian's original contributions and my own present convictions are each respected in their specificity and integrity.

The way the present manuscript is set up is similar to the projected original with two main exceptions. First, I have significantly trimmed the content, condensing the main argument into 5 rather than the originally planned 8 chapters. Rather than try to say something about everything, I have decided that our case would be best served by brevity and a more readable approach. The existing text is thus at times more exploratory and conversational in nature than the first, and may be thought of more as an experiment in the hermeneutics of conjugal politics rather than an exhaustive systematic treatise on the theme.

Second, I have distinguished between my voice and Brian's in the text. From the beginning, the main brunt of Brian's contribution was an article he had published in 2011 in the Heythrop Journal on the topic of Trinity and male headship. This was to have been integrated with my own contribution, which largely consisted of revised material from my licentiate thesis on a similar theme. In the present manuscript, Brian's above contribution will appear largely unaltered in chapter 2, which I intend to leave as a will and testament to his thinking which can also be thought of as an important experimental foil for my own thinking. The rest of the book will consist of my own creative re-framing of the topic in line with my own developing insights, which I will present in my own voice. What I will thus reframe is both new material and material that I had already mostly written with Brian's critical feedback and ultimate approval. I cannot of course seek his approval from him for this re-write, but I hope and pray that inasmuch as I think it represents an intensification of my (perhaps our?) earlier thinking rather than its repudiation, that he would be happy enough with the changes.

Precisely what I will add to my re-write is my present working argument that if we wish to know what it might mean to speak of a trinitarian conjugal politics, we must first much more deeply clarify the sacramental conditions of what it means to belong baptismally to Christ. If, as I have started to argue elsewhere, baptism is in it own right a fundamental ontology and anthropology, then any question that one might ask about conjugal politics whether from "below" (nature, reason) or from "above" (grace, faith) must first be crucified along with the baptized person's old identity and self, and then asked only from the point of view of the full sacramental "now" or "within" of adopted and deified existence in the Son. The extent to which this, in my estimation, will constitute a radicalizing perhaps of the entire task of theological anthropology, is the extent to which I feel the need for a re-write of my original contribution to this book.

This all means that, aside from chapter 2, I take full responsibility for the content presented in this text, and ask the reader not to automatically presume that what is presented here necessarily reflects Brian's own view (especially what could be regarded as the more radical elements of my new contribution). What this does not mean, however, is that Brian has not in important ways influenced reworked parts of the text. In this, my creative re-framing will still feature and reflect keenly made (and deeply appreciated) points and clarifications offered by Brian when he was still with us. Overall, I believe there to be a deep affinity between our respective ways of thinking, and if I may be so bold, express my hope that this present manuscript be an occasion for Brian's own voice to live on in and through a further living dialogue with mine.

In the end, I remain honored to have worked with Brian for the short time that I was able. And I hope that this book in some small way does justice to Brian's deep, faithful, and courageous conviction that the conjugal politics contained in St. Paul's witness to Christ still have something important to say to us today.

Acknowledgments

Thanks is owed, first, to Margaret Pargeter for encouragement and patience as this project matured. I am also grateful for feedback and conversations with my colleagues, particularly Dr. Colin Patterson, Associate Professor Adam Cooper, Dr. Owen Vyner, and Dr. Anna Silvas. Thanks also to Rev. José Granados for his guidance during my early forays into the topic of this book. Any errors or oversights in the text are mine. A thank-you to the Heythrop Journal for permission to re-produce Trainor's contribution. Finally, a big thanks to Wipf and Stock for bringing this project, my second with them, to print. Their warmth and professionalism do them credit. To my wife Jaclyn, and our children Finnian, Elle (who expects great personal fame to come from being acknowledged herein), Thea, Oliver, and Ava, thank-you for your love and patience.

Introduction: Reframing the Question

It was, and from my point of view still is, a shared conviction of Brian T. Trainor and myself that the Trinity has a fundamental role to play in adequately articulating a Christian anthropology. More specifically, it was and is our conviction that the mystery of love revealed in the trinitarian mystery of Father, Son, and Holy Spirit has something important to say to and about marriage and the family, and what can be referred to as the "conjugal politics" therein; namely, in this instance, the apparently divinely ordained order of relation between husband and wife in marriage.

From the beginning, we were in agreement that a God who is in himself a unity of three Persons cannot be inconsequential in regard to both sexual difference and "gender" identity, and to the particular expression of this difference and identity that is to be found in the sacrament of marriage and in the "domestic church" that is marriage and the family in the Lord. This must be the case if, following Pope St. John Paul II, it is true that marriage belongs properly and fully to the plan of God from all eternity. The primordial "form" of marriage from "the beginning," brought to sacramental completion in the new economy in Christ, is of properly trinitarian origin and provenance, and via the "Great Analogy" of Ephesians the spousal relationship can thus be said in a certain (albeit qualified) sense to "mirror" and "participate" in the intratrinitarian relations.

This includes what can at this point be referred to with unavoidable ambiguity as the "hierarchical" or "political" parts of the marriage relationship, specifically the Pauline teaching that the husband is head of the wife in marriage, a distinctly uncomfortable teaching in an age of equality. Typically, traditional Christian interpretation of this teaching has been to read it as a theological affirmation of what was regarded as a fairly self-evident truth of the natural created order. Our argument in the present work is that within a more adequate hermeneutics what have typically been regarded as the hierarchical and political dimensions of married life become properly speaking in fact *anything but* hierarchical or political, at least according to how these terms have commonly been understood in this context. Instead, we argue that when marriage as a whole is re-cast in a properly baptismal and trinitarian light, a power-centered or rank-dominated analysis of spousal relations cannot be sustained. Instead, a baptismal and trinitarian hermeneutic will present an opportunity to reread the political significance of sexual difference in a surprisingly theological manner, one that will undermine certain premises and conclusions of both "conservative" and "progressive" approaches to the question.

What drove our initial consensus was the conviction that a trinitarian hermeneutics, more radically conceived, could in the end out-narrate both so-called "complementarian" and "egalitarian" framings of conjugal politics current today by exposing a much deeper sacramental grammar upon which spousal relating is grounded and flows. I remain committed to this approach, but to it I now append a more explicitly expressed qualifying frame.

In my estimation, a potential ambiguity of our approach previously was that our trinitarian hermeneutic had not yet been grounded as deeply and radically in the sacramental forms of the new economy of salvation as it could have been. While we were acutely aware of and tried to qualify the fact that trinitarian "transpositions" are never univocal or static imitative affairs, I do not think that, at least in my own thinking and in the supplementary material that I had written at the time, that an adequate *methodological* expression of this qualification had in fact been sufficiently articulated and embedded at a deep level. Even if one rehearses the common truism that divine and creaturely predications always carry an infinitely greater dissimilarity than similarity in relation to each other, the fact remains that if this qualifier does not deeply penetrate into the structure or deep logic of one's hermeneutical approach, the language and arguments of that approach will always risk serving another master, thus eliding the *maior dissimilitudo*. Put differently, unless the fundamental logic of the *approach itself* undergoes a sort of *death by greater difference*, as it were, that prompts the radical re-creation of said approach as a whole under new conditions, one cannot expect that qualifying invocations against idolatry will be enough to safeguard the *maior dissimilitudo* on their own terms.

What I have attempted to add to our endeavor, therefore, is a more radical framing of trinitarian possibilities by recourse to the (also more radically framed) baptismal conditions of Christian faith articulated as a fundamental ontology and anthropology herein. "Fundamental" in this regard for my thinking is that these conditions are discovered via the analogy of the *theological person*; that is, in the perspective of the self who by baptism receives adopted personhood in the Son, and who in and according

INTRODUCTION: REFRAMING THE QUESTION

to the measure of the new history and genealogy received here, embodies a dramatic, existential, *sacramental* form of existence that is *existence properly speaking*. Through the baptismal adoption received from the Father by the work of the Son and the Spirit, conceived and generated in the nuptial womb of Mary-Church, *the natural self dies* so that a radiant sacramental person can be born, a person who lives and moves and has his or her being within and according to the *single* sacramental "now" that is an adopted identity fed at sacramental and liturgical springs.

This approach takes its point of departure, first from the perspective on person suggested by Hans Urs von Balthasar[1] and Joseph Ratzinger,[2] and then from Cardinal Marc Ouellet's[3] methodological application of this perspective in his work in the theology of marriage and family, all of which are animated and framed by the original approach to body, sex, and person found in St. John Paul II's "Theology of the Body."[4] Broadly typical of all four authors' anthropological approach is the determination to treat human identity *dramatically*, as an historical and personal gift of adoptive belonging to the Father in Christ, and not as something produced at the level of natural beings or, concomitantly, simply copied from a static divine archetype. What this provides the impetus for is an approach to anthropology where the unique personhood of Christ, in its full hypostatic glory, is not an ontological or speculative exception distinct from anthropology, but is rather as Ratzinger puts it "the true fulfillment of the idea of the human person,"[5] without for all that presupposing a process of merely exemplary transposition. This is thus to say, with Balthasar, that human identity properly speaking is not something that can ever be generated or discovered "from below," but is rather discovered in the drama of the discovery of the self in Christ: "if we want to ask about man's 'essence,' we can do so only in the midst of his dramatic performance of existence. There is no other anthropology but the dramatic."[6] It is to insist, with Ouellet, "on placing anthropology within the framework of a Trinitarian theocentrism."[7] And within this perspective of a theological person shaped by the dimension of theological event and

---

1. See Balthasar, "Concept of Person"; *Person in Christ*, 202–8; *Creator Spirit*, 307–15.
2. See Ratzinger, "Notion of Person"; Ratzinger, *Introduction to Christianity*, 181–84. An approach to person very similar to both Ratzinger and Balthasar—but in an Orthodox perspective—can be found in Lossky, *Image and Likeness*, 111–23.
3. See Ouellet, *Divine Likeness*; *Mystery and Sacrament*; "Christian Ethics."
4. See John Paul II, *Theology of the Body*.
5. Ratzinger, "Notion of Person," 450.
6. Balthasar, *Man in God*, 335.
7. Ouellet, *Divine Likeness*, 16.

time, we can thus speak of an approach that more radically integrates the historical and theological dimension into John Paul II's embryonic trinitarian claim that "Man becomes an image of God not so much in the moment of solitude as in the moment of communion."[8]

Now, what might it mean if the analysis of conjugal politics is moved fully within the ambit of a human identity more radically constructed according to the hypostatic character and trinitarian ground of Christ's own person, communicated to the creature via baptism? If it is true to say that within the lens of faith it is "person" rather than "nature" that is the fundamental criterion for determining what belongs properly to the *humanum*, then if we want to get to the heart of what is going on in the question of conjugal politics, we must do so from within the person's existential and dramatic participation in the trinitarian relations as they are mediated baptismally and sacramentally; not, therefore, according to any species of a "one foot in nature, one foot in grace" or merely formalistic perspective. I suggest that if this hermeneutic can in fact be more fully established, then it will be here that conjugal politics will either stand as a properly theological datum or fall as a secular interpolation.

Beyond establishing this point follows the pressing question of just how the baptismal person might encounter and participate in the trinitarian relations. And it is here that I propose the significance of a specifically *baptismal* (ecclesial, sacramental, liturgical) personhood for both supercharging and qualifying the theological notion of person by strengthening the conditions under which that person's participation in the relations takes place. Precisely what I think that baptism adds to a trinitarian hermeneutic is a fundamental sacramental infrastructure that will deeply qualify the mode of that participation. What I call a "baptismal theology of relation"—a kind of first or fundamental anthropology—more robustly clarifies how the person's incorporation into and representation of the divine life is not something that happens superficially, extrinsically, imitatively, partially, nominally, or according to any species of abstraction or formalism.[9] A person generated directly from the font, as it were, is one whose deepest existential coordinates are the sacramental conditions of their adoptive existence. Other coordinates of identity certainly exist, but after baptism none of them can be regarded as hermeneutically fundamental in the sense of a meta-narrative. If, for instance, myth, symbol, nature, science, or art say something about human identity (as they clearly do), they can no longer purport to offer the

---

8. John Paul II, *Theology of the Body*, 163.

9. My first published attempt to articulate a sustained account of this thesis can be found in Sweeney, *Abiding the Long Defeat*, esp. 115–55.

last word or the ultimate organizing frame; even if they are capable of saying some pretty remarkable things which do not cease to have fundamental value for the task of Christian anthropology, and which in some cases may shed more unexpected light than conventional approaches.[10] Nevertheless, the last word can belong only to Christ, if Christ is in fact who he says that he is. This is what I will mean when I speak of the priority of (baptismal) person over nature, of (salvation) history over ontology.

This is thus to say in the strict (that is theological) sense that the human individual no longer bears the nature that they bore before they took the plunge. Rather, according to the absurdity and scandal of faith—but without dualistically abrogating the sacramental-symbolic value of their pre-baptismal being, many elements of which will carry over into their baptismal identity (but by way of baptismal re-creation)—the "nature" the baptized person *now* bears is the personalized and reconstituted hypostatic "nature" of divine adoption, where relation to God the Father, through the Son, sealed and actualized in the Spirit constitutes their new history, genealogy, present reality, and eschatological horizon in a fundamentally original and constitutive way. And it is thus to say that if one wishes to speak of a christological and trinitarian notion of the anthropological person, one must do so from within its rigorous baptismal framing, according to the liturgical and sacramental grammar discovered there.

To view person in this way is to eschew any use of a trinitarian hermeneutics that would employ the Trinity as a merely formal, metaphysical ideal that one might then abstractly import in any number of diverse ways into the lifeworld of the *humanum*. The Trinity is not an idea or a concept that furnishes an array of interesting insights that can then be sociologically (or ideologically) applied to human relations. In its fundamental anthropological implications, the Trinity can only be interpreted via the radical and existential specificity of *the place within which is given*: the liturgical and sacramental place of the person's adoptive belonging to God the Father in the Son and the Spirit in the ecclesial economy of salvation. In other words, if we want to speak of any trinitarian possibility or significance of the claim that the person is created in the image of God, we can do so only within a baptismally generated hermeneutics of the person, one that begins on the altar and in the font.

Perhaps this might not at first glance appear particularly radical or original. At a certain level, it simply represents being properly restrained by the economy of salvation when we attempt to speak of God and God's

---

10. See, for example, Jordan Peterson's 12 session lecture series, Peterson, "Psychological Significance of Biblical Stories."

relation to us. But at a deeper level I mean it to represent a radicalizing of what is meant when we speak of the precise *manner* in which persons belong to and participate in that economy, of how we describe a person whose "nature" has been plunged into the font and rewritten in adoptive terms. It is to specify that the person belongs to the economy and relates to the living God not simply as a theistically colored natural being; that is, not simply at a natural, moral, psychological, or merely intentional level, whether this be conceived in "substantialist" or "gnostic" terms. Grace does not produce a Frankensteinian juxtaposition of divine and human elements that inhere in the one particular instantiation of human nature that is the individual. It does not merely "top up" natural human identity. It does not merely supercharge one's moral ability, disposing one to live a more recollected or mindful spirituality. Nothing about it is conditional or relative, able to be gotten out of in a pinch. Adoptive sonship does not mean that I become a child of God in some other world or at some deferred time yet to come.

Rather, it means—quite literally—that I am a son in the Son *now* and according to a new principle of integration and totality, a new hermeneutics: according to the single sacramental "now" of full adoption into the Father via the pneumic efficacy of Christ's gift of himself to the Church. This is so, literally speaking, inasmuch as baptism first involves the *real death and resurrection* of the individual[11] who is in the baptismal rite "crucified with Christ" (Gal 2:20), and who *only after this death* can arise as a new, radiant sacramental person: a new creation in Christ (2 Cor 5:17), a full son of the Father (Gal 4:4–7) who now bears and expresses "nature" or "Being" in a new way. St. Cyril of Jerusalem's words are apt in relation to the death dimension of baptism that bears new life:

> Then you were conducted by the hand to the holy pool of sacred baptism, just as Christ was conveyed from the cross to the sepulchre which stands before us. Each person was asked if he believed in the name of the Father and of the Son and of the Holy Spirit. You made the confession that brings salvation, and submerged yourselves three times in the water and emerged: by this symbolic gesture you were secretly re-enacting the burial of Christ three days in the tomb.[12]

The point I am making thematic here is not that baptism represents some "magical" transformation and justification of the person once for all

---

11. In this, it is enough to say that "baptism marks the death of the old man and the miraculous beginning of a new life under the banner of the resurrection" (Käsemann, *Perspectives on Paul*, 8).

12. Cyril of Jerusalem, "Mystagogical Catechesis," 31.

in the sense that the Christian is automatically conformed to Christ from the moral or psychological point of view. No, what I am claiming here is that the baptismal birth of "water and Spirit" (John 3:5) has been given as a radical existential and ontological gift to the Christian *here*, *now*, in a way that literally creates a new self and a new dimension for the self (even if this self's inhabiting of this new dimension remain susceptible to relapses into the perspective of the "old man's" captivity to the law of sin). You are "in Christ" (Gal 3:26), as St. Paul expresses it; a "new creation" (2 Cor 5:17). You belong to Christ, and through Him you belong to the Father (cf. 1 Cor 3:23). And in the Spirit that gift of divine adoption finds is deepest potential and fullest actualization (cf. Acts 2:38, 19:5–6).[13] All of this happens within the sacramental economy of the Church, paradigmatically constituted and embodied in the image of Christ the Bridegroom's love for his Bride, the Church. And all of this thus constitutes the new horizon of the radiant sacramental person who now lives and moves and has his being within the single perspective or "now" of divine adoption mediated by life in Christ and the Spirit in the Church.

What I am arguing thus is that in the baptismally generated person there emerges a kind of existential hypostatic unity of nature and grace within that new radiant personhood, and that it is here that exists reality itself for that person. This person's new being *in Christ* is an existential "hinge" of nature and grace, as it were, its living and immediate realization, one that eschews all possibilities of abstraction. This person is neither pure nature nor pure divinity, but rather their consummated sacramental unity. This person thus receives the criteria for its existence from this sacramental "middle" or *metaxu*, as it were. The person is no longer a "natural" being whose existence can be parsed in any way, shape, or form "from below." And nor can the divine "addition" to the being of this person in any way, shape, or form either replace or simply be applied in an *ad hoc* manner outside of the concrete blueprint of baptismal existence. From the unique dramatic perspective of the baptized person, both nature and divinity are, as it were, "crossed out" and rewoven into a *personalized* re-dimensioning in the spirit and flesh of the Christic person.

---

13. "Christ is buried and rises 'with' the baptized, and actually lives only as the exalted *Pneuma*-Lord. . . . This *Pneuma*-Lord also draws the baptized to himself and imparts his *Pneuma* to him. The process of dying etc. with Christ, in so far as it takes its rise from God and brings the baptized into relation with the *Pneuma*-Lord, is to be characterized as 'pneumic'—borne by the *Pneuma*" (Schnackenburg, *Baptism in St. Paul*, 165). "Then by the words of the priest and by his hand the presence of the Holy Spirit flies down upon you and another man comes up out of the font, one washed from all the stain of his sins, who has put off the old garment of sin and is clothed in the royal robe" (Chrysostom, "Stavronikita Series," 46).

This means that when we seek to ask *who* the person is (and this should be *the* question, as it is for Balthasar), we can do so only from within the perspective of the *baptized* person, within their lived "habitat" or "environment": and herein is my explicit sacramental-existential intensification of the notion of person. When we seek to ask what fundamental meaning—whether of nature and grace, faith and reason, history and ontology, body and soul, male and female—is for that person, we can do so fully only from the point of view of sacramental existence. And this means that when we seek to ask about what *conjugal politics* is all about, we can do so only from the point of view of the same coordinates. The answer to the interpretation of conjugal politics will be found, then, not in the "above" or "below" per se, but *inside the within* of the consummated union of the above and the below in the sacramental "now" of the radiant sacramental person's inhabiting of the hypostatic forms of baptismal adoption.

What I think this accentuates in the perspectives of John Paul II, Ratzinger, Balthasar, and Ouellet is a more robust and qualified sense that becoming a person (and *remaining* a person) belongs fundamentally to the baptismal and liturgical architecture of Christian existence in its basic givenness, i.e., according to the architectonic character of the sacraments, understood as the definitive anthropological blueprint. What I seek to flesh out more strongly, then, are the concrete conditions that baptism thus places on what it means to be and understand oneself as a person, conditions that arise within a baptismal relation that we could describe as a kind of *analogia baptismi*. If it is true, as Balthasar claimed, that Christ is the "concrete analogy of Being,"[14] and if it is further true that in baptism, this analogy deeply penetrates the existential subjectivity of the person, making those who receive baptism the radiant bearers of Christ's transformative work within a re-dimensioned personal being, then I suggest that it must be within and according to the concrete conditions of the analogy of the *baptismal being* given in Christ that we seek to understand Scriptural passages that propose a conjugal politics.

All of this, then, constitutes a fundamental hermeneutics for framing what the Trinity might have to offer for our conjugal politics—for how we conceive of the dimension of difference and "roles" in marriage. With this frame in mind, our narrative will unfold in the following manner. Chapter 1 will explore the state of play of conjugal politics today, tracing its development in the Tradition. Particularly important here will be to clarify the hermeneutical conditions of the question, exposing the two major camps of interpretation that emerge on the basis of different questions and answers

---

14. Balthasar, *Theology of History*, 69.

to the hermeneutical question. Rather than attempt to give an exhaustive account of this scene, my goal will be to simply expose the main lines of thought and the commitments that feed into them. Along the way, I will bring these lines and commitments into a developing dialogue with the baptismal thesis that has been presented here in this introduction.

Chapter 2 consists of the bulk of Trainor's contribution. While more integration would have been ideal, this is no longer a possibility. So here, I simply allow Trainor to submit in his own words that it is preferable to regard the inner life of the Trinity (God *ad intra*) as consisting of "three sovereignties *for* each other," rather than to regard the Trinity as, for example, a "functional hierarchy" or a "chain of subordination" in the manner suggested by complementarians.[15] "Triple sovereignty" for Trainor expresses the notion that there is *both* (i) a legitimate sense in which there is a "sharing" of the "difference" in the intratrinitarian relations, such that it becomes misleading to speak of an *absolute* authority on the part of the Father or an *absolute* submission of Son or Spirit, *and* (ii) an equally legitimate sense in which there is an absolute irreducibility of the specific "missions" of each trinitarian Person. From this, Trainor articulates his position on how this translates into the spousal relationship.

Beyond this, chapters 3 and 4 move back to my baptismal thesis, considering the possibility of a theological anthropology constructed within the space of a baptismal theology of relation. Chapter 3 builds especially on John Paul II and Ouellet's fundamental anthropology, and through this, engages with Ratzinger and Balthasar's radical take on person as relation. I then propose a baptismally supercharged version of this anthropology, thus strengthening and deepening the perspective of the radiant sacramental person and establishing a more theologically robust hermeneutical foundation for the *humanum* in general according to the sacramental "now" of adopted existence. Chapter 4 then applies this anthropology more specifically to the question of sexual difference, consciously placing this question inside the same baptismal relation exposed in chapter 3.

The final chapter advances a critical (though by no means exhaustive) re-reading of conjugal politics from a point inside the baptismal anthropology shaped in the prior two chapters. I suggest that at their heart, both headship and submission are united and shaped first by a shared theological mission to offer the spousal relationship as a living sacrifice of praise to the Father. In this, already "inside" the trinitarian relations via the dramatic sacramental forms of life in Christ as son and daughter and brother and sister, the specifically masculine and feminine tasks or missions within a conjugal

15. Cf. Ware, "How Shall We?," 270; Knight, *Role Relationship*, 33.

politics—the call and answer of baptismal masculinity and femininity in a sacramental marriage—will emerge, not as a merely natural or fallen paradigm of "first" and "second" or a flattened egalitarian sameness, but as the genuine grammar of love in Christ, one that corresponds in a real way to the relations of love discovered in the Trinity—but only through baptism.

1

Conjugal Politics: Taking Stock

To encounter commentary on the theme of conjugal politics—especially the Pauline and Petrine motif that the husband is head of his wife (cf. Eph 5:23; 1 Cor 11:3; 1 Pet 1)—is to very quickly discover that claims regarding the validity or invalidity of the teaching turn on the question of hermeneutics. Paul Ricoeur's understanding of hermeneutics as "the theory of the rules that preside over an exegesis—that is, over the interpretation of a particular text, or a group of signs that may be viewed as a text,"[1] or Hans Georg Gadamer's contention that hermeneutics functions to "clarify the conditions in which understanding takes place"[2] are thus particularly relevant for the present study. This is to say that to view the politics implied in the *Haustafeln* texts of the New Testament according to the rules of historical-critical scholarship, biblical literalism, or through a more theological and ecclesial lens has everything to do with the conclusion that one will arrive at.

For example, in the case of a purely historical-critical hermeneutic, we find that the rules (implicit or explicit) governing the interpretation of a particular text (in this case the *Haustafeln*), lead in the main to the dismissal of the teaching, whereas a "plainer" or more literal reading of the same text produces the precisely opposite result. Clearly, then, we need to further investigate and thematize this hermeneutical "fork" and inquire more deeply into the methodology and motivations that feed into the different interpretations of the New Testament *Haustafeln*. This chapter will thus survey some of the dominant hermeneutical options exercised both historically and in contemporary readings, with the broader aim of establishing the importance of a baptismal-trinitarian theory of the rules of interpretation for conjugal politics.

---

1. Ricoeur, *Freud and Philosophy*, 8.
2. Gadamer, *Truth and Method*, 295.

Complementarians and Egalitarians, Maximalists and Minimalists

Very roughly speaking, there are two main interpretive camps across Christian denominations when it comes to the particularly vexing question today about whether some kind of "priority," "leadership," or "authority" position should be afforded to the man over the woman in the spousal relationship; or, stated from the reverse, whether some kind of "receptivity," "obedience," or "submission" should be imputed to the woman vis-à-vis her husband, each thus implying certain distinct spousal and perhaps social roles. Put simply, to use the language of the contemporary debate, the "complementarian," "subordinationist," or "pro-difference" interpretation answers in the affirmative, while the "egalitarian," "anti-subordinationist," or "equal regard" interpretation answers in the negative. The egalitarian position broadly assumes that one should not read sexual difference as denoting divinely sanctioned hierarchical connotations where there is a "first" and a "second" or "roles" that would forbid women a role in ministry or suggest a submissive posture on the part of a wife in relation to her husband in their shared married life. By contrast, the complementarian position holds that sexual difference *is* a divinely sanctioned hierarchical ordination, where masculinity and femininity come attached with determinative ministerial and spousal vocations and restrictions, e.g., headship and submission.

The above terms and framing of the debate presently plays out in the liveliest, often acrimonious terms within Evangelical forms of Protestantism, which tend to be today's "hot zone" as regards the question of conjugal politics. Here, the question is very much alive and up for debate, and much ink has been spilled in recent debates between complementarian[3] and egalitarian[4] foes. Across Protestant denominations in general, the particular question of the role of women in liturgical ministry continues to be a point of contention that dominates discussion. Distinguishing Evangelical

---

3. A Protestant think-tank representing the complementarian position is the "Council on Biblical Manhood and Womanhood," established in 1987. The vision statement on their website is "Proclaiming God's Glorious Design for Men and Women." Some important sources are: Grudem and Piper, *Recovering Biblical Manhood and Womanhood*; Grudem, *Evangelical Feminism*; Piper, *Momentary Marriage*; Knight, *Role Relationships*; Ware, *Father, Son, and Holy Spirit*.

4. A Protestant think-tank representing the egalitarian position is "Christians for Biblical Equality," established in 1988, consisting of 100 Protestant denominations in 65 countries. A vision statement on their website reads, "Advancing a biblical foundation for gift-based rather than gender-based ministry and service." Some key representatives of the egalitarian camp and their works are: Giles, *Trinity and Subordinationism*; Grenz, *Women in the Church*; Bilezikian, *Beyond Sex Roles*.

Christianity from older mainline denominations is their particular concern with not only the ministerial dimension of gender, but also with the pastoral implications of difference in a conjugal setting. Driving the conjugal question in certain Evangelical contexts is the complementarian position, which places great pastoral stress on the importance of distinctly male headship as ingredient to the unity and stability of the marriage, a role thought to flow directly from the will and ordination of God as embodied in the Scriptures. Against this, more egalitarian strains of Evangelicalism have begun to resist this more classical reading, arguing for a levelling of gender roles in both ministerial and domestic spheres.

As the debate has continued, the doctrine of the Trinity has emerged as a key question in the debate, an ultimate horizon by which both Evangelical camps have sought to defend their claims. Complementarians have accented the perceived status of the obedience and subordination of the Son to the Father as exemplary for the position of the wife in relation to her husband, while egalitarians have stressed the equality and mutuality of the trinitarian persons as an ultimate frame of reference thought to be ultimately corrosive of a rigidly hierarchical and exclusionary interpretation of difference. In the following chapter, Trainor will consider and engage many of the arguments adduced in the Protestant context of the debate particularly as regards the use of the Trinity.

The situation in a Roman Catholic context is somewhat more ambiguous and—at least on the question of spousal roles—decidedly less "hot." Given that Catholics share the same core Scriptural foundation and much of the same interpretive tradition with Protestants, there is a similar range of theoretical questions in play here, although when we descend deeper into the hermeneutics of it all some key differences will emerge. Ministerially speaking, the question regarding gender roles within Catholicism is more or less settled, at least at the formal or doctrinal level. Pope St. John Paul II's 1994 apostolic letter *Ordinatio Sacerdotalis*, published in an effort to put the debate about the ordination of women to rest, concluded with the pope's judgement "that the Church has no authority whatsoever to confer priestly ordination on women and that this judgment is to be definitively held by all the Church's faithful."[5] Sara Butler contends that there is little or no scope within the constraints of the received tradition to seriously entertain the possibility of the ordination of women.[6]

---

5. John Paul II, *Ordinatio Sacerdotalis*, 4.

6. See Butler, *Catholic Priesthood and Women*. Cf. also Manfred Hauke's exhaustive study in Hauke, *Women in the Priesthood?*

Of course, the letter has provoked hermeneutical gymnastics and dissent similar to that which characterized the response to other contentious documents such as *Humanae vitae* in 1968. At a de facto level, there is ongoing grumbling and malcontent from various quarters about the ongoing exclusion of women from sacramental ministry. Movements agitating for women ordinations have waxed and waned in the Church since the Second Vatican Council. There has been, and continues to be produced reams of liberal and feminist theology that seeks to give credibility to an alternative conclusion, but by and large by going well beyond the formal constraints of the apostolic tradition. More recently, under the papacy of Pope Francis, however, the "revolution by praxis," so to speak, that has recently swept through the Church has fostered hope that a more radical rethinking of traditional gender roles and distinctions could be possible. At a deep level, it seems, many faithful simply do not buy or understand the rationale for the restriction of the ministerial priesthood to men. While there might be an established "official" position, the teaching of a priesthood restricted to men belongs to a suite of theological and anthropological issues typified by deep subterranean conflict within the Church, thus making the Catholic situation analogous to the Protestant when it comes to questions related to sexual difference.

When it comes to the somewhat less pressing pastoral question of politics and roles within marriage, however, the Catholic situation is at present decidedly less conflictual, at least as regards the level of practice. Indeed, the whole question almost seems dead, and both the mainstream left and right seem more or less comfortable with this state of play. To find a clear statement on whether in fact St. Paul's words carry a more than symbolic weight or whether they might have some important place in how the marriage relationship is conceived and successfully realized, one has to go all the way back to Pope Pius XI's *Casti connubii* in 1930. His articulation of "the primacy of the husband with regard to the wife and children" and "the ready subjection of the wife and her willing obedience"[7] represents the last full-throated voicing of a broadly complementarian interpretation that—as we will see—had more or less reigned in the tradition up to that point.

Since then, the closest formal Church teaching has come to the question of male priority and female submission in marriage has been John Paul II's *Mulieris dignitatum* in 1995. John Paul's twist on the traditional tendency to elevate verses dealing with a difference of rank and role in Ephesians 5 (verses 22–24) was to back up and read this difference through the command of mutual subordination in verse 21. He submits that Ephesians

---

7. Pius XI, *Casti connubii*, 26.

5:22–23 must, according to the "Gospel 'innovation' " be "understood and carried out in a new way: as a 'mutual subjection out of reverence for Christ.'"[8] While this does not in principle represent an abrogation of the fact that some real vocational difference between the spouses remains, it seems at first glance to effectively scrub out possible implications of that difference, certainly any cruder political or subordinationist possibilities. As a consequence, according to a more robust hermeneutic of equality, the most John Paul II seemed willing to say regarding the question of headship and submission at this teaching level was to acknowledge the textual fact of the man's headship. But at all times this fact is framed and conditioned by the imperative of kenotic love and mutual self-giving based on the model of Christ as articulated in verse 21.[9]

The closest the pope came to a more direct exegetical stake on the meaning of the difference seemingly implied by St. Paul comes in his *Catechesis on Human Love*, his Wednesday audiences delivered in Rome between September 5, 1979 and November 28, 1984 that become known as the "Theology of the Body" (which cannot strictly speaking be given the same authoritative weight as, say, *Mulieris dignitatum*).[10] Here, after clarifying that the love implied in mutual subordination and in the kenotic element of Christ's offering of himself for the Church "excludes every kind of submission by which the wife would become a servant or slave of the husband, an object of one-sided submission,"[11] John Paul II arrives at a more direct confrontation with verses 22–23. He concludes that yes, there is a distinct vocational difference implied, but specifies that this difference

---

8. John Paul II, *Mulieris dignitatum*, 24.

9. *Mulieris dignitatum* reads thus: "The author of the Letter to the Ephesians sees no contradiction between an exhortation formulated in this way and the words: 'Wives, be subject to your husbands, as to the Lord. For the husband is the head of the wife' (5:22–23). The author knows that this way of speaking, so profoundly rooted in the customs and religious tradition of the time, is to be understood and carried out in a new way: as a '*mutual subjection out of reverence for Christ*' (cf. Eph 5:21). This is especially true because the husband is called the 'head' of the wife *as* Christ is the head of the Church; he is so in order to give 'himself up for her' (Eph 5:25), and giving himself up for her means giving up even his own life. However, whereas in the relationship between Christ and the Church the subjection is only on the part of the Church, in the relationship between husband and wife the 'subjection' is not one-sided but mutual" (John Paul II, *Mulieris dignitatum*, 24)

10. My own preference is not to get too hung up on the extrinsic question of how authoritatively defined or expressed a teaching may or may not be. This can easily degenerate into archaism, objectivism, and ultramontanist tendencies. I am more interested in the *intrinsic* grounds for authoritativeness, i.e., its truth within the geography of its theological givenness, than whether or not it has been "authoritatively" defined.

11. John Paul II, *Theology of the Body*, 473 (89.3).

is a difference *within* the same mission of love. The pope admits that the author of Ephesians seems to speak of a greater responsibility imputed to the husband in regard to this love, and concludes that verses indicating this priority or extra responsibility on the part of the husband should be read as indicating that "the husband is above all the one who loves and the wife, by contrast, is the one who is loved."[12] Further, he speculates that "One might even venture the idea that the wife's 'submission' to her husband, understood in the context of the whole of Ephesians 5:22–23, means above all the 'experiencing of love.'" With this, the pope saves a notion of the priority of the husband, but radically transforms it by apparently excising it of any other content than that of love.

This maneuver has the benefit of both affirming sexual difference—there is a real difference, but it belongs more to existence in Christ, and less to nature or fallen existence—while lessening the extent to which this difference could designate a conception of woman as *ontologically* inferior to man at the level of nature or reason. Furthermore, in fidelity to the received tradition, it does not go beyond its scope regarding the bases for a male-only ministerial priesthood. Of course, the mere fact that there remains a qualitative identity and vocation-differentiating *difference* here at all—specifically, a continued linkage with the feminine as characterized by a receptive act (the woman defined in the passive as the one who "is loved") and a "greater" responsibility from the point of view of the husband—is enough for critics to assert that John Paul II does not go nearly far enough. Alternatively, from a more complementarian point of view, the question might be raised whether the pope in fact gives *enough* to the difference to prevent it from simply being collapsed generically into identity and therefore the homogenization of difference in the direction of something like allowing women to the priesthood after all.

Be that as it may, the long and short of this recontextualization of the notion of male priority and female subordination is that the *specific point of masculine difference* seems to have more or less fallen out of favor in Catholic discourse and teaching. John Paul II himself would seem to have hedged his bets here, likely on the grounds of trying to correct a perceived lop-sided or misplaced emphasis on wifely subordination in the tradition. Most telling is the absence of any mention at all of a specifically masculine prerogative or responsibility for the husband in the *Catechism of the Catholic Church*. This perhaps explains why to mention the word "headship" in casually Catholic circles is to be greeted either by a blank stare or a puzzled "do we still believe in that?"

---

12. John Paul II, *Theology of the Body*, 485 (92.6).

In what follows, we will move to a deeper consideration of the hermeneutical and exegetical factors that influence contemporary interpretation, first by considering the approach of the earlier tradition.

Patristic and Scholastic Hermeneutics and Exegesis

The present Catholic tendency to recontextualize, downplay, or dismiss a clear emphasis on a functioning notion of male priority and female submission in marriage has not always been in vogue. As mentioned above, it is not until the modern era that we see a departure from what has by and large been consistent affirmation of a certain fundamental priority, preeminence, or authority role for the husband and a clearly subordinate status for the wife, even if the way this is parsed may vary somewhat from thinker to thinker. Generally speaking, this is thought to flow from divine ordination as it is expressed in both the natural created order (both in its fallen and unfallen state) and in the Christ-Church revelation.

For example, St. Augustine understands it to be "more consonant with the order of nature that men should bear rule over women, than women over men. It is with this principle in view that the apostle says, *The head of the woman is the man* and, *Wives, submit yourselves unto your husbands*."[13] Elsewhere he stresses that "Just as Christ is head of the Church, and the Church is ordered to follow its head and, as it were, walk in the footsteps of its head, so everyone's household has as its head the man, and as its body, the woman. Where the head leads, there the body ought to follow."[14]

St. Jerome states that "Husband and wife should be bound to the same relationship as that of Christ as head and the Church as subject" and speaks of how "the wife is subjected to her husband, *since your desire shall be for your husband and he shall rule you* [Gen 3:16]."[15] Pseudo-Jerome tells a woman named Celantia that the upholding of her husband's authority is co-extensive with her own honor.[16] St. John Chrysostom understands St. Paul to be teaching that "the husband occupies the place of the 'head,' and the wife the place of the 'body.'"[17] Each have been assigned "their proper role, to the one that of

---

13. Augustine, "Marriage and Concupiscence," 267.
14. Augustine, "Sermon 9," 269.
15. Jerome, "Epistle to the Ephesians," 243.
16. "See that your husband's authority is upheld and that the entire household learns from your example the degree of respect due to him. Show by your obedience that he is the master and indicate his importance by your humility, since the more abundantly you honor him the more you will be honored yourself. For, as the Apostle says, *the husband is the head of the wife*" (Pseudo-Jerome, "Letter to Celantia," 300).
17. Chrysostom, "Epistle to the Ephesians," 320.

authority and provision, to the other that of submission." The wife must not "demand equality, for in fact she is subjected to the head."[18]

St. Thomas Aquinas refers to how the "wife is naturally subject to her husband as governor,"[19] and speaks of how "the relation of a husband to his wife is, in a certain way, like that of a master to his servant, insofar as the latter ought to be governed by the commands of his master."[20] Further, on the basis of the relationship of Christ and his Church, "the wife must be obedient to her husband as the Church is subject to Christ."[21]

We may summarize the above selections by making the initial observation that the teaching tends to be read through a heavily hierarchical or "political" lens, in which clearly defined roles are given where the husband is tasked with authority, leadership, and ruling, while the woman is tasked with listening, obedience, following, and subjection. The scriptural text is generally understood to be indicating a clear ruler-ruled relationship of superior (male) and inferior (female).

Exactly how this relationship is understood and defended is something to be explored in more depth in a moment, but we should note here that there is perceived to be much at stake in this issue for these Christian thinkers of the past. For them, this particular husband-wife ordering is an important prerequisite for a harmonious family life lived in fidelity to the order laid down by the Creator. Origen believes that "concord and unison and harmony between husband and wife" are the product of a domestic situation "when he is as ruler and she is obedient to the word, [']He shall rule over you.[']"[22] Augustine queries, "do you want your household to hang upside down?" The preventive measure: "*The husband is the head of his wife.*"[23] Chrysostom claims that when wives are subject to their husbands "the children are well brought up, and the servants are in good order, and neighbors, and friends, and relations enjoy the fragrance."[24]

Conversely, to ignore St. Paul's admonitions leads to familial chaos: "all is turned upside down, and thrown into confusion," continues Chrysostom, "and just as when the generals of an army are at peace with one another, all things are in due subordination, whereas, on the other hand, if they are at variance, everything is turned upside down; so, I say, is it also

18. Chrysostom, "Epistle to the Ephesians," 328.
19. Aquinas, *Summa Contra Gentiles,* 123.4.
20. Aquinas, *Epistle to the Ephesians,* 217.
21. Aquinas, *Epistle to the Ephesians,* 218.
22. Origen, "Gospel of Matthew," 192.
23. Augustine, "Marriage and Concupiscence," 267.
24. Chrysostom, "Epistle to the Ephesians," 319.

here." This conviction that the headship of husband over wife is an essential prerequisite for familial harmony is shared strongly by the tradition at least up to the issuance of *Casti connubii*, after which the notion of familial order grounded in a hierarchical interpretation of the man-woman difference tends to disappear from view.

Just what is going on in these interpretations requires consideration of a number of factors. As we have seen, both the Fathers and Scholastics generally affirm the scriptural teaching of headship at face value, and it is to them that we owe the main body of premises that support this conclusion. To fully understand what the Fathers and Scholastics mean when they speak of conjugal politics as consisting of a more or less unambiguous ruling of husband over wife requires an understanding of how bodiliness, temporality, and eternity are thought to function in relation to anthropological existence. In other words, how are these factors and their place within anthropological discourse shaped, ordered, and interpreted by what we would in contemporary language describe as early Christian thinkers' "worldview," specifically, the placing of "nature" vis-à-vis "grace" in relation to the human person? Clearly, if we compare the way that John Paul II treats conjugal politics as belonging to the perfection of love with the way the earlier tradition tends to describe especially the woman as being the imperfect inferior of the man by reference to a hierarchically interpreted natural order, we see that something has changed quite dramatically at the "worldview" level here.

While for patristic and scholastic interpretation the spiritual and the eschatological represent a new source of at least part of the form of the man-woman relationship and most certainly a new "spirit" for it, it is typical for them to first base their arguments on an understanding of the temporal sphere understood from within a more naturalistic and fallen perspective, and in more airtight terms. This means that when attempting to interpret difference and the roles presupposed therein, patristic and scholastic exegesis easily reverts to common cultural norms and truisms about masculinity and femininity, which are then qualified and framed by recourse to revealed insights. The cumulative result is at times a somewhat uncomfortable alliance between faith and reason, nature and grace, where any organic integrating principle of unity is lacking. We might say today that what they lack is a properly "dramatic" or "sacramental" starting point, a principle of unity that transcends both the aporias of temporality and the limitations of a revealed framework read through said aporias.

But before we get too far ahead of ourselves with critical evaluation, let us begin our deeper exploration of fundamental patristic and scholastic exegesis and interpretation by considering first the more basic presuppositions about masculinity and femininity that inform their approach. On the one hand, there is in the Fathers and Scholastics a very traditional argumentation which equates the male with perfection, with a greater degree of originating activity and priority, illustrated by its association with terms such as source (*arche*) and head (*kephale*). Read according to a typically Greek backdrop of empirical and metaphysical interpretation, this tends to be a largely a solitary perfection, i.e., it does not require the woman for the perfection of man; in most cases its proper spiritual realization deliberately excludes her. And in this sense, we can see the influence of metaphysical analyses that read *actus purus* in solitary rather than relational or social terms.

On the other hand, according to the same Greek lens, the corresponding argument for femininity as co-extensive with receptivity usually associates it with imperfection, even if scriptural and theological perspectives in one way or another strongly mitigate and qualify the at times negative effects of this emphasis, e.g., with the new valuation of feminine receptivity according to the Marian dimension. In the more metaphysical and naturalistic categories of scholasticism in particular, the feminine is linked to a deficient mode of Being represented by the potency of subsistent Being, being the flipside of masculinity as representative of the *actus purus*. Consequently, the perceived imperfection of the feminine is often linked to speculations that a sexually differentiated *humanum* is not per se original to the plan of God but somehow the effect of sin; or if original, on a qualitatively lower hierarchical rung than the solitary spiritual male individual or the female individual in a spiritualized perspective. A subsequent inability to link up the masculine and feminine in the context of a theology of marriage largely results in headship being spoken of as a temporal and not so much a strictly theological matter, except extrinsically, in the sense perhaps of a moral-psychological trope ordained in some way by the Creator, perhaps by way of a legal decree.

In this perspective, speaking of headship as a "natural" dictate pertaining mostly to household politics and eminently explicable by human reason tends to be the norm. Patristic and scholastic exegesis often simply presupposes a kind of "how could it be otherwise?" attitude, and simply assumes (correctly) that none of their contemporaries could think otherwise.

More deeply understanding the anthropology of the Fathers and Scholastics thus requires a keen awareness of the effect of the neo-Platonic division—especially present in the Fathers and still operative in the Scholastics—between so-called temporal and spiritual man. For example, a triple and dual perspective informs the anthropological thinking of Augustine and Aquinas respectively, in which temporal imperfection tends to be contrasted with spiritual perfection.[25] Here, a vibrant consciousness of the

---

25. See Roberts, *Creation and Covenant*, 71. Regarding Augustine, Roberts observes

correlation between sin and certain anthropological givens of temporal human existence makes it difficult to integrate the more temporal and physical elements of marriage seamlessly into the fabric of the logic of faith. To some extent influenced by Platonic and Neo-Platonic thought, consciousness of the limitations of temporality extends particularly to the corruptibility of the corporeal nature of man which is contrasted with the perfection and supernatural destiny of man's incorruptible spirit: "Spiritualization," notes Balthasar, "presented in a thousand different colorations, is the basic tendency of the patristic epoch."[26]

Yet, it is certainly erroneous to accuse the Fathers or the Scholastics of a basic Gnostic denial of the goodness of bodiliness.[27] It can rather be suggested, with the benefit of hindsight, that they were challenged and limited by a certain theological and philosophical methodology which prevented them from speaking of the bodily component of human existence as a *full* perfection of Being in its historical instantiation, as we might be accustomed today.[28] Balthasar highlights just how difficult coming to grips with bodiliness (including in its sexually differentiated character) has been historically, calling it one of the fundamental "riddles" of human existence. Of the three constitutive polarities of the human condition which he identifies—spirit-body, man-woman, and individual-community—it is the first two that are most clearly a result of embodiment.[29] The historical dialectic between

---

how Augustine treats sexual difference within the matrix of the perspectives of creation, earthly pilgrimage, and eschatology. See also Allen, *Concept of Woman*, 219–20, 385–86. Regarding Thomas, Allen notes how he works within a more simplified schema of nature and grace.

26. Balthasar, "Fathers, the Scholastics, and Ourselves," 375.

27. "In the authentic Judeo-Christian vision, sexuality is never seen from the point of view of a 'phobia of sex.' Thus, every causal link between sin and sex, which would present sex as the negative heritage of sin, is to be excluded. This position cannot be deduced either from Scripture or from the tradition. The position of the Cappadocian Fathers . . . did not derive from any such phobia; if anything, it arose from an attempt to elaborate the contents of a theology of the original state" (Scola, *Nuptial Mystery*, 47). Similarly, Adam G. Cooper notes how both "the Greek and Latin Fathers, bound to biblical revelation, were consistent in affirming the goodness of marriage and in denouncing certain gnosticizing tendencies in which its integrity was compromised" (Cooper, "Marriage and the 'Garments,'" 217).

28. Again speaking of the Greek and Latin Fathers, Cooper suggests that it nevertheless "may be asked whether they ever broke free from such [gnosticizing] tendencies themselves" (Cooper, "Marriage and the 'Garments,'" 217).

29. "These constants are part of his [humankind's] nature, his essence, which does not mean that they solve his riddle; in fact, they render it more profound and more pressing. In all three dimensions, man seems to be built according to a polarity, obliged to engage in reciprocity, always seeking complementarity in the other pole" (Balthasar, *Man in God*, 355).

materialism and spiritualism demonstrates the difficulty of coming to grips with the first polarity. The challenge of the second polarity[30] is illustrated by the historical tendency to either uncritically regard sexual difference as a copy of divine sexuality, which leads, as Balthasar tersely observes, "to the realm of the fantastic"[31] or to regard sexual difference as an inessential, merely horizontal aspect of human nature, a move which locks man in the cosmos, trivializing sexuality, and obscuring his transcendence.[32] Consequently, Balthasar goes on to speak about "what a difficult task 'pre-Christian' anthropology must have had in finding the correct locus of sexuality within a total interpretation of being." He emphasizes further that this "will remain a sensitive area even when given a Christian interpretation."

This tension and the methodological lens inadequate to its full resolution is clearly evident in early Christian treatment of sexual difference. It is present in its most extreme form in Greek Fathers such as St. Gregory of Nyssa, Origen, St. Maximus the Confessor, and St. John Damascene, all of whom, with various degrees of nuance, escape the problem of bodiliness by flirting with an ideal androgynous *humanum*, beyond all sexual difference, and consequently tend to regard sexual difference as a contingent manifestation within historical time caused by or at least associated with the fall into original sin.[33] For them, notwithstanding God's sovereign ability to draw good from this alleged imperfection of fallen human nature,[34] the relationship between the *imago Dei* and the bodily dynamic of human existence remains tenuous—man is most clearly the image of God as an individual through his rational and spiritual faculties and the *transcending* of his body.

In the Christian West, Augustine and especially the more Aristotelian Aquinas, while perhaps more clearly affirming the natural created goodness and essentiality of bodiliness and sexual difference, nevertheless continue to register lingering suspicion of the vertical significance of these dimensions of anthropological existence, as exemplified in their firm rejection of the man-woman-child triad as an *imago Trinitatis*,[35] and their continuing stress

---

30. The tensions of the body-spirit polarity "recur, and in a deeper form, when we go on to examine human nature's sexual differentiation into man and woman" (Balthasar, *Man in God*, 365).

31. Balthasar, *Man in God*, 368. Cf. Benedict XVI, *Deus Caritas Est*, 4.

32. Balthasar, *Man in God*, 2:368.

33. Scola, *Nuptial Mystery*, 46–47.

34. Explaining Gregory of Nyssa's position, Scola says that "since God foreknew that man would rebel, man was created with sexual traits in order to attain the total unification of humanity by means of human reproduction" (Scola, *Nuptial Mystery*, 47).

35. Scola, *Nuptial Mystery*, 284–85. Cf. Augustine, *De Trinitate* 12.5.5; Aquinas, *ST* 1.93.6. Balthasar explains Augustine's refusal: "In his great work on the Trinity,

on the rational or spiritual imaging of God over against any bodily or relational aspirations to that imaging. For them also, then, the alleged imperfection—even if it is relative—of a purely temporal bodiliness prevents them from including the sexed body and the relational triad that it perpetuates as full created participants in the *imago Dei*.[36]

In general, Christian thinkers in the patristic and scholastic ages tend to have an acute consciousness of man's bodily and sexual nature in the following sense: (i) as an "elementary bio-instinctual dynamism"[37]; (ii) part of the "animal and intracosmic sphere"[38]; (iii) of the relation between sexuality and ontological dependence/creaturely contingency[39]; and (iv) of the "reciprocity of generation and death."[40] One also thinks of the keen Augustinian awareness of the close connection between sin and sexual intercourse, where the latter is somehow implicated in the former. The tendency to downplay marriage in favor of virginity in some ways reflects this general concern,[41] and of course, beyond these concerns about temporal

---

Augustine certainly understood the relational and dialogical character of the persons in God, but he placed the image of the Trinity in created man completely in the single individual—certainly from fear of polytheism—in that he wanted to see this image only in the individual's spiritual faculties (memory, knowledge, and will)" (Balthasar, "Concept of Person," 22).

36. Thomas contends that "God's likeness in the manner of an image is to be found in man as regards his mind; but as regards his other parts only in the manner of a trace" (Aquinas, *ST* 1.93.6). The likeness of "image" extends by way of direct cause only to the rational mind. Because the likeness of "trace" is to be found in things by way only of an effect, Aquinas concludes that the human body cannot properly be called an image of God. The fact that man has an upright constitution "must not be understood as saying that God's image is really to be found in man's body; only that the shape and posture of the human body portrays God's image in the soul, in the manner of a trace" (Aquinas, *ST* 1.93.6). Servais Pinckaers observes that for Thomas "the body, with its sexuality and particularly the human face, cannot properly be considered as being images of God, but rather traces or reflections of God" (Pinckaers, "Ethics and Image of God," 134). All of this should be somewhat familiar to us now, operative as it is in complementarian logic about the image of God.

37. Scola, *Nuptial Mystery*, 26.

38. Scola, *Nuptial Mystery*, 28.

39. Scola, *Nuptial Mystery*, 23–24. "This [sexual] nature, which makes its presence known by imposing on the consciousness an 'other' different from the self, indicates finitude, but more precisely ontological dependence" (Scola, *Nuptial Mystery*, 23).

40. Balthasar, *Man in God*, 374. Balthasar notes Hegel's three reasons for why death is implicated in the process of generation: one: reproduction anticipates the death of the one generating; two: division of species promotes violence, and ultimately, death; three: the self-preservation of the species requires death (Balthasar, *Man in God*, 375).

41. "In the early Church, while virginity was associated with immortality and accordingly exulted as an especially worthy vocation, marriage was often associated with sin and death" (Cooper, "Marriage and the 'Garments,'" 217). Again, however, there are

human existence, is an overriding fear that drawing a similarity between man and God based on anything other than spirituality and rationality will return us to pagan ideas about the Godhead.[42]

This general context has important repercussions for the patristic and scholastic conception of the specificity of masculinity and femininity. First, for them, the ideal person is one who perfects his or her rational or spiritual imaging of God—"Since man is said to be after God's image in virtue of his intelligent nature, it follows that he is most completely after God's image in that point in which such a nature can most completely image God. Now it does this in so far as it imitates God's understanding and loving of *himself*"[43]—and who thereby possesses the fewest possible links to temporality. For most thinkers, this ideal person can, according to an eschatological perspective, be either a man or a woman. For example, Allen references Augustine's notion that the worship of God is most a function, not of the embodied person as a whole, but of the spiritual soul. In this context, both male and female may "equally reflect the image of God by transcending their sexual identity."[44] Similarly, Aquinas advances the notion that in the ideal form of the soul, both man and woman can be said to be the image of God: "God's image is found equally in both man and woman as regards that point in which the idea of 'image' is principally realized, namely an intelligent nature."[45] For Augustine and Aquinas, then, in a spiritual and eschatological perspective, notwithstanding certain differences, both man and woman can be said to be the image of God. In this sense, both man and woman most perfectly live up to this image insofar as their temporal existence is lived eschatologically, something that in its perfect form requires "the Christian to cease from the typically 'worldly' activity of marriage and procreation."[46] Thus, in this perspective, virginity and celibacy most closely approximate and anticipate this ideal spiritual state.

Howsoever things may be on this spiritual and eschatological plane as it regards the essential equality of spiritual capacity in masculinity and femininity, things change when the Fathers and Scholastics move to make sense of embodied temporality. In this perspective (i.e., in temporal history) it is the male human being who is regarded as the most perfect image of God. St.

---

other important *theological* reasons not related to the alleged imperfection of the body for why virginity has always been held in such high esteem (cf. Matt 19:11–24). See John Paul II's detailed discussion in John Paul II, *Theology of the Body*, 412–57 (73–85).

42. Allen, *Concept of Woman*, 223.
43. Aquinas, *ST* 1.93.4.
44. Allen, *Concept of Woman*, 221.
45. Aquinas, *ST* 1.93.4.
46. Gasparro et al., *Human Couple*, 63.

Thomas says that "as regards a secondary point, God's image is found in man in a way in which it is not found in woman; for man is the beginning and end of woman, just as God is the beginning and end of all creation."[47] For the Fathers and Scholastics the male is thought to have fewer ties to the limitations and corruptions of temporality and more ties to source and actuality than the woman and is therefore in some sense understood to be paradigmatic of the more perfect human being prior to sin. The man is, as it were, in this sense *less* fallen than the woman, ontologically speaking, even if sin is said to be transmitted through him: "For as in Adam all die" (1 Cor 5:22).

This conception of the male is closely tied up with the revealed typology of Adam-Christ and a stress on the absolute, self-contained, fully actual, simple oneness of God. In the beginning, the human race is organized corporately in Adam, for it is man who is the source of woman, Eve being taken from his flesh (cf. Gen 2:21–24). For this reason, "no one was born except through Adam"[48]; "Because the first Principle made man in His image to be an expression of Himself, He created the bodily element of man in such a way that all men would stem from the first man as from a single radical principle."[49] And consequently, it is through Adam also that sin is transmitted: "The first man fell, and all who were born of him from him derived the concupiscence of the flesh"[50]; "The soul itself is not handed down, but original sin did pass from the soul of Adam into the souls of his descendants through the flesh born of concupiscence."[51] As source, Adam is also head just as Christ, as source of the Church, is her head, as the references cited earlier attest. Because of this priority of Adam who was "the type of the one who was to come" (Rom 5:14), it was therefore "fitting" that Christ would become incarnate as a man:

> let us consider how rightly Paul compared Adam to Christ, not only considering him to be the type and image, but also that Christ Himself became the very same thing, because the Eternal Word fell upon him. For it was fitting that the first-born of God, the first shoot, the only-begotten, even the wisdom of God, should be joined to the first-formed man, and first and first-born of mankind, and should become incarnate."[52]

---

47. Aquinas, *ST* 1.93.4.
48. Augustine, "Lectures or Tractates," 22.
49. Bonaventure, *Breviloquium*, 123.
50. Augustine, "Lectures or Tractates," 12.
51. Bonaventure, *Breviloquium*, 123.
52. Methodius, "Banquet of Virgins," 318.

For these reasons, man can be called the "glory" of God (1 Cor 11:7). All of this indicates to the Fathers and Scholastics that it is the man who is the image of the transcendence and glory of God to the most acute degree. Methodius speaks of "the innocent and unbegotten Adam being the type and resemblance of God the Father Almighty, who is uncaused, and the cause of all."[53] This similarity to God the Father Almighty is often taken to imply the self-sufficiency of the male on his own. In this perspective, the "help" of woman is often seen more functionally in terms of the necessity of procreation—"If one should ask why it was necessary that a helper be made for man, the answer that seems most probable is that it was for the procreation of children"—and not because the man might need the woman on an interpersonal, relational level. Augustine's rhetorical question communicates this effectively: "How much more agreeably could two male friends, rather than a man and woman, enjoy companionship and conversation in a life shared together?"[54]

As a general rule, as suggested, this stress on the transcendence and self-sufficient actuality of the male is very often supported, not only by the witness of Scripture, but also by the strength of converging empirical claims of the day. For example, Aquinas adopts elements of the Aristotelian theory of generation to illustrate this point, holding that while the man contributed the active part of the generation of the child (its form), the woman was merely the passive vessel that provided the matter.[55] Even if he believes the conception of a female to be in some sense intended by God,[56] like Aristotle he regards the conception of a male child as the more perfect conception, as most perfectly reflecting "the image of God as pure act."[57] Consequently, in this perspective of the perfection of masculine representation of the "active power"[58] of God, it is not surprising that authors see little reason to doubt that in the context of marriage it is the man who is fit to be head.

53. Methodius, "Two Fragments," 402.

54. Augustine, "Literal Meaning of Genesis," 265. Perhaps the sense of the perfection of all things masculine explains something of the prevalence of pederasty in Greek and Roman antiquity. Cf. Harper, *Shame to Sin*, 19–79.

55. Allen, *Concept of Woman*, 386.

56. Allen explains Aquinas's rather dubious and convoluted conclusion "that God willed this [the conception of a female] to happen so that the human race might have continuity. God intended woman to be generated and arranged for the mark to be missed approximately half the time" (Allen, *Concept of Woman*, 393).

57. Allen, *Concept of Woman*, 392. "The male, having a closer approximation to the actuality of God through his more perfect generation and capacity for providing principle or act to his offspring, was superior to the female" (Allen, *Concept of Woman*, 389).

58. Allen, *Concept of Woman*, 395.

The Fathers and Scholastics thus tend to regard temporal woman as a less perfect image of God, who is thought to have more ties to the limitations and corruptions of temporality and less to source and actuality.[59] In this regard, the Eve-Mary-Church typology in relation to the Adam-Christ typology is paradigmatic: "Adam [is] in the figure of Christ, Eve [is] in the figure of the Church."[60] There is an affinity between how Eve is dependent on Adam as source and subject to him as "helper" and the way in which the Church is dependent on Christ as source and is subject to Him as head. This subordination of the female has numerous biblical attestations in its support, in both a spousal and liturgical setting.[61] Regarding subordination generally speaking, flirtations with theories of an androgynous origin of the *humanum* greatly affect the concept of woman because woman, being the apparently imperfect being who must be subordinate to man, is always understood as the version of humanity not exactly original to the thought of God which has fallen furthest away from the original ideal of creation. Consequently, patristic and scholastic thought persistently equates woman with potency in need of masculine act in a manner that does not have nearly so great a counterpoint in any non-instrumental masculine need for femininity. Summarizing the Augustinian view, Allen explains that "since woman was taken from man's side, she is not complete in her own identity, she cannot present the image of God by herself; while man, the complete being, perfectly represents the image of God."[62]

In the context of life after the Fall, the need for the subordination of woman becomes even more acute. Man must "rule" over woman because

> [']you [woman] have not made a right use of the faculty of command, pass now to a condition of subordination; you have not known how to maintain liberty; be submissive now to servitude. You have not known how to command and have not given proof with your operation. You will be one of the subjects and will

---

59. "The fathers, guided by Platonic principles, associate the female body with sense and matter. Women are intellectually and morally inferior to men because of the limitations of their physical sex" (Miller, *Sexuality and Authority*, 28).

60. Augustine, "Expositions," 131.

61. 1 Corinthians 11:13 deals with the question of head coverings, and teaches that men should not pray or prophesize *with* their heads covered as they are the image and glory of God (4, 7), while women should not pray or prophesize *without* their heads covered as they are the glory, not of God, but of man (5-6, 7-10). 1 Corinthians 14:34-36 admonishes women to be silent in the churches and if they wish to learn anything, to ask their husbands at home. 1 Timothy 2: 9-15 tells woman that she is to be quiet and submissive and have no authority over man because it was Eve and not Adam who was deceived.

62. Allen, *Concept of Woman*, 225.

recognize man as your master.' *Your urge shall be for your husband and he shall be your master* [Gen 3:16].[63]

This theme of feminine moral frailty and susceptibility to sin accompanies most patristic and scholastic reflections on women. The prototypical example of this is to be found in Eve, who "was the first to be deceived and was responsible for deceiving the man."[64] Jerome is convinced that woman is constituted "of a substance of inferior worth and less importance"[65] and Chrysostom indicates that woman is the "frailer vessel"[66] to whom "the lesser and inferior part" is given.[67] This is highlighted indirectly by an observation of St. Bonaventure, who suggests that because of her possession of this lesser part, it is Adam who actually bears responsibility for Eve's sin: "Because he did not rebuke where he should have rebuked, the woman's sin was imputed to him."[68] Further, where "the woman was deceived, the man was not," something that imputes more guilt onto the male, inasmuch as it implies his greater responsibility; the woman's guilt is lessened because of her more limited capacity.

Feminine moral frailty is also present in Augustine, who understands women to be outstripped by the man when it comes to the ability to battle concupiscence. Addressing husbands who expect their wives to be chaste, he points out that "You are demanding self-discipline from the weaker sex; both of you have the urgings of the flesh to deal with; let the stronger be the first to overcome them. . . . The man is stronger than the woman; the man is the head of the woman."[69] Advising husbands, Chrysostom says "she is the woman, the weaker vessel, whereas you are a man. For this reason you were ordained to be ruler; and were assigned to her in place of a head, that you might bear with the weakness of her that is set under you."[70] All of this tends to lead to a view of woman as a passive, less actual partner designed to submit to the greater actuality and self-possession of the male: "St. Thomas argued that the more passive something was, the better it could yield to the active power."[71] Therefore, this would seem to provide ample warrant for the straightforward conclusion that woman is as a consequence not rightly

---

63. Chrysostom, "On Genesis," 316–17.
64. Ambrose, "On Paradise," 219.
65. Jerome, "Epistle to the Ephesians," 250.
66. Chrysostom, "On Genesis," 329.
67. Chrysostom, "In Praise of Maximus," 340.
68. Bonaventure, *Breviloquium*, 3.
69. Augustine, "Sermon 132," 271.
70. Chrysostom, "Epistle to the Corinthians," 334.
71. Allen, *Concept of Woman*, 395.

the image and glory of God, but rather, according to a hierarchical scale, the glory of man (cf. 1 Cor 11:7).

And yet, one would be remiss not to qualify the above by affirming that patristic and scholastic reflection on femininity can by no means be characterized as deliberately or crudely misogynistic, the perennial temptation of any retroactive exegesis conducted from the perspective of an "enlightened" age. In fact, when compared to the cultural norms of the day Christian teaching is radical and revolutionary.[72] Whatever the ontological and theological status of woman presupposed here, it is important to understand how often the above is circumscribed by appreciation of the way the newness of Christian faith challenged the concrete manner in which the social and cultural status quo was interpreted. Don S. Browning observes that in what he calls the "Stoic-Christian" synthesis, we nevertheless have "the mitigation of male agency, a funneling of male sexuality into procreation, an enhanced respect for women, a counting of wives as friends, and a connection of sexuality with having and caring for children."[73] Even if in the perceived order of nature and creation woman is regarded the second to the male first, there are many indications that for Christian interpretation she is a second not to be treated according to typical patterns of domination and injustice, that she possesses a distinct feminine dignity and importance, that genuine love is present between the spouses, and that marriage is indeed "good."

Augustine's understanding of the natural hierarchy flowing from the alleged inferiority of woman is nevertheless robustly Christian in character when it comes to how it is to be interpreted. Roberts suggests that the hierarchy affirmed by Ephesians 5 is understood by Augustine to be "modified by a sense of mutuality."[74] Whether men or women are "superior and inferior, they are all good." This is amplified by Augustine's sharp rebuke of male chauvinism. He contends that headship "undermines male license," and implies that unfaithful men "ought to have been punished more severely, since it is their role to surpass women in virtue and guide them by example."[75]

---

72. Kyle Harper provides an excellent treatment of this point in Harper, *Shame to Sin*.

73. Browning, *Marriage and Modernization*, 83.

74. Roberts, *Creation and Covenant*, 65.

75. Roberts, *Creation and Covenant*, 65. Augustine has many blunt words directed to husbands exhorting them to live up to the demands of their role as head: "Man, you expect your wife to be chaste; show her by example how to be so, not just by words. You are the head; watch your step. You should be going, after all, where it won't be dangerous for her to follow. You are demanding self-discipline from the weaker sex; both of you have the urgings of the flesh to deal with; let the strong one be the first to overcome them. And yet the sad fact is that many husbands are surpassed in this matter by their wives. . . . If you are looking for a wife who is undefiled, do not be impure yourself" (Augustine, "Sermon 132," 271–72).

The task of headship is such that it places particularly heavy demands on the husband: "If the husband is the head, the husband ought to live better and outdistance his wife in all good deeds, so that she may imitate her husband and follow the lead of her head."[76]

St. Ambrose bids the man to

> lay aside the inordinate emotions of your heart and the rudeness of your manners when you meet your patient wife. Get rid of your obstinacy when your gentle consort offers you her love. You are not a master, but a husband. What you have acquired is not a handmaid, but a wife. God designed you to be a guide to the weaker sex, not a dictator. Be a sharer in her activities. Be a sharer in her love.[77]

Chrysostom admonishes the husband not to despise his wife because of her subjection, "for she is the body—and if the head despises the body, it will itself also perish. But let him bring in love, on his part, as a counterpoise to obedience on her part. . . . Nothing can be better than this union."[78] He points out how "a wife is a member which is related to us, and because of this we especially ought to love her."[79] Bringing the Christ-Church relationship to the fore, Chrysostom asks husbands: "do you wish to have your wife obedient unto you, as the Church is to Christ? Make then the same provision for her; take care of her, as Christ takes care of the Church."[80]

There are also flirtations with views suggesting possibilities other than a view of the ontological imperfection of woman. St. Clement of Alexandria submits that "as far as regards human nature, the man does not possess one nature, and the woman another, but rather both have the same."[81] Referencing the book of Proverbs, he praises woman, saying that

---

76. Augustine, "Sermon 9," 269.

77. Ambrose, "Hexaemeron," 225.

78. Chrysostom, "Epistle to the Ephesians," 328.

79. Chrysostom, "In Praise of Maximus," 324. "We must love our wife not only because she is part of ourselves and had the beginning of her creation from us, but also because God made a law about this when He said, For this reason a man shall leave his father and his mother, and shall cleave to his wife, and the two shall become one flesh [Gen 1:21–22]" (Chrysostom, "In Praise of Maximus," 324). "And to you husbands also I say this: make it a rule that there can be no such offence as to bring you under the necessity of striking a wife. And why do I say 'a wife'? since not even upon his handmaiden should a free man endure to inflict blows and lay violent hands. But if the shame be great for a man to beat a maidservant, much more so is it to stretch forth the right hand against her that is free" (Chrysostom, "Epistle to the Corinthians," 333).

80. Chrysostom, "Epistle to the Ephesians," 346.

81. Clement of Alexandria, "Stromata," 171.

> *a treasury of virtue is the brave woman, who has not eaten her bread hesitatingly* [Pr 31:27], *and the laws of mercy are on her tongue* [Pr 31:26], *who hath opened her mouth wisely and justly, whose children rising up have called her blessed* [Pr 31:26; 31:28], as the Holy Spirit says through Solomon, *and her husband has praised her* [Pr 31:28]. *For a pious woman is praised, let her praise the fear of the Lord* [Pr 31:30], and again *a courageous wife is the crown of her husband* [Pr 12:4].[82]

Implying the importance of a distinctly feminine mode of existence, Ambrose stresses the positive importance of the role of woman as helper in procreation, pointing out that

> If we take the word 'helper' in a good sense, then the woman's co-operation turns out to be something of major importance in the process of generation, just as the earth by receiving, retaining, and fostering the seed causes it to grow and produce fruit in time. In that respect, woman is a good helper even though in an inferior position."[83]

Recognizing the possibility of women outstripping men in perfection, Origen asks, "How many of the female sex are counted among the strong men before God, and how many men are reckoned among the languid and sluggish women?"[84]

A theme of the intrinsic goodness and beauty of marriage and spousal love is also present in some authors. Tertullian asks,

> What kind of yoke is that of two believers, united in one hope, one desire, one discipline, one and same servitude? Both (are) brethren, both fellow servants, no difference of spirit or of flesh; no, (they are) truly two in one flesh. Where the flesh is one, one only is the spirit too. Together they pray, together prostrate themselves, together perform their fasts; mutually teaching, mutually exhorting, mutually sustaining."[85]

Paulinius of Nola argues that

> a harmonious marriage-alliance is at once a holy love, an honorable love, and peace with God. God with His own lips consecrated the course of this alliance, and with His own hand established

---

82. Clement of Alexandria, "Paidagogos," 175.
83. Ambrose, "On Paradise," 222.
84. Origen, "Homily on Joshua," 191.
85. Tertullian, "To His Wife," 157.

the coupling of human persons. He made two abide in one flesh, so that He might confer a love more indivisible.[86]

In all of this, then, even though there usually tends to be a vibrant and enduring emphasis on the natural inferiority and weakness of woman, there is also abiding precedence for recognizing that she is nevertheless a person who possesses her own dignity, and that her husband's headship therefore ought always to be conditioned and motivated by love. Thus, this distinguishes the sexually differentiated hierarchy of Ephesians 5 from the hierarchies of the earthly city.[87]

Nevertheless, notwithstanding attempts to integrate bodiliness and femininity into the faith as perfections of being, overall the tradition has found itself largely unable to integrate all of these "raw materials" of marriage into an integrated and sustained sacramental perspective; to that perspective that we might now take to be normative, at least after John Paul II. While on the one hand, Scripture and Tradition affirm that marriage is a sacrament of the order of grace, on the other, experience reminds the Fathers and Scholastics that it is also clearly rooted in a nature stained by the consequences of sin. Consequently, the tradition has persistently found it difficult to reconcile these two horizons effectively.

Ouellet speaks of "strange vicissitudes and much groping in the dark"[88] in the history of the sacramentality of marriage, and notes the tendency to understand marriage "almost exclusively from the point of view of 'nature,' even if one affirmed that this nature was 'elevated' by Christ to the dignity of a sacrament."[89] Similarly, noting an impasse in the sacramental theology of marriage in the 1950's, Scola observes how "the theme of the sacramental nature of marriage, as well as that of the link between matrimonial grace, the person of Jesus Christ, and the ecclesial dimension of marriage and the family, were left in the shadows."[90] Like Ouellet, Scola believes the problem to lie in an inability of the tradition to integrate so-called "natural" marriage, with all of its temporal riddles, with the Christ-Church thematic:

> This impasse may have been born of a certain extrinsicism in understanding the connection between the sacrament of marriage and marriage as a natural phenomenon, beginning with a certain way of understanding sacramentality as a pure *superadditum*. This explains, as a consequence, why so little attention

---

86. Paulinius of Nola, "Carmen," 290.
87. Roberts, *Creation and Covenant*, 66.
88. Ouellet, *Divine Likeness*, 217.
89. Ouellet, *Divine Likeness*, 214.
90. Scola, *Nuptial Mystery*, 204.

was given to a direct consideration of the relationship of marriage to the mystery of Jesus Christ."[91]

By the time we arrive in the twentieth century, theological manuals are primarily treating marriage in terms of its hierarchical "ends," the primary end being procreation (*proles*), the secondary, mutual help (*fides*) and the perspective of the sacrament (*sacramentum*).[92] These secondary were further supplemented with the "remedy for concupiscence" (*remedium concupiscentiae*).[93] Given all that we have seen, it was the *sacramentum* which always found itself only awkwardly incorporated into the matrix of marriage, especially in a hierarchical and teleological perspective. While this is not to say that sacramental reflection was lost altogether, the salient point is that the tradition has always found it difficult to reconcile and integrate the sacramental perspective on marriage with the perspective of marriage perceived originally as a properly natural reality and one moreover stained by sin. Even if there have always been verbal affirmations to the contrary,[94] when it comes to the practical task of integrating the two, the sacramental perspective has to varying degrees always tended to be understood as *extrinsic* to the temporal perspective.

Given this puzzle of patristic and scholastic perspectives, it is not surprising that headship more often than not tends to be spoken of as a truth of the relative goodness of a temporal existence drastically affected by sin. That is, it is an operation most often thought of in relation to a femininity marked by imperfection and inferiority and a theology of marriage where sacramentality has not intrinsically and therefore effectively penetrated into the relationship of the spouses. Headship is thus often spoken of as a

---

91. Scola, *Nuptial Mystery*, 204–5.

92. Cf. Augustine, "Excellence of Marriage," 33–61; Aquinas, *Commentary on Corinthians*, 122.

93. "The manuals of moral theology in most common use before the Second Vatican Council unanimously propose the *remedium concupiscentiae* as *one* of the secondary ends of marriage" (Burke, "'*Remedium Concupiscentiae*,'" 498–99). See also Burke's opinion on why the term *remedium concupiscentiae* should be expunged from the tradition (502, 536). Augustine describes the *remedium concupiscentiae* as follows: "When the performance of the marriage duty is insisted on unreasonably, so that they have intercourse even when it is not for the purpose of having children, the apostle allows this as something that can be excused, thought it is not something he lays down as a command. So even if a perverted morality motivates them to have intercourse like that, marriage still saves them from adultery or fornication" (Augustine, "Excellence of Marriage," 37).

94. "Nothing can be further from the truth than to say that the sacrament is a certain added ornament, or outward endowment, which can be separated and torn away from the contract at the caprice of man" (Leo XIII, *Arcanum Divinae*, 24).

remedial measure designed to hold in check the impulses and inclinations of woman's imperfect identity.

This presupposition, when viewed under the auspices of scriptural passages dealing with headship and coupled with the perspective of the curse in Gen 3:16—"because it was in woman that sin first began, her punishment was twice as heavy; for having risen in her pride, she incurred subjection"[95]— makes it easy for commentators to understand St. Paul to essentially be affirming a natural truth of the temporal world. There is little chance left for seeing in the scriptural text itself any indication that headship is a *specifically and originally theological norm*, with roots in the much more than natural and temporal "beginning" of Genesis, and intrinsically and constitutively shaped by Christ's relationship with his Church as opposed to just being extrinsically underwritten and guaranteed by that relationship. Certainly it is informed by the Christ-Church analogy, but since it is already regarded as fully constituted *in naturalibus*, all that grace adds are suggestions concerning the spirit of its interpretation precisely within its temporal domain.

For example, it is true that Aquinas recognizes that "the wife must be obedient to her husband *as the Church is subject to Christ*"[96] but, as we have seen, the potential novelty of this Ephesians passage appears to be lost on him, as he proceeds to explain headship by means of (what we would today call unfortunate) secular illustrations: the "wife is naturally subject to her husband as governor,"[97] and "the relation of a husband to his wife is, in a certain way, like that of a master to his servant, insofar as the latter ought to be governed by the commands of his master."[98] Although he recognizes the dissimilarity between the relationship of master and slave and the relationship of husband and wife—"The difference between these two relationships is that the master employs his servants in whatever is profitable to himself; but a husband treats his wife and children in reference to the common good"—there is little to otherwise indicate that Thomas's understanding of headship is little more than a theistically-colored analogue of an essentially temporal norm.

This approach to headship, conducted within a temporal space understood in some sense to be a fall away from the plan of God, therefore precludes the possibility of a full-blown, archetypal approach from the perspective of an anthropology conceived as a "new creation" (2 Cor 5:17). It makes problematic a distinctly theological-sacramental logic which might radically

---

95. Bonaventure, *Breviloquium*, 6.
96. Aquinas, *Epistle to the Ephesians*, 218 (emphasis added).
97. Aquinas, *Summa Contra Gentiles*, 123.4.
98. Aquinas, *Epistle to the Ephesians*, 217.

transform the logic of temporality and therefore of headship from within. Thus, on the grounds of certain patterns of argumentation employed by the Fathers and Scholastics, there appears little reason to dispute an observation made by Daniel Mark Cere that for them a "woman's state of subordination in marriage is not a theological assertion, but a natural pattern of social relationships that needs to be acknowledged and accommodated."[99]

What can be gained from this exercise is better understanding of the intricate range of theological and anthropological questions that confront the question of the interpretation of conjugal politics. In particular, we have seen how crucial for the question of the divine provenance of fundamental aspects of conjugal politics is the way time, temporality, and bodiliness relate to the creature. If each of these factors are in some sense interpreted as a "fall" from some timeless, eternally, and purely spiritual source rather than a full creation properly speaking, then there can be no *properly theological* place—indeed, no *trinitarian* place—for a conjugal politics. If this is the case, then we end up with either a temporal politics of difference propped up by a divine ordinance, whose hierarchical mandate is at least to some extent forced by the effects of sin (a phenomenon which leads to the male's temporal priority), or we end up with an historical-critical reexamination of time, temporality, and bodiliness, which feeds into the contemporary trend of an egalitarian demythologization of a politics of difference.

Ironically, many of the tenets of both positions, in stressing the relative and temporal dynamic of difference (albeit from "traditional" and "progressive" perspectives respectively), tend to lead in the end to a reduction of any genuinely "ontological" significance of the difference. It is just that one heads in a "traditional" direction and the other in a "progressive" direction; and there are problematic tendencies in each. And both, it would seem, deny in some measure that difference can in fact ascend to the heights of the ontological difference, thereby denying trinitarian analysis anything more than a moral and psychological function, either for or against headship and submission, depending on one's bent.

Before assessing all of this in more depth, we turn now to consider how more historically and culturally conscious modes of exegesis today tackle the question of conjugal politics.

---

99. Cere, "Marriage, Subordination," 103.

An Historical-Critical Exegetical Test Case

It should come as no surprise that it was the historically conscious nineteenth and twentieth centuries that began to question the dominant way of interpreting texts by accenting the time-bound and context-informed character of their framing and contents. German liberal Protestantism turned this into an art form in its historical-critical approach to the Scriptures. With regard to the question of Scriptural texts dealing with conjugal politics, it took little imagination to perceive that here we are obviously dealing with a whole range of time-bound cultural assumptions, whatever we make of any possible broader significance. It is now commonplace for exegetes of all confessional stripes to recognize that the biblical authors, like the early Christian thinkers we just explored, appear to have presumed a whole range of cultural understandings of the politics of spousal difference.

For example, John Paul II is quite comfortable speaking of how the "author of Ephesians is not afraid to accept the concepts that were characteristic of the mentality and customs of that time; he is not afraid of speaking about the submission of the wife to the husband."[100] Elsewhere, he observes here a way of speaking "profoundly rooted in the customs and religious traditions of the time."[101] Speaking of St. Paul's command for wives to be submissive to their husbands, Raniero Cantalamessa claims that "it is true that on this point, St. Paul is at least partly conditioned by the mentality of his time."[102] Benedict Ashley sees in the texts a certain conditioning of the times by "the sinful injustices of sexism" and by "the pastoral gradualism" of St. Paul, and therefore concludes that these texts are "no longer literally normative for us."[103] Cere notes how the author of the social codes of Ephesians and Colossians "seems to be drawn to one particular formulation—the Aristotelian household code."[104] Joseph A. Fitzmyer suggests that "Paul echoes the contemporary view of women in the society of his day when he speaks of the 'husband' as the 'head of the wife.'"[105] These are only several examples, which could today be multiplied indefinitely.

Precisely what one does with this information is of course the ultimately relevant point. For those who go more or less all the way with historical-critical analysis, the above becomes the basis for a maximalist *reduction*

---

100. John Paul II, *Theology of the Body*, 474 (89.5).
101. John Paul II, *Mulieris dignitatum*, 24.
102. Cantalamessa, *Loving the Church*, 72.
103. Ashley, *Justice in the Church*, 47.
104. Cere, "Marriage, Subordination," 94.
105. Fitzmyer, *Paul and His Theology*, 104.

of the significance of a politics of difference, if not its total dismissal. The egalitarian interpretation of difference depends fundamentally on this kind of reading. As a paradigmatic example of how this approach works in a Catholic exegetical context, we turn now to Edward Schillebeeckx's sustained historical-critical exegesis of the text in 1965, which remains a classic example of this approach.

Schillebeeckx begins his study by employing a "form-critical analysis"[106] which immediately draws the exegetical eye to the "secular" character of the household codes [*Haustafeln*] of the New Testament: "These codes were modeled on the secular household codes of the Hellenistic, and especially of the Judeao-Hellenistic, world."[107] He goes on to accentuate how these codes reflect dominant views of women in the ancient world. For example, women were expected to remain silent, to stay in the home, and most importantly, to be subject to their husbands.[108] Schillebeeckx is at pains to stress that the views expressed in the household codes are already derivative, not from categories of divine revelation, but from one particular, contingent culture, a fact which he believes St. Paul himself to be aware of: "Paul's view of woman certainly contains elements which were without question determined by existing social conditions, and . . . to some extent the apostle was undoubtedly aware of these himself."[109] Schillebeeckx must then explain how this body of apparently secular teaching came to be in the biblical text in the first place, what theological weight it may nevertheless carry, and whether or to what extent it might therefore remain normative for Christian spouses of all times and places.

Schillebeeckx argues that St. Paul tries to ground this secular code in a "theological superstructure."[110] He suggests that St. Paul saw in these secular norms something of lasting value, and something that fit nicely with the theme of Christ being the head of his Church:

> In Paul's own time the man, as husband and father, was the head of the wife and of the whole family. For this reason Paul was able, in his revelation of the relationship between Christ and his church, in which Christ was in fact the head, not only to disclose the very profound meaning of Christian marriage as 'one flesh' but to use this reality as a suitable image of the ethos

---

106. Schillebeeckx, *Marriage*, 172.
107. Schillebeeckx, *Marriage*, 171–72.
108. Schillebeeckx, *Marriage*, 178.
109. Schillebeeckx, *Marriage*, 185–86.
110. Schillebeeckx, *Marriage*, 192.

generally accepted at the time of the wife's complete subjection to her husband.[111]

Note here the ground-up approach, one already committed to a view of the proximate cultural foundation of headship and submission as merely secular. And having staked his claim thus on the *secular* character of the code, Schillebeeckx must then treat the christological dimension as a mere add-on superimposed over-top of the human aspect.

In an attempt to justify his use of the Christ-as-head theme, St. Paul adduced scriptural data. "It is clear," observes Schillebeeckx in relation to the Genesis accounts, "that Paul regards the actual [inferior] social status of woman as something ordained by creation."[112] The most important aspect of St. Paul's argument for the support of headship and subordination is made on the basis of the order of creation in the so-called Yahwist creation account of Genesis (Gen 2). Here, the male is created first and the female is created "from" the man "for" the man. But if one reading of St. Paul is to say that he thinks this has an abiding theological origin and value, for Schillebeeckx it indicates to the contrary that the Yahwist account is also conditioned by the same kind of contingent social reasoning he supposes is at play in New Testament texts. In Schillebeeckx's estimation, the Yahwist account presents an "andocentric" view of creation,[113] and "was, in its very formulation, [also] dependent on the actual social status of woman which was prevalent at the time when the tradition gained its form." On this basis, Schillebeeckx sees St. Paul essentially trying to theologically justify one socially contingent body of ideas with another. Schillebeeckx argues that Paul is unsuccessful in this attempt, seeing as he confuses the content of the *imago Dei* with "a social and historical datum which conditioned the Old Testament view" and by this conflation proceeds to the New Testament error of mistaking social and historical data with theological truth.[114] In

---

111. Schillebeeckx, *Marriage*, 195–96.

112. Schillebeeckx, *Marriage*, 189.

113. "The view revealed by this account of creation without a doubt relies on the actual, historical conditioned status of woman at the time" (Schillebeeckx, *Marriage*, 190). Schillebeeckx accepts that it "is a biblical view, but the assertion [about women] itself is not biblical, in the sense that it is revelatory, but rather a framework within which divine revelation could come to men." Schillebeeckx pits this account against the so-called Priestly account of creation, which he apparently regards as the more "biblical" of the two accounts. Here, "there is no mention of the man being the first being and the woman being the second, 'taken out of the man.'" This stands in stark contrast to John Paul II's interpretation of the so-called Yahwist account.

114. Schillebeeckx, *Marriage*, 191.

Schillebeeckx's estimation, Paul's attempts to *theologically* justify headship and subordination subsequently fail.[115]

All of this leads to Schillebeeckx's final judgment about the doctrinal and pastoral status of the teaching of headship and subordination. For him, New Testament teaching about headship and subordination ends up being a contingent pastoral judgment rather than an enduring dogmatic imperative:

> It is quite clear, then, that the Pauline (and for that matter, the Petrine) assertions concerning the subjection of the woman to the man are not dogmatic reactions on Paul's part, but a question of ecclesiastical and hierarchical pastoral guidance within a definite historical setting—a policy in pastoral matters which required arguments to substantiate it and to make it meaningful.[116]

The strongest normative meaning that Schillebeeckx believes may be derived from the text is that the household codes remain a perennial intentional and moral call to live whatever nuptial and familial ordering in which one finds oneself "in the Lord": "We are bound to conclude, therefore, that Paul is saying no more than that Christians should experience the existing social structure of marriage and the family 'in the Lord.'"[117] The biblical text only lends the *impression* that we are dealing with timeless norms because of St. Paul's—ultimately unsuccessful, in Schillebeeckx's estimation—attempts at theological justification. In actual fact, once one strips away the contingent cultural accretions, it can be seen how "Paul inwardly transformed this human fellowship, and saw the woman, though subject to the man, as his 'sister' in Christ."[118] On this basis, St. Paul actually provides a broader basis for an ethic of equality. Once we expose the teaching of headship for what it really is—"a fact determined by social and historical conditions"[119]—we can then free ourselves to be struck by the newness of the Gospel message concerning women.[120]

With a few swift exegetical blows Schillebeeckx is thus able to topple the entire edifice of the Fathers and Scholastics that allowed them to

---

115. Schillebeeckx, *Marriage*, 192.

116. Schillebeeckx, *Marriage*, 200.

117. Schillebeeckx, *Marriage*, 193. In the Protestant context, a similar view is pointed out by Cere: "W. Shrage, Rudolph Schnackenburg, and James Dunn argue that the Pauline and Pastoral *haustafeln* texts represent an exhortation to live under the Lordship of Christ with the institutions of the secular world" (Cere, "Marriage, Subordination," 107).

118. Schillebeeckx, *Marriage*, 198.

119. Schillebeeckx, *Marriage*, 196.

120. See Schillebeeckx's New Testament references in Schillebeeckx, *Marriage*, 199–200.

support headship. One can see how adopting the foregoing analysis essentially means that we no longer need to talk about headship at all, at least in its anthropological iteration. For according to Schillebeeckx, once we recognize the social and historical factors at play in the biblical text, we are obliged to disqualify headship from inclusion in the genuine deposit of faith.[121] Accepting Schillebeeckx's exegetical approach bids one to conclude that headship has nothing to do with immutable truths of anthropological and theological truth. On this reading, then, one could again justifiably invoke Cere's conclusion that a *theological* politics of spousal difference, one that goes all the way down, is a contradiction in terms.

Schillebeeckx's rather ingenious exegetical exercise is a good example of how large swathes of contemporary Catholic and Protestant exegesis stress the perspectival and gradualist dimensions to the Pauline teaching, and thus emphasize the way in which the "spirit" of the text actually serves to undermine any determinate hierarchical content that might otherwise appear to be present. Of course, it varies from author to author as to the extent of this relativization. However, in general, while there may often be a desire to safeguard the biblical text's ability to transcend cultural relativity—"It is always wrong, however, to dismiss any biblical text as a mere relic of the past"[122]—many commentators effectively use this alleged cultural relativity to downplay the importance of the text and soften what are commonly regarded as its more rigid and unappealing contours. All of this we will return to consider (and contest) again in more detail in chapter 4.

New Interpretive Horizons

There can be no question that the above hermeneutical strategy offers a challenge to traditional interpretation, at least if you accept its fundamental terms of engagement. In making their claim for the abrogation of the lasting anthropological and theological significance of spousal and sexual difference, egalitarians capitalize on the perceived *relative* and *temporal* character of conjugal politics—a premise supported with new intensity by historical-critical research—and thus exploit many of the weaknesses and ambiguities (real or imagined) of the preceding tradition.

---

121. Hans Schürmann implies much the same thing: "When the New Testament writers see *the wife as subject to her husband* . . . a view which we can understand as being of its time, we feel that the Holy Spirit has led Christians today, along with the contemporary environment, into a deeper understanding of the moral obligations of personal relationships than that enjoyed by the primitive Christian generation" (Schürmann, "How Normative," 40).

122. Ashley, *Justice in the Church*, 47.

As suggested earlier, we thus discover a paradoxical affinity between the older tradition that reads conjugal politics maximally and the newer that views it minimally. In certain respects, the hermeneutical divide that one might suppose yawns like an abyss between the two positions is in fact not quite so wide as might appear at first glance. In the end, neither position has (at least up until recently) been willing to posit conjugal politics as a properly theological and ontological phenomenon with a fully created, redeemed, and eschatological significance, a datum that belongs in a real way to the very Godhead itself. Both interpretive traditions have begun from the premise that its sharper edges belong more substantially to a relative temporal stage and order than it does to an absolute eternal order, even if in one the relative temporal stage is caught up in the eternal in some real, if extrinsic and somewhat unclear way. That is, the way that a politics of difference works its way out temporally in the context of bodily difference will even for traditional interpretation in some manner eventually be exceeded in a relativizing movement of "spiritualization" in the eschaton. Gender differences and roles will only in the eschaton be overcome: "there is not male and female; for you are all one with Christ" (Gal 3:28).

Very simplistically put, the *divergence* between the two camps tends to arise only at the point where the earlier tradition at least in part interprets the parameters of the temporal order according to the cultural theory and philosophical presuppositions of *that* day (e.g., Greco-Roman culture and philosophy), while the contemporary historical-critical tradition interprets the parameters of the temporal order according to the cultural theory and philosophical presuppositions of *this* day (e.g., Western historicist categories). In the former, the domain of conjugal politics is shaped by a world of clearly defined and intelligible substances, essences, and ends, in a context where the time of Galatians 3:28 has not yet arrived in any substantive way, and hence a maximalist conjugal politics reigns; whereas in the latter, the domain of conjugal politics is shaped by a world of constructed meaning and cultural historicism where the time of Galatians 3:28 *has* in some sense already arrived, and hence a *minimalist* politics holds sway.

However, a new development has appeared in recent years with the introduction of more systematic recourse to trinitarian theology in an effort to try to prop up competing interpretations of conjugal politics. With both contemporary camps of interpretation attempting to adduce greater support for their positions in an embattled context of trenchant debate with much at stake (this is so particularly in evangelical debates), we have seen more willingness to appeal to a more eternal and immutable foundation for the dynamic of conjugal politics. We thereby see both complementarians and egalitarians each inching towards an ontologizing of an otherwise intuitively experienced and regarded temporal and conditionally valid phenomenon—whether this ontologization presupposes an "egalitarian" Trinity or a "hierarchical" Trinity.

What makes this new trinitarian turn potentially problematic is not just that its proponents continue to presuppose many of the unresolved ambiguities and aporias of the patristic and scholastic heritage, but that in then proceeding to invoke the ultimate in divine discourse (*viz*. the Trinity), they more definitively paper over or even rubberstamp these problem areas. While perhaps the most common and overt use of the Trinity is of a merely extrinsic moral and exemplary nature it is also the case that a surreptitious and unexamined kind of analogical thinking has brought ontologizing trends into the evaluation of conjugal politics without sufficiently examining the deeper infrastructural ground of such trends.

So, the complementarian position wants to base the wife's submission to her husband on the Son's eternal subordination to the Father, while the egalitarian position wants to defend the wife's equality with her husband on the basis of the eternal mutuality of the trinitarian persons. Now, this is not to categorically deny that there might well be a trinitarian foundation for "subordination" or that the Trinity will not in some way qualify or indeed erase certain features that belong to temporal constructions of the spousal relationship. But if we do not at a far more basic level first clear up the historical ambiguities associated with the way that temporality interacts with and mediates eternity in the context of the spousal relationship, then we risk importing insufficiently clarified data and imperatives from "below" which then may begin to impose their logic (with all its inadequacies) onto the Trinity, and vice versa. One cannot help but think that much of the trinitarian theology performed today in light of the imperatives of hostile debates over conjugal politics will bear such motivational pollution.

The other risk is that in an attempt to short-circuit the ambiguities of temporality, we instead employ a top-down approach which invokes the doctrinal purity of systematic perspectives of the immanent Trinity, forcing them overtop of the anthropological sphere. In each case, we would do violence to the *maior dissimilitudo* that ought to govern the relation between human and divine predications.

As I see it, the problem with the above is that any insight generated will not have taken seriously enough the question of the "sacramental middle": the way that *both* human *and* divine concepts and understandings are in their anthropological theater crucified and reborn in an original way—such that in the context of the baptized person they are no longer either "human" or "divine" strictly speaking—before they can be employed in the interests of a theological anthropology that seeks to ascend to trinitarian heights. This is as simple as saying that all speech about both human and the divine predicates can only take place from within the economy of salvation. But this must be much more than a merely nominal verbal or mental nod from a subject who otherwise still aspires to an order of knowledge other than his or her adoption, a risk even in the best forms of analogical speech; Barth should be listened to carefully (though not uncritically) here.[123]

I thus want to further specify and radicalize the "form" of this speech by suggesting that it must be a robust and existential *baptismal* speech. It must be speech that bubbles up from within the given conditions of the adopted subjectivity of the child of God the Father who is immersed in this "hybrid" space and time of baptismal existence which is for this child the *only* space and time. I thus think there is something profoundly important about the *who*, the *how*, and *where* of this speech. *Who* is this person who speaks? *How* does this person speak? And *where* does this person speak from?

Here, it is appropriate to employ certain insights from Heidegger's phenomenological approach to Being via his notion of *Dasein*, but with the critical addition of baptismal and sacramental variables as genuinely phenomenological variables therein. Jean-Luc Marion's category of "givenness," similarly more radically inclusive of the dramatic forms of baptismal and sacramental experience, is also an important horizon.[124] In this space, I would speak of baptism as providing the ultimate existential and personal condition of human questioning inasmuch as it has for the one who has received (and nurtured) it radically changed the infrastructure or "geography" of that which informs the thinking, loving, remembering, and willing self. Baptism imposes a sacramental form on the horizon and capacities of the self, one that in a certain sense exceeds the limitations of both the *analogia entis* and the *analogia fides*. This *baptismal "Dasein,"* as it were, is for the baptized believer the horizon of faith that penetrates into the core of the theological person, in some sense re-dimensioning all binary oppositions (faith versus reason, nature versus grace, humanity versus divinity, body versus soul, man versus woman etc.) inside the new microcosm of the baptized subjectivity of the one called, named, loved, redeemed, sanctified, and adopted into the divine life itself through the work of Christ and the Spirit.

Commenting on Heidegger's notion of *Dasein*, David Farrell Krell suggests that Heidegger's central aim in *Being and Time* "is to resist the inclination nurtured by the metaphysical tradition to interpret the Being

---

123. Barth, CD 1/1:26–47. See also Balthasar's sympathetic reading of Barth in Balthasar, *Theology of Karl Barth*. Barth makes his famous pronouncement that "I regard the *analogia entis* as the invention of the Antichrist, and think that because of it one can not become Catholic" (Barth, CD 1/1:x). I certainly do not reject the *analogia entis* per se. Rather, I contend that all possible "analogies" (*analogia entis, analogia fides, analogia relationis, analogia amoris, analogia Trinitatis*) belong inside a prior *analogia baptismi*. This claim will be explicated further in subsequent chapters.

124. Marion, *Givenness and Revelation*.

of *Dasein* by means of categories suited not to human being but to other entities in the universe."[125] For our purposes, this can be revised as *resisting the inclination to measure any existential phenomenon—especially those touched in a specific way by faith—by means of categories suited, not to the being of the baptized person, but to unincorporated possibilities outside baptism*. "Da-sein means," said Heidegger, "being held out into the nothing."[126] Exceeding Heidegger somewhat, to be a Christian is to be willing to hold our being out into the *baptismal* nothing beyond all temporal temptations of abstraction. That is, baptism is the unanticipated and unsupportable historical "nothing" that becomes the radical "something" of faith, an event, a givenness that no human category could conceive on its own, that becomes the new foundation of existence for the believer, allowing a much richer reconciliation of human and divine in the hypostatic personhood of the One in whom they are perfectly balanced.

In this way, I will attempt to nuance and/or outmaneuver the premises supporting both complementarian and egalitarian positions, past and present, by going beyond an a-sacramental temporal domain interpreted either by closed metaphysical or historical-critical theorizing. Ultimately, if the Scriptural text and the Trinity speak to us about conjugal politics, *they will speak to us through baptism*, through the existential subjectivity of the adopted child of the Father who in the Son—and only in the Son—is brought inside the trinitarian relations.

In the meantime, however, we move now to Trainor's attempt to navigate beyond the complementarian and egalitarian framing of the debate, especially as it concerns the trinitarian question. Where I will evade a direct confrontation with this debate, Trainor deals with it head-on. Here, he will offer what I take to be an important and fundamental step in re-imagining a trinitarian discourse more adequate to a baptismal framing. While Trainor does not use this language or attempt to develop the problem in the direction that I am now suggesting, he nevertheless presupposes a kind of "fontal" conception of Christian existence wherein the question of spousal politics can never be held hostage to a dialectical conservative-liberal either-or. This is to say I think that Trainor has what I would call deeply baptismal instincts. His fundamental instinct and *modus operandi* are to approach the question at hand with a keen sense that conjugal politics can in its fundamentally revealed character be neither complementarian or egalitarian. To his contribution we now turn.

---

125. Krell, "General Introduction," 19.
126. Heidegger, "What is Metaphysics," 103.

2

The Trinity and Male Headship of the Family

This chapter is an attempt to break through the current impasse between egalitarian and conservative Christians on the Trinity and male headship of the family.[1] "Egalitarian" Christians broadly assume that to take differences seriously is to endorse inequality and that to even speak of men and women having different but complementary roles in family and community life is to employ a kind of "ideological/religious" language whose real intent is to subordinate women to men and to legitimize unequal and oppressive power relations between the sexes. "Conservative" Christians are aware that there is a very real danger that the language of Scripture ("Wives obey your husbands"), when selectively and selfishly employed against the whole spirit and intent of the Pauline teachings, could be manipulated in just this way, but they are convinced that to hold that these teachings are "all about unequal power relations and the justification of male hegemony"—we might call this the "deep anti-subordinationist conviction" of egalitarians—is to miss altogether the beauty and truth of what St. Paul says and the liberation that it promises.

It is no secret that deep suspicion has arisen between the "anti-subordinationist" egalitarian camp and the "pro-difference" conservative camp. The fact that the anti-subordinationist conviction has sunk so deeply into the unconscious roots of egalitarian theology and become a kind of unquestionable and untouchable "holy cow" may tempt conservative evangelicals to conclude that serious dialogue with the "egalitarian camp" is impossible, just as the pro difference convictions (and their depth) of

---

1. Trainor's contribution here was originally published under the same title in *Heythrop Journal* 52.5 (2011) 724–38. It is reproduced here with kind permission and just a few minor adjustments, mostly of a stylistic nature. For a helpful commentary on Trainor's article, see Peter J. Leithart's review, Leithart, "Trinity and Headship"–CS.

conservatives may similarly lead egalitarians to conclude that dialogue with the "conservative camp" is unlikely to bear much fruit.[2]

Against this backdrop, the recent work of Kevin Giles is important and engenders hope, because even though it is thoroughly permeated by the deep anti-subordinationist conviction of egalitarian theology, and despite the fact that his main critical target is ideologies of subordinationism (of the Son eternally to the Father in the Trinity and of wives to their husbands in the family), Giles at least takes seriously the "equal but different and complementary" position of the conservative camp. For example, he takes note of Raymond Ortland's insistence that the allocation of different roles to men and women by God does not infer the inferiority of women[3] and that, in Ortland's own words, there is "no necessary relation between personal role and personal worth,"[4] before proceeding to offer his reasons as to why he thinks the "equal but different and complementary" position should be rejected. Hence, it is important for conservatives to acknowledge and applaud the fact that he is very open to serious dialogue and invites communication "across the borders," so to speak. His work may serve then as a meeting-point for direct, tension-reducing "peace" discussion between two hostile camps hitherto largely accustomed to dealing with each other from afar and to delivering blows (or slogans) against each other from a safe rhetorical distance. This chapter is my own contribution to this discussion.

I will argue that many conservative Christians have been too heavily hierarchical in their approach, too strongly and narrowly focused on what they see as the "single sovereignty" of the Father (the eternal subordination of the Son to the Father in authority in the inner life of the Trinity) and insufficiently attentive to what I call the "triple sovereignty" of the Trinity (the sovereignty of each of the Persons of the Trinity in different and balancing respects). I will suggest that this narrow and one-sided focus on their part actually obfuscates and derails (and is certainly not of critical importance for or essential to) their two main contentions, that is, first, that the egalitarian denial of any real differentiation in the inner life of the Trinity leads, to use Robert Letham's expression, to "a thoroughgoing homogenization of the

---

2. In chapter five of my *Christ, Society, and the State*, I hold (i) that only a common consciousness of the importance of our membership of a single political community can help us to deal with the "culture wars" that currently plague modern pluralist societies and (ii) that the key task or challenge of public policy and debate is to transform divisions within the body politic into complementary aspects of the social whole (the single political community to which we belong). The same holds true when dealing with the "culture wars" within the community of the Church.

3. Giles, *Trinity and Subordinationism*, 158.

4. Ortland, "Male-Female Equality," 111.

[divine] persons in fully mutual relations"[5] and, secondly, that the kind of differentiation we find in the inner life of the Trinity is echoed (expressed in human terms) in the "inner life" of the "father-headed" family.

I begin in section one by making an important distinction between the use of ontological and immanent language to refer to the inner life of the Trinity, for with this distinction in mind we can more clearly see a major weakness in the egalitarian approach to the Trinity, the deleterious effect of which is that Christians find that they are impeded from saying important things about the Trinity that they need to say. In section two, I argue that conservatives are right to criticise the egalitarian approach to the Trinity for "homogenising" the three Divine Persons and that Giles in particular, as a prominent representative of the egalitarian point of view, fails to substantiate his claim that he endorses true or genuine differentiation in the inner life of the Trinity just as much as his conservative opponents do. However, in this section I also argue that it is a mistake to hold, as many conservative Christians do, that the Father exercises a kind of sole, single sovereignty and has a kind of overall priority in the inner life of the Trinity, and in section three I hold that, on the contrary, the inner life of the Trinity (God *ad intra*) consists of "three sovereignties *for* each other." I suggest that the Father is sovereign as the "author-ial" source of all that is, that the Son is sovereign as the supreme, absolute "object" of the Father's Being and disposition and as the eternally beloved object of his being as Father, and that the Spirit is sovereign in the sense that love, or the Spirit of Love, is the supreme, sole and eternal "origin and end" of the life of the Trinity. I then argue in section four that the inner life of the Trinity (the "three sovereignties for each other") is imaged in a family where the Spirit of love is sovereign, where the wife/mother is the sole, sovereign, absolute end of her husband's being as husband/father, and where the father, because he is, as father, none other than "consciousness of his wife (and child)," bears the sovereign, loving presence of the Father, through Christ, into the life of the family as a whole.

Ontological and Immanent Language

Ever since it became widely acknowledged that a distinction needs to be made between the triune God as he is in Himself apart from history (God *ad intra*) and the triune God that is revealed to us in history and Scripture (God *ad extra*), commentators have used expressions such as "the immanent Trinity," "the essential Trinity," "the ontological Trinity," and "the transcendental Trinity" to distinguish the former (God as he is in Himself)

---

5. Letham, *Holy Trinity*, 392.

from the latter ("God acting in the world for us," "God *pro nobis*," "God for us"—the economic Trinity). However, it would be helpful, I believe, if we made a further distinction between "the essential Trinity" (and "the immanent Trinity") on the one hand, and "the ontological Trinity" (and "the transcendental Trinity") on the other. What I am suggesting is that (i) where possible, our talk of "the ontological Trinity" should refer to *God's being*, to God's *ousia*, to the reality or substance shared by the Persons of the Trinity by virtue of which (that is, by virtue of their shared participation in this one Being), they are each fully God, and that (ii) where possible, our talk of "the essential Trinity" should refer to *God's communal mode of being*, to God as he is in Himself (*Esse in se*), to the inner communal life of Father, Son and Spirit which is God's eternal way of being.

In this way, our ontological language, as applied to God, would refer more strictly to his Being or "that-ness," whereas our immanent/essential language, as applied to God, would refer to his Being-in-itself, to his living "whatness" or, for want of a better expression, to the infinite riches of the inner triune life, the differentiated life of the Trinity as "experienced" by Father, Son, and Spirit. In our use of ontological terms, we would be focusing on the Being of God, whereas when we seek terms to convey the inner life of God, we would use the language of essence, in the sense of "being-in-itself" (*esse-in-se*) or "inner differentiated being," and not in the sense of *ousia* or substance. It must always be borne in mind, however, that both types of language, as they refer to God, are attempts to convey "what fundamentally is," (namely (i) God's Being and (ii) God's tri-personal mode of Being) and that it is both proper and understandable (indeed inevitable) that these two types of language should converge and overlap. God *in se*, we need to recollect, is God's "Being *in se*' or '*Esse in se.*" Ultimately, the two types of language/meaning must converge, for God's Being is the eternal, living, real universal (God) that embraces and differentiates the three divine Persons (subsistences).

With this distinction in mind, we can more clearly see a general weakness in the Giles/egalitarian approach to the Trinity. "What fundamentally is" is the Being of God, God's Being as shared by Father, Son and Spirit, and "what fundamentally is" is God's mode of Being, God's threefold, inner life or essence (God's *esse-in-se*, being-in-itself, or the communal being of Father, Son and Spirit for each other). As Cornelius Van Til once remarked, in the Trinity, "the one and the three are equally ultimate."[6] However, a major problem with the egalitarian analysis of the Trinity is that it allows us to speak of "what fundamentally is" in the ontological sense but not in the

---

6. Van Til, *Defence of the Faith*, 25.

immanent or essential sense, and thus hampers Christians from saying what they need to say. Concerning God, Christians believe and want to say (and to use whatever ontological terms they find to be adequate) that he is One, that "what fundamentally is" is Unity or the One Being of God and that this One Being is shared by three Persons. At the same time, they also want to say (and to use whatever immanent terms they find to be adequate) that God is somehow internally differentiated into three distinct Persons, that he is "threefold," that "what fundamentally is" is Diversity or Differentiation in the inner (immanent) life of God, but this is precisely what Giles hampers us from saying. Since, for Christians, God is eternally "Unity and Diversity," or "Unity-in-and-through-Diversity," we need the most appropriate terms we can find to express the aspect of diversity or inner differentiation in God (the mode of God's Being or threefold inner life) but this is where the egalitarian approach is distinctly unhelpful, as we shall see by considering Giles's criticism of John Frame and Letham.

Frame rejects unequivocally "the ontological subordination of Arius"[7] but maintains that the Son willingly submits to the Father's authority and, concerning the inner life of the Trinity, he speaks quite unselfconsciously and unapologetically of "the eternal nature of the persons, the personal properties that distinguish each one from the others" and of "the distinctiveness of each."[8] Giles believes that Frame is here saying that the "divine persons are ontologically differentiated" and that "they are not one in being as the Nicene Creed affirms,"[9] whereas in fact what Frame says is entirely innocent and orthodox. He quite routinely employs one type of language to refer (ontologically) to God's Being or oneness of Being, to the sameness of Father, Son and Spirit as God, and another type of language to refer (immanently or essentially) to the differences that constitute the inner life of the Trinity. Thus Giles will allow us to use only one kind of language (ontological) to speak of the Trinity and fails to acknowledge the appropriateness and necessity of the second kind of language (immanent or essential).

Likewise, when Letham says that "it is impossible to separate the human obedience of Christ from who he is,"[10] Giles is persuaded that Letham here means "his being,"[11] whereas what Letham in fact means is not the Son's Being as God, in which case he is identical to, or the same ontologically as, the Father and the Spirit, but the Son's Being as Son, in

7. Frame, *Doctrine of God*, 720.
8. Frame, *Doctrine of God*, 723.
9. Giles, *Jesus and the Father*, 23.
10. Letham, *Holy Trinity*, 396.
11. Giles, *Jesus and the Father*, 24.

which case he is different immanently, or in the inner life of the Trinity, from the Father and the Spirit. Finally, when Giles takes issue with the Sydney Anglican Diocesan Doctrine Commission Report for making the (in his view) startling claim that the Athanasian creed clearly witnesses to a belief in "differences of being" of Father, Son, and Spirit, he fails to realize that that there is nothing startling or unorthodox in speaking in this way of "differences of being," provided that this expression is taken in the immanent sense that the authors of the report clearly intended and not in the ontological sense that Giles supposes. It is both interesting and highly significant that when Giles quotes the report as saying that the Son's submission to the authority of the Father "arises from the very nature of his being as Son,"[12] he italicizes the words "very nature of his being"[13] and thereby (i) attempts to give the expression an ontological meaning that the report's authors never intended and (ii) overlooks the immanent/essential meaning that the authors of the report clearly had in mind and that could have been highlighted by italicizing the words "as Son."

The same "error of ontologism" appears when Giles, commenting on Robert Doyle's assertion that he [Doyle] cannot see how terms "like 'essence,' 'being,' 'eternal nature'" can be avoided "in talking about who they [the Divine Persons] are in their differences,"[14] states that here "we have divine differentiation ontologically grounded."[15] Again, he misses Doyle's point (and the point broadly made by the conservative camp) that divine differentiation "fundamentally is," not in the ontological sense, but in the sense that it is grounded (immanently) in the inner life of the Trinity itself, that is, in the way in which the three Persons of the Trinity are collectively God in their "being-for-each-other." We could perhaps summarise all of the above by saying that "Subsistence is immanent; Being is ontological," meaning that subsistence (existence in or as, or being in or as) is an immanent, rather than an ontological category/term, that Being (Being as such) is an ontological, rather than an immanent category/term and that the two terms, though different in reference and meaning, are relative to and complement each other.

---

12. Sydney Anglican Diocesan Commission, "Doctrine of the Trinity," 18.
13. Giles, *Jesus and the Father*, 25.
14. Doyle, "Are We Heretics?," 13.
15. Giles, *Jesus and the Father*, 27.

Homogenization and Differentiation

In this section, I argue that the conservatives are right to criticise the Giles/egalitarian approach to the Trinity for "homogenising" the three Divine Persons and that Giles in particular fails to substantiate his claim that he believes in true or genuine differentiation in the inner life of the Trinity just as much as they do. Indeed, I would go so far as to say that in the Giles/egalitarian account of the Trinity, the terms "Father" and "Son" are virtually evacuated of any real meaning; it is readily conceded in the Giles/egalitarian account that they love each other as "Persons" but no attempt is made to articulate their distinctiveness or the mode of their "inner-relatedness" and differentiation. In this account, the distinction between "Father and Son" becomes virtually indistinguishable from the distinction between "A1 and A2" or between "Person A and Person B"; that is, the distinction becomes virtually a merely numerical or nominal one. (Interestingly, this homogenization of the Trinity is duplicated in Giles's account of the family, for though he describes himself as an "egalitarian complementarian," yet for him the biblically informed "egalitarian-complementary ideal" envisages "men and women standing side by side, equal in dignity and authority in the world, the church and the home"[16] which certainly tells us how he thinks men and women are the same in marriage but not how they are different from each other or have complementary roles.)

One can imagine these homogenized Divine Persons of the Trinity having a profound regard and respect for each other, like human persons sharing a common humanity and exhibiting mutual respect, regard and a warm "fellow-feeling" towards each other, but one simply cannot understand or imagine how Divine Persons, reduced to their sameness as God, their sameness as Divine Persons (their "ontological sameness"), but deprived of any real differentiation in their mode of being and their inner relations (this is what I mean by "homogenized Persons"), can eternally love each other with a love so intense that the Holy Spirit eternally proceeds therefrom. Indeed, a curious effect of the Giles/egalitarian analysis is that everyday human love in the family is more intelligible than the divine love of Father and Son. We can understand a human father loving his son, or a wife loving her husband, but we can only regard with dismay, and acknowledge as unintelligible ("mysterious" in a derogatory rather than a sublime sense), the divine love for each other of the Father and Son (now effectively reduced to undifferentiated Persons, and viewed only in terms of their sameness as God).

---

16. Giles, *Trinity and Subordinationism*, 157.

It is, I would submit, insufficient for Giles to concede that "Scripture tells us the first two persons of the Trinity are in some ways like human fathers and sons,"[17] for whilst he certainly tells us a great deal about why he thinks conservatives are mistaken in their view of the way in which the first two persons of the Trinity are like human fathers and sons (that is, in differing in authority), he fails to provide us with a positive account of the ways in which they substantively are, in his view, like human fathers and sons.

When Giles agrees (i) that the Father "is the Father of the Son, and the Son is the Son of the Father,"[18] that there is an operational order among the divine persons, as expressed in Basil's formula ("Each act of God is initiated by the Father, effected by the Son, and perfected by the Spirit"), and that the "divine three work inseparably but not identically"[19] and (ii) that there is also complementarity and differentiation in the human family, he believes that this is sufficient to silence his conservative opponents. He cannot, it might be said, be criticized for "homogenizing" the Persons of the Trinity when he avows that that the "divine three work inseparably but not identically." He certainly insists that he believes in a real differentiation within the inner life of the Persons of the Trinity (and in the life of the human family) just as much as his conservative opponents do.

However, the criticism still stands, for the "promise" of these concessions is not delivered in his work on the Trinity and the human family in the way in which it is delivered in the work of his conservative opponents. Concerning the human family, the only differentiation he will allow is sexual differentiation/complementarity; he holds that men and women "are differentiated by their God-given sexual nature"[20] but this, he insists, does not imply any other kind of differentiation or complementarity and hence he leaves himself open to the charge generally levelled at the egalitarian position, namely that of advocating "an unqualified equation of the sexes"[21] and of misusing and misunderstanding the concept of equality itself.[22]

With regard to the Trinity, the contrast between the two opposing camps is clear and strong. Giles believes that "differing the divine persons by nature, being, essence or subsistence denies the homousian principle enshrined in the Nicene Creed" and that if the three Divine Persons are "one in

---

17. Giles, *Jesus and the Father*, 176.
18. Giles, *Jesus and the Father*, 51.
19. Giles, *Jesus and the Father*, 50.
20. Giles, *Trinity and Subordinationism*, 186.
21. Ortland, "Male-Female Equality," 99.
22. O'Donovan, *Desire of the Nations*, 280.

being, they cannot be divided in work/function or authority."[23] In contrast, the conservative Christians that Giles criticises believe that to distinguish the Divine Persons by nature, mode of being, essence or subsistence is not only fully consistent with, but is actually required by a true understanding of, the homousian principle enshrined in the Nicene Creed. This is because, as I shall now proceed to explain, Giles is thinking (wrongly) in terms of "unity-despite (or against)-differentiation" (absolute sameness or oneness), whereas the conservative evangelicals are thinking (rightly) in terms of "unity-through-differentiation" (relative sameness or oneness).

In the Giles/egalitarian account of the Trinity, the three Persons have an (illusory, false) "absolute" rather than a (real, true) "relative" sameness. Though you and I are identical (the same) as persons, yet since I am Irish, sexually embodied as male, married to Marie, etc., my personhood, though the same as yours, is not absolutely so. "Persons" do not actually exist as (absolutely) identical monads separated from each other in space and time [X + X + X] and nor do the Persons of the Trinity subsist in eternity [X + X + X] in such a fashion. We are the same as persons or share the same personhood but this sameness (universality) always exists in and through differentiation (relative sameness), rather than uniformly in all instances (absolute sameness).

In the same way, when we say that the Father and the Son have or share the same will, we should not have in mind two absolutely identical, though separately entertained, wills [X + X] but rather the same will "differenced" into the subsistences of the Father and Son. With regard to the one will or "common family will" of Father and Son, we have, or should have, relative rather than absolute sameness in mind, and we certainly should not say that in the immanent (*ad intra*) Trinity the Son is eternally submissive or obedient to the Father or the Father's will; Father, Son and Spirit share the same trinitarian will. The unity of will of the Persons of the Trinity is a differentiated unity. Each Person of the Trinity entertains the same "family will" or "trinitarian will" but they entertain it differently. (Personally, I am not persuaded that the Cappadocians, when grappling with what it meant to say that the will of the Father and the will of the Son are one and the same, were helpful in speaking of a coincidence of willing in the Persons of the Trinity, for this to me implies separate, absolutely identical "wills" entertained by non-differentiated Persons [X + X + X].) Giles speaks as if God's "sameness" (the sameness of Father, Son and Spirit as one God) could be directly and uniformly inserted into God's "differences/diversity" (the mode of being of the Father as distinct from the mode of being of

---

23. Giles, *Jesus and the Father*, 60.

the Son, etc.) or as if God's "Being-in-unity" could be directly transposed into, or superimposed upon, his "Being-in-relation"; he is convinced that "what God is as being-in-unity he is as being-in-relation,"[24] whereas his opponents hold that what God is as Being-in-unity, he is through Being-in-relation. Because they appreciate that the unity of the Christian God is a "unity-in-and-through-diversity," the conservative camp can clearly see what Giles fails to see, namely that the three Divine Persons can and must be distinguished in terms of work/function and authority; otherwise, it is simply pointless and vacuous to concede, as Giles appears to do, that the "divine three work inseparably but not identically."[25]

In a similar fashion, the problem with Giles maintaining (quite correctly) that if "the divine persons eternally coexist in perfect communion and self-giving love, they must be always of one mind and one will"[26] is that he has "absolute sameness of will" in mind (an absolutely identical will duplicated, so to speak, in each of the three Persons) and he believes that it is only with this kind of sameness in mind that we should speak of the one mind and one will of the Trinity; he assumes that advocates of the "social-familial" model of the Trinity, since they believe in three persons of the Trinity, must subscribe to the view that there are three (absolutely) different wills in the inner life of the Trinity.[27] What he fails to see is (i) that when Jürgen Moltmann says that the Trinity is "three Persons-one family"[28] or when exponents of the "social/familial" model of the Trinity speak of the divine Persons submitting to each other, they are thinking in terms of "relative sameness," that is, of one trinitarian or triune will that is differently entertained, and (ii) that their "relative" understanding of the "one will and mind" of the Trinity (that is, in terms of "relative sameness") is consistent with and reinforces true differentiation in the inner life of the Trinity, whereas his own "absolute" understanding of the "one will and mind" of the Trinity is inconsistent with and undermines any real differentiation in the Trinity.

The central insight of the conservative camp is well expressed by Doyle when he insists that the Father is a "real father" and that the Son "is a real son" (neither names are "metaphorical"[29]) and by Letham when he speaks against "a thoroughgoing homogenization of the [divine] persons in fully mutual relations."[30] Certainly, conservative evangelicals are right to

24. Giles, *Jesus and the Father*, 60–61 (emphasis added).
25. Giles, *Jesus and the Father*, 50.
26. Giles, *Jesus and the Father*, 238.
27. Giles, *Jesus and the Father*, 238.
28. Moltmann, *Trinity and the Kingdom*, 199.
29. Doyle, "Are We Heretics?," 10.
30. Letham, *Holy Trinity*, 392.

forthrightly reject the kind of homogenization of the Persons of the Trinity effected by the Giles/egalitarian analysis and its minimalist approach to diversity and differentiation within the inner life of the Trinity. However, not every kind of differentiation is acceptable; for example, it is surely a mistake to hold, as many conservatives do, that the Father has a kind of overall priority in the inner life of the Trinity and to suggest, as Norman Geisler does, that in the Trinity the Father's "function is superior"[31] or to speak, as Doyle does, of "the priority of the Father in intraTrinitarian relations."[32] To speak in this way of the priority of the Father, and of the Son's eternal submission to the Father's will, is surely to give the impression that Father, Son and Spirit do not share the same trinitarian will (one common will differentiated into three divine subsistences) but that they each have their own "separately entertained" wills. Now this, surely, is to set us on a pathway leading to tri-theism (three Gods; three wills) or else to the idea that the one will of God is the will of the Father, to which Son and Spirit are subject, in which case the Father is alone "truly God" (one God; two "lesser gods" or the one "modalistic" God, known as Father, Son or Spirit as the occasion requires). Giles is surely right to point out that "orthodoxy with one voice insists that the three divine persons have one will and always work in perfect harmony and unison,"[33] even if he has the wrong sense of unity (absolute rather than relative) in mind.

A difficult question that arises at this point is whether or not it is proper to identify the unbegotten Father with the self-contained intelligibility of God, the universal God containing all within "itself" but not "itself" contained or included within the life of a higher universal. My own response is to say that in so far as we, as Christians (and not just as Eastern Christians), think of the Father as unbegotten and the Son as begotten, our minds naturally tend to associate the Father with the source of divinity and this tendency is, I think, both sound and orthodox. The Cappadocians, for example, held that the Father is the source (*arche*) or cause (*aitia*) of the being of the Son and is the *monarche* of divinity, and many Western Christians regard the Father as the first principle or *principium* of the Godhead. However, as well as allowing our minds to take proper account of the term "begotten" as applied to the Son, we must also dwell on and appreciate the full significance of the qualifier "eternally," for we will then see that the Son is eternally in the heart of the Father and, as such, is eternally and equally divine. God is eternally unity-in-diversity; there is no unity prior to diversity.

---

31. Geisler, *Systematic Theology*, 290.
32. Doyle, "Are We Heretics?," 9–10, 14.
33. Giles, *Jesus and the Father*, 30.

God is one Being eternally expressed in three Persons. We must do our utmost to somehow rid our minds of the temporal residue that clings to the term "begotten," for the more we succeed in doing so, the more we will be able to properly grasp the full eternal divinity of the Son and the Spirit and the more we will appreciate that the Son is ever in the heart of the Father. The Father is indeed the first principle of the Godhead but he is never alone. He eternally subsists as Father of the Son. As Athanasius remarks, the Son "is the Father's Image and Word eternal, never having not been, but being ever, as the eternal Radiance of a Light which is eternal."[34]

To identify the Father with God, with God as such or with "true" divinity, or to speak of "the priority of the Father in intra-Trinitarian relations,"[35] especially if this priority is understood in a general or "over-all" sense, is in effect to undermine the Fatherhood of God, for it is part of the essence of "being a father" to be included in, or to be an integral part of, an enveloping reality (the "family" life of the Trinity). To be in relationship with another is constitutive of a person's (or Person's) identity as father (or Father). God, not Father, is the inclusive, enveloping universal or reality. Indeed, "God," considered as a universal (or whole) containing its three particulars (or parts/Persons), is in this respect not unlike "family," for just as the "parts" (father, mother, son) of the latter are unintelligible apart from their enfolding "whole" or universal (the family), so too the divine Father and Son are unintelligible apart from their enfolding "whole" or universal, namely the "family" or "communion" of God, the inclusive unity and reality that enfolds the Persons of the Trinity and makes them who they are.

The Trinity: Single Sovereignty or Triple Sovereignty

Rather than thinking in terms of the priority of the Father, it is preferable, I wish to maintain, to regard the inner life of the Trinity (God *ad intra*) as consisting of "three sovereignties for each other," rather than to regard the Trinity as a "functional hierarchy" in the manner suggested by Bruce Ware. He claims that the position or proper role of the Son of God in this functional hierarchy vis-à-vis the Father is to be "equal in being, eternally subordinate in role," for there is an "eternal relationship of authority and obedience grounded in the eternal immanent inner-Trinitarian relations of Father, Son and Holy Spirit."[36] In a similar vein, George Knight speaks of a

---

34. Athanasius, "Four Discourses," 314.
35. Doyle, "Are We Heretics?," 14.
36. Ware, "How Shall We Think?," 270.

"chain of subordination" in the inner life of the Trinity,[37] Letham refers to the Son as submitting "to the Father in eternity,"[38] and Wayne Grudem holds that while the Father and the Son are both divine, yet the Son is eternally subordinate in role and authority to the Father, for the Father has "the role of commanding, directing, and sending" and the Son has "the role of obeying, going as the Father sends, and revealing God to us."[39] Geisler, as we have seen, goes so far as to say that the Father's "function is superior"[40] and that the functional subordination of the Son to the Father in the Godhead "is not just temporal and economical: it is essential and eternal."[41] In contrast, my recommendation is that we should acknowledge that the Son is sovereign as the supreme, absolute "object" of the Father's Being and disposition. What is in the "mind" of the Father is sovereign but what is in the mind of the Father is the Son, the eternally beloved object of his being as Father, in much the same way as a mother "is" (almost, indeed, is nothing but) the "consciousness of her new-born child." The Son is the "eternal, absolute end" of his (God's) being as Father; the Father is the "eternal, absolute origin" of his (God's) being as Son, and this "sovereignty" of each in the "divine consciousness/perspective" (for want of a better term) of the other "is" (or eternally generates) the Holy Spirit. The Spirit is sovereign in the sense that love, or the Spirit of Love, is the supreme, sole and eternal "origin and end" of the life of the Trinity, whereas the Father is sovereign, not so much in authority, as in the sense that he is the "author-ial" source of all that is. The Father has what Tom Smail refers to as "originating" or "initiating" sovereignty.[42] He is the original Author in the sense that he creates the world of time through the Son, who may be said to "author" the will of the Father into existence. The Father is Author; the Son Authors; the Son is the "verb" of the Father's "noun." The Son is the Word of God and very God.

This idea of the triple sovereignty of the Persons of the Trinity, or of what Millard Erickson calls their "mutual submission" to each other[43] and what Frame calls their "mutual deference" to each other,[44] is present in the work of conservative Christians but it is not emphasized and it seems that it has, indeed, become increasingly de-emphasized. Grudem, for example,

37. Knight, *New Testament Teaching*, 33.
38. Letham, *Holy Trinity*, 495.
39. Grudem, *Systematic Theology*, 250.
40. Geisler, *Systematic Theology*, 290.
41. Geisler, *Systematic Theology*, 291.
42. Smail, *Like Father, Like Son*, 102–3.
43. Erickson, *God in Three Persons*, 333.
44. Frame, *Doctrine of God*, 695.

who is perhaps the most well-known exponent of conservative evangelical theology at the present time, holds that "supreme authority always belongs to the Father"[45] and that the expression "seated at the right hand of the Father" indicates that Jesus is second to God the Father in authority. However, I would suggest that we should think, rather, in terms of the Son having all authority and the Father having none. Jesus is not second to the Father in authority, for Jesus is the Word of the Father, is the authority of the Father as original Author, is the One who conveys, "authors," makes present, bears, crystallises and expresses in his Person, the Father as original Author. The Father is the original, eternally begetting Author of all, the font whence his initiating sovereignty flows through Christ into the universe, the "Author-as such" whose author-ial presence is eternally borne or expressed by the Son; it is his authorial presence, eternally begetting the Son, that lives in and is expressed in the Son. As Athanasius remarks, for "as the Father is first, so also is he [the Son] as the image of the first."[46] Athanasius regards as wholly unscriptural the suggestion that the Son came into being by the Father's "will and pleasure," for he "is himself the Father's living counsel (*patros agathon boulema*) and power."[47] As Alvyn Pettersen notes, for Athanasius "The Logos is the Father's will, and is not the consequence of the Father's will."[48]

Corresponding to the eternal flow of the initiating sovereignty of the Father through the Word to the world, there is, so to speak, an eternal reverse flow, empowered by the Spirit, from the world, through the Son back to the Father. In this scheme, Christ's death and burial ends the "incarnational flow" from the Father to the world through the Son, and Christ's resurrection begins the reverse flow from the world through the Son to the Father, culminating in 1 Cor 15 24–28 where Paul speaks of Christ returning all rulership and authority to the Father, the original "initiating" Author. In all of this, I think, we can hear distant echoes from the inner life of the Trinity itself or the "heartbeat" of God himself. Through the economy of salvation (God *ad extra*) or through our sense of the "twin flows" we have just considered, perhaps we can catch a glimpse of this inner divine life (God *ad intra*), that is, of the never beginning/never ending flow of the love of the eternally begetting Father to the Son in the Spirit and of the eternal reverse flow of the love of the eternally begotten Son to the Father through the Spirit.

---

45. Grudem, *Evangelical Feminism*, 412.
46. Athanasius, "Four Discourses," 398–99.
47. Athanasius, "Four Discourses," 428–29.
48. Pettersen, *Athanasius*, 172.

The Trinity and the Family

The inner life of the Trinity (God *ad intra*) consists of "three sovereignties for each other" and the "outer" life of the Trinity (God *ad extra*) consists of "three sovereignties for each of us and our worlds."[49] This inner life of the Trinity (the three sovereignties for each other) is imaged in a family where the Spirit of love is sovereign and bears new life through the love of husband and wife for each other, where the wife/mother is the sole, sovereign, absolute end of her husband's being as husband/father, and where the father, because he is, as father, none other than "consciousness of his wife (and child)," bears ("author-ially" carries, represents, and expresses) the sovereign, loving presence of the Father, through Christ, into the life of the family as a whole; *this, and only this, is the true, ultimate meaning and purpose of the father's authority.*

Interestingly, what Basil says of the "transmission of will" between Father and Son—that a commandment of the Father is not a "peremptory mandate" that "gives orders to the Son," but "the transmission of will, like the reflection of an object in a mirror, passing without note of time from Father to Son"[50]—could be said just as truly of the "transmission of authority" between Father and Son, and, ideally, even, of the "transmission of authority" between father and family; in each case, there is a differentiation of the same authority into a series of different forms (the authority of Christ, of the father, of the mother) or a series of successive crystallizations of the Authorial presence of the Father into the authorial presence (authority) of the Son, of the father and of the mother. Perhaps we could also view the "operational order" of the inner differentiated life of the Trinity described by Basil—"Each act of God is initiated by the Father, effected by the Son, and perfected by the Spirit"—as the ultimate "paradigmatic" source of the "operational order" of the inner differentiated life of the family. Thus, what Basil refers to as the initiating or headship role of the Father—what we might call the Father's original, eternal, unbegotten "author-ial" presence—would be reflected and imaged, through Christ, in the headship role of every father in the life of the family; what he refers to as the effecting role of the Son would be reflected and imaged by the mother through whom the life of the Father is borne forth or "effected"—mirroring the role of the Son in Creation as a whole—and what he refers to as the perfecting role of the Spirit would

---

49. The term "*ad intra*," as applied to God, is immanent rather than ontological in meaning, since it refers to God's inner differentiated life (his mode of Being) rather than to his Being as such but the term "*ad extra*" as applied to God refers to the essential/immanent life of God as it is revealed to us and for us.

50. Basil, "On the Spirit," 14.

be reflected in the birthing of new life in the family and bringing it to the fullness of life intended by the Father.

Because, ultimately, all life and holiness comes from the Father and returns to the Father, there is an important respect in which God the Father is dissimilar to an earthly father. Since the latter has authority, whose whole purpose is to serve the well-being of his wife and children, he is unlike our Heavenly Father, who has no authority but who is both its source and its ultimate point. This means that a wife, when viewed in this way as the end or final purpose of authority (male headship), is more akin to the heavenly Father than her husband, and that a daughter is more akin to the heavenly Father than her father. Seeing his wife and child in this way, a father will not exercise "authority over" in the sense of issuing commands and "peremptory mandates" to members of his family but will exercise "authority through," in the sense of transmitting (differentiating, crystallizing) the authority (the authorial presence) of Christ into the life of the family. This is the kind of servant headship a husband is obliged to exercise and which, in a good home, is routinely and unselfconsciously exercised.

However, the fact of fallibility and sin in the father means that he will at times grasp the "authoring" or "authority-bearing" will of Christ only darkly or dimly, that he will exercise what he thinks is "authority through" when it is in truth "authority over" and that he will at times exercise "his" authority in a distorted and self-serving way, just as the fact of fallibility and sin in the mother likewise means that she will often grasp the "authoring" or "authority-bearing" will of Christ only darkly or dimly and that she will encounter what she thinks is "authority over" exercised by her husband when it is in truth "authority through."

This inner life of the Trinity is, I believe, also imaged in the family in another way, for what we might call the relational/supra-relational life of the inner Trinity is, I think, reflected in the relational/supra-relational inner life of the family. God's being or inner differentiated life is both relational and supra-relational (or "post-relational"), by which I mean that it is relational but that it is also more than relational, that it transcends its own relationality. God (the three persons of the Trinity) is one in Being but God is also one in the fullness or perfection of inner differentiation. Indeed, (i) "Being" (the one-ness of Being) and (ii) the fullness of each of the three distinct modes of being (of Father, Son and Spirit) in Unity, actually coincide. Athanasius saw that the term *homousios* referred both to the unity of God's Being and also, since only different things or persons can be said to be *homousios*, to the differentiated life of the Trinity, the inter-weaving of the eternal distinctions between the three Persons.[51] God is both three (relational) and one (supra-

---

51. Athanasius, "Four Discourses," 395–96.

relational) but the family is also plural (consisting of several members related to each other) and yet also one (supra-relational), what Basil calls an indissoluble union of will.

In marriage, a man and woman are related as husband and wife through a legal contract but as Hegel observed, the point of the marriage contract establishing this relation is to transcend the standpoint of contract and to "birth" a real unity, a common "family world." In moments of the most intense intimate personal communion (*koinonia*), husband and wife become one, and transcend, in a sense, the duality of the husband-wife relation. In this way their intimacy echoes the mutual "self"-transcending of the Persons of the Trinity. Likewise, in truly being a husband, a man is, or becomes, more than a husband, for his "truly being a husband" carries him into the living unity, the inner citadel, the arc of the covenant, of family life. To the degree that he participates in the supra-relational unity or reality of family life, and to the extent that he is a servant-husband, the headship of his family is no more than the ready, natural and unself-conscious exercise of responsibility for its well-being as a whole.[52]

This idea of "triple sovereignty" in the family has also been expounded by Pope John Paul II in his *Mulieris dignatatem*. He says that the author of Ephesians sees no contradiction between his (Paul's) strong affirmation of the unity and mutuality in marriage and the words: "Wives, be subject to your husbands, as to the Lord. For the husband is the head of the wife" (Eph 5:22–23). He says that Paul well knew that this way of speaking was "profoundly rooted in the customs and religious tradition of the time" but that it "is to be understood and carried out in a new way: as a mutual subjection out of reverence for Christ (Eph 5:21)."[53] Husband and wife are to be subject to each other and to Christ. The husband is called the "head" of the wife as Christ is the head of the Church; however, the husband is so, John Paul II insists, in order to give "himself up for her" (Eph 5:25), and "giving himself up for her means giving up even his own life."[54] The husband is, then, in a sense, subject to, or the servant of, his wife's "sovereignty," that is, her absoluteness in his life as the object of his affections and as the one whose welfare is his sole concern as father and husband, requiring, if need

---

52. A holy Christian husband of my acquaintance once told me that he could only think of two occasions in the whole of his married life (some thirty years) when the issue of authority/male headship between him and his wife actually arose and when he actually felt as if he was "exercising his authority" as head of the home. The tragedy is that the Giles/egalitarian understanding of the point and purpose of this authority is the complete opposite of the truth; it is not domination but service.

53. John Paul II, *Mulieris dignitatum*, 24.

54. John Paul II, *Mulieris dignitatum*, 24.

be, even the sacrifice of his own life. John Paul II calls this an "innovation of the gospel,"[55] and likens the newness of this proclamation concerning the status of women in marriage to the newness of the gospel proclamation in relation to the custom of slavery, which was not overcome in history for centuries after the proclamation.

> The awareness that in marriage there is mutual 'subjection of the spouses out of reverence for Christ,' and not just that of the wife to the husband, must gradually establish itself in hearts, consciences, behavior and customs. This is a call which from that time onwards, does not cease to challenge succeeding generations; it is a call which people have to accept ever anew.[56]

Clearly, then, John Paul II unequivocally (and with remarkable courage in the current cultural climate) endorses what Paul teaches in Ephesians 5:22–23 concerning the authority of the father as head of the home, but he (John Paul II) also insists on "mutual subjection" or on a kind of "triple subjection," that is, on the subjection of the wife to the husband as "head" of the house, of the husband to the wife as the "heart" of the home, and of both to Christ as their common Lord and Saviour. In so strongly recommending differentiated roles for husbands and wives in family life (the "twin poles" of their mutual subjection), John Paul II echoes the differentiated inner life of the Trinity. We must then be faithful to the Gospel and take care not to remove or render optional one of the "poles of subjection" that St. Paul regards as pivotal to good family order and functioning. We (especially husbands) must endeavour, with God's help, to leave behind the kind of "headship and submission" that seemed to be necessitated by the Fall, that is really no more than heartless one-way domination and that is suggested by "Your desire shall be for your husband, and he shall rule over you" (Gen 3:16).

Finally, the flow of authority, by which I mean the successive expressions or "presences" of the Father's original Authorship (in the Son in whom all authority is eternally vested, in the state, in the headship of the father, etc.) needs to be approached and understood from the perspective of the woman. As she grows to maturity, a young woman will become reverentially aware of her awesome potential to bear life and will regard giving birth to new life as the climactic event of being a woman. At that climactic period before and after birth, her whole being as mother and woman will, ideally, be focused on her child and at that time, her husband's whole being as father

---

55. John Paul II, *Mulieris dignitatum*, 24.
56. John Paul II, *Mulieris dignitatum*, 24.

and man will, ideally, be focused on his wife and child. (This is humorously referred to by John Cleese as "the parental emergency.")

These roles do not define who we are as men and women; these roles flow from the heart of who we are as men and women, and the authority of the father as head of the household likewise flows from the differentiated positions of fathers and mothers within the family, that is, from the mother's proper focus on the needs of her child and the husband's proper focus on the needs of his wife and child and the needs (food, shelter, security, etc.) of his family as a whole. Through Christ, the father "authors" the order, love and peace of the Father into the household as a whole, and in so doing facilitates his wife's being as mother, as co-creator with the Father.

This is our "gender subsistence," our mode of being as men and women, fathers and mother[57] and it is completely misunderstood by the Giles/egalitarian analysis. Giles, for example, states that in the evangelical literature supporting what he calls "the permanent subordination of women in the home and the church," the term "role" (as in woman's role) is employed as a "gender-and-person-defining-category."[58] A woman's role, he insists, "defines who she is. She *is* the subordinated sex. Her role and function defines her being; it can never change."[59] Here, he completely reverses the true order of causality or sequence, for in fact our gender subsistence, our being as men and women, as mothers and fathers, engenders or gives rise to our roles; the latter (roles) flow from the former (our being as men and women). What Giles, and egalitarians generally, see as "our current gender socialisation imbued with a sinister subordinationist intent" is in fact "our universal gender subsistence imbued with a divine loving, liberating intent." Giles believes that for conservative evangelicals, "role determines being" whereas in fact they are saying that "relational being precedes role[s]." He fails to understand that what the headship of a husband actually means is that, in a deep and profound sense, he is "at the command" of his wife,[60] though at one point he

---

57. Margaret Mead, in *Male and Female*, outlines the "gender subsistence" of woman as mother as follows: "The mother's nurturing tie to her child is apparently so deeply rooted in the actual biological conditions of conception and gestation, birth and suckling, that only fairly complicated social arrangements can break it down entirely. ... Women may be said to be mothers unless they are taught to deny their child-bearing qualities. Society must distort their sense of themselves, pervert their inherent growth-patterns, perpetrate a series of learning-outrages upon them, before they will cease to want to provide, at least for a few years, for the child they have already nourished for nine months within the safe circle of their own bodies" (Mead, *Male and Female*, 183–84).

58. Giles, *Jesus and the Father*, 45.

59. Giles, *Jesus and the Father*, 46.

60. In the classic song "The first time ever I saw your face," Roberta Flack reveals

seems to come very close to conceding precisely this point, surely the single most important and "precious" point made by conservative evangelicals. He agrees that Paul "calls the husband the 'head' of the wife" and that this involves sacrificial, self-giving love on his part[61] but he holds that to be "head" does not involve or convey "rule/authority."[62] Giles simply does not see any link between "rule/authority" in the family and the loving service of the husband's headship. Curiously, then, at the end of the day, the difference between Giles and the conservative evangelicals boils down to the crucial difference between a "not" (mutual service/submission, not the rule/authority of the husband) and a "through" (service through this rule/authority).

The Courage to be Counter-Cultural

In 2004 then-Cardinal Ratzinger made the following point in his letter to the Bishops of the Catholic Church:

> The obscuring of the differences or duality of the sexes has enormous consequences on a variety of levels. This theory of the human person, intended to promote prospects for equality of women through liberation from biological determinism, has in reality inspired ideologies which, for example, call into question the family, in its natural two-parent structure of mother and father, and make homosexuality and heterosexuality virtually equivalent, in a new model of polymorphous sexuality."[63]

Conservative Christians are well aware that this "obscuring of differences" and its deleterious effects on the family is the major challenge before us today.

In facing this challenge, however, many have pressed too hard in the opposite direction and have argued for the sole sovereignty of the Father and the eternal obedience of the Son. As we have seen, many conservative authors, when referring to the inner life of the Trinity, speak in terms of the (single) sovereignty of the Father, rather than of the triple sovereignties of Father, Son and Spirit. Their account, I am convinced, (i) needs to be amplified by including the two "missing sovereignties" and to avoid any suggestion that one sovereignty or "function" is superior to the others and (ii) needs

---

the open secret that eludes the Giles/egalitarian analysis when she compares her true love to "the trembling heart of a captive bird that was there at my command."

61. Giles, *Trinity and Subordinationism*, 206.
62. Giles, *Trinity and Subordinationism*, 206.
63. Ratzinger, "Letter to the Bishops," 2.

THE TRINITY AND MALE HEADSHIP OF THE FAMILY 65

to be rephrased or reformulated to avoid subordinationist (and thoroughly relational) language which poorly and misleadingly represents the inner life of the (supra-relational) Trinity. As Basil remarks, when focusing upon what I call the supra-relational aspect of the Trinity, the Son's "will is connected in indissoluble union with the Father" so that we should not "understand by what is called a 'commandment' a peremptory mandate delivered by organs of speech, and giving orders to the Son, as to a subordinate, concerning what he ought to do."[64] In the supra-relational inner life of the immanent Trinity, there is, surely, only spontaneous loving response and empathic union, and nothing remotely corresponding to our human notion of obedience. It is, indeed, because Barth failed to appreciate this supra-relational dimension of the Trinity—and especially of the inner life of Father and Son—that he could be brought to the point of saying that we must regretfully acknowledge "the offensive fact that there is in God Himself an above and a below, a *prius* and a *posterius*, a superiority and a subordination [that] belongs to the inner life of God."[65] If even Barth can be so "radically wrong" on such an important matter, it is imperative that we do our utmost to "get it right," especially given the plight of the family at the present time to which Benedict XVI refers and which we are all only too aware of.

Certainly, since the 1970s the family as ordained by God and as portrayed in Holy Scripture has been under severe attack; the quality of family life, and of life in general in the Western world, has not improved as a consequence. Youth suicide, drug addiction, and mental depression are certainly complex problems in our society at the present time, but there can be little doubt that the demise of the family (and in particular the decline in the belief that men and women have different but complementary roles within the family) has contributed significantly to the problems currently faced by our young people. In the western world, in broad terms, they no longer know how to relate to each other as sexual beings; our society offers no socially approved rules of sexual engagement provides very few significant role models, and offers inadequate support and encouragement to young people who express an interest in marriage and family life.

And yet, as God is our witness in Holy Scripture, at the deepest level of their being and spirit, the family is what our young people want and need, and what God has ordained for them in his gracious love. The unspeakable tragedy is that the true face of the family, its beauty, dignity and true freedom, has been hidden from our youth and what they see instead is an ugly, repellent, oppressive thing. This is what they have been told and this is what they

---

64. Basil, "On the Spirit," 14.
65. Barth, *CD* 4/1:200–1.

believe; in their eyes, it is the Pauline understanding of marriage (God's eternal plan) that is dark and demonic. However, God asks us, not to be popular or successful, but to be counter cultural, to witness through our lives to God's Truth, to keep it alive as a light in the darkness and enable it to prevail in the minds and hearts of this lost generation of our youth. We, the faithful remnant that clings to Christ, owe this to them. In brief, this is not a time for a paradigm shift in our thinking; it is a time to be faithful.

3

A Baptismal Anthropology of the Acting Person

Trainor's contribution represents a rich effort to transcend many of the features that typify the question of conjugal politics across the ecumenical spectrum. In many respects, he can be read as proposing a resetting of this particular debate in a way that attempts to transcend the limitations both of traditional/complementarian and egalitarian interpretation. Guided above all by what I would say is a deep commitment to read the revealed text first and foremost as the word of God—that is, at face value until proven otherwise—he engages the concepts and frames that typify complementarian and egalitarian discussion and on these grounds offers an original alternative interpretation.

What he ends up with is a proposal regarding a politics of difference grounded in the "politics" of the Trinity where questions of authority and obedience are adequately understood only when they are placed within the context of the relationship between the three Persons understood as "three sovereignties for each other." Simply put, Trainor here seeks to eliminate any sense that there could be something in the trinitarian relations akin to competitive and rank-based notions of authority and obedience where such terms embody uninflected distinctions of *rank and stature* between persons. Because any difference in the relations of the Persons is in the service of the unity of the Divine Substance itself, no relational "role" can be thought to be inferior or superior. Each must be thought of as a function "within" the greater unity of the whole organism. Indeed, distinct Personal missions serve each other so totally that it becomes impossible to think of each as discrete, self-contained units that do not bear a more fundamental relation to one another. But far from flattening the significance of difference, it is instead theologically purified and intensified.

As suggested at the end of chapter 2, the specific contribution I seek to make to this discussion of the role the Trinity might play as regards the question of conjugal politics is in relation to a baptismally deepened anthropological vision of man and woman thought according to the "sacramental middle" of existence in the "hypostatic" measure offered to the person in the baptismal font. My hope is that building up this middle will complement Trainor's contribution, providing a systematic anthropological basis with which his insights into the trinitarian dimensions of conjugal politics may be further supported and explicated. To this end, I hope specifically to establish a more adequate hermeneutics from which to consider how by the spousal bond husband and wife are incorporated into the *sacramentum magnum* that is Christ's union as Bridegroom with the Church. With the existential reality of divine adoption as my lens—the conditions and essence of which it will be the intention of this chapter to flesh out—I hope to further address and move beyond some of the anthropological aporias that have typified both patristic and scholastic reflection on the theme of conjugal politics, as well as seek to resolve some of the more recent permutations of these aporias in contemporary historical-critical approaches.

In advancing a baptismal hermeneutics for anthropology, I recognize that not all comers will be comfortable either with my starting point or what might be some of my more radical suggestions and conclusions. There are many reasons why one might rather prefer an anthropology more independent of robust divine investiture. The classical Thomist, perhaps, might think that the relationship of difference and similarity between God and man is best served by thinking of grace more as a modification of nature and less as its radical structural re-creation. Perhaps "human nature" as an abstract category of creation is thought to be a sufficient guide to the "structure" of human existence, its fundamental ends and goods. Here, if we want to talk about what existence in Christ adds, then, we would do so more in moral and eschatological terms, not in structural sacramental ones.

Alternatively, for many of our cultural contemporaries, perhaps the relative independence of anthropology is desired so that it might be kept exempt from a grace that might claim everything and thereby shake nature's aspirations to autonomy to the core. Maybe this is seen as a way to insulate us from the apostolic tradition and doctrinal formulations of faith. In this case, the more anthropology can be kept methodologically distinct from the claims of faith the better.

However, my basic presupposition—which I hope to be the presupposition of *faith*—is that an existential starting point in baptism, one that begins by seriously accepting the fact that by baptism we become adopted sons in the Son, children of God the Father, will inexorably lead us much deeper into the mystery of salvation than we could ever imagine, slaying every kind of demon and idolatry. To begin by "throwing" ourselves into the mystery—presuming that when Scripture speaks of our new life in Christ and the Spirit, of our election and adoption, of our putting off of the old man and putting on the new, it *really* means what it says—should in the end call us to much more than an account of faith and grace as only "adding" (whether conservatively or progressively) to the structure of our existence without in fact having already first crucified and resurrected it according to the hypostatic measure of Christ's own person. And so, my hermeneutical "gamble" will be to "bet the farm" on the ontological realism of Scripture, particularly on the realism of the "three words of Christ" (cf. Matt 5:8, 27–28; 19:3–8; 22:23–33)[1] and the baptismal and nuptial theology of St. Paul (cf. Rom, Eph).

In gambling thus, I am suggesting that a fundamental conditioning factor for the interpretation of conjugal politics is an "adequate anthropology,"[2] one ultimately adequate only in a baptismal key, and one first generated, not from either the historical-critical minutiae of source criticism or the merely theistically colored observations of "human nature" *in abstracto*, but from the sacramental and liturgical description of the person in Christ, from the *living* text of the Scriptures borne and made manifest in the baptized flesh of the son and daughter of God the Father.

Perhaps this is naïve, but I am more and more convinced that the viability and credibility of faith can in the end rest only on and begin in the *a priori* confession that in Christ we have become a new creation, a child of God, and that it is only from a vantage point already deeply and existentially *inside the mystery*—indeed, perhaps then even *inside the Trinity*—that the mystery can be encountered in any depth or fidelity. From this point of origination, I suggest that rather than contracting and narrowing the scope of human possibility, it will instead expand it infinitely beyond the flat horizons of either nature or historical context as the hermeneutical structure within which theological thinking about anthropology takes place. Baptism will give the new person—man and woman—their nature and their history properly speaking. Today, particularly in an historical epoch that

---

1. This is a reference to the structure of the first part of John Paul II's *Theology of the Body* (General Audiences starting from September 5, 1979 through July 21, 1984), which explores Christ's teaching on marriage according to *the Beginning* (Matt 19:3–8), *the Heart* (Matt 5:8, 27–28), and *the Resurrection* (Matt 22:23–33).

2. This term is John Paul II's. An adequate anthropology "seeks to understand and interpret man in what is essentially human" (John Paul II, *Theology of the Body*, 178 [13.2]). Michael Waldstein offers the important clarification that John Paul II's use of "adequate" (from the Italian *adeguato*) does not carry the sense of only "fulfilling the minimum requirement" as it does in English. Cf. John Paul II, *Theology of the Body*, 678.

has plumbed the depths of possibility of existence without God, perhaps almost to the point of its nihilistic consummation, neither pure nature nor pure history can suffice as an hermeneutic to the question of existence in its deepest post-nihilistic specification. In the first movement toward the mystery, there must be, especially today, an existential leap into the living God, the radical response to the *personal* invitation to participate in the divine life itself through adoption.

Thus, by seeking to refresh the fundamental bases of anthropology, I hope to begin to move towards addressing some of the problems associated with the interpretation of conjugal politics throughout the ages.

From Imitation to Incorporation

To be a person, is to be with and in Christ. It is to be a son or a daughter. It is to be incorporated as a living agent into the divine life through the Spirit-filled generative mediation of Christ in his fruitful relation to the Church. It is to have been *nuptially* generated from a real union of love, and it is to have come to share in Christ's filial relation to the Father as Son. It is to thus have had one's self and nature rewritten as a *living* image of the Son (as distinct from image as a static ontological imprint that merely represents or mimics the archetype morally or psychologically), to have received one's identity *in history*, *in relation*, in the *sacramental time of Jesus Christ*. As a son, it is to have discovered the Father. It is to perceive the infrastructural meaning of one's existence as *filial belonging*, as submission to the Love that conceived and generated the world, and that personally called, named, and adopted *you*.

The above vision presupposes that the first act of cognition and thought for the baptized Christian comes after *immersion in the font*, from inside a bodily, sacramental vision of what life in Christ is as a reality shared wholly, entirely, and existentially with the new believer. The thinking of the baptized person is the thinking of one who is already inside the mystery, one whose ultimate and organizing measure of existence is the mystery itself, the mystery that now pervades and surrounds *this* child of God the Father, the mystery that now feeds *this* child through the sacramental life of the Church.

All of this is to say that for this person, strictly speaking there can no longer be a "below" (nature) or "above" (grace) as pure, extrinsic, or discrete measures distinct from their new baptismal existence. These sources are of course present in any act of defining the person who belongs both to this world and the next, but in *baptismal, adopted* existence, their fundamental contexts are now read through a new dramatic, existential, and sacramental prior hermeneutics, one that has been archetypally made flesh in the hypostatic personhood of the Son. We could say that in baptism, the natural and the supernatural are "married" for the person who receives it: natural and supernatural become "one flesh" in the flesh of the person and a new reality is thus brought into existence. Each informing pole is now filtered through the new reality of adoption, the new existential subjectivity of this person who by the death and life of the baptismal font now occupies the sacramental middle, a new sacramental "now."

The baptized person occupies this middle as a radiant sacramental icon, one who—again, strictly speaking—lives neither in nature nor in the eschatological fulfilment, but rather in and according to a "hybrid" existence that is sacramental participation in the hypostatic personhood of the Son in this life, one that plays out within the sacramental time of the new economy of salvation in the Church. For this person, therefore, there can be no definitive "natural" structure of existence that remains as a formal law sufficient in itself, and nor is there some divine reality or object towards which this natural structure might then be intentionally directed or imitated by powers natively internal to the natural self. The only "structure" of this person's existence is the structure of baptismal childhood within which nature and grace, humanity and divinity, have been remade, re-transmitted, or recapitulated according to the fundamentally new conditions of the incarnate Son's hypostatic identity as human and divine in his Person.

What I hope is made clear here is the way this constitutes an approach to anthropology from a robustly "dramatic" point of view, one that seeks to outwit the pretensions of both rationalism and fideism. It is a perspective developed within and according to what we might call that of the *sacramental* acting person. It eschews an "objective" or "formal" approach to the mystery of human existence from any point external to the question of *who this person* is as chosen and named by the Father in and through the Son and the Spirit. This is not to deny the historical validity—and indeed in certain respects and within certain conditions the *necessity*—of other, more classical hermeneutical approaches to anthropology. However, regarding the fundamental question of *WHO* the person—*this* person—is, there can only be one answer, one starting point: this person is an adopted child of God the Father. This is the animating and originating point, the fundamental ontology, the framing and constituting "now." This is the perspective of what could be called a baptismal actualism, an *analogia baptismi* without which the person must remain a being locked in the shadows of the intracosmic condition of alienated humanity, a being who cannot hope for and attain more than a nominal and extrinsic intimation of theological identity.

The question we need to address with more rigor is *how exactly* to move from an approach that considers man and woman more as natural imitators of the mystery who do so while remaining largely still within their own "natural" skins, as it were—the approach that has mired anthropology in many of the dualisms and partial perspectives that we saw in chapter 1,— to one in which the single, baptismal sacramental "now" determines them completely and entirely, incorporating them into full "family" participation in the mystery, overcoming the riddles of temporality, but without thereby stripping man and woman of their unique human specificity or imprisoning them in new dualisms and distortions.

Ratzinger on Person

We can note, against the thesis being proposed here, how most of the *Wirkungsgeschichte* of historical Christian reflection—despite many nuances and qualifications—has, at least in its consideration of embodied, temporal man, treated the question of the *humanum* as more or less functionally distinct from the *theological* mode of personhood that might be thought to be a horizon implied by the trinitarian relations.

For example, Ratzinger famously lamented the fact that the West generally chose to treat anthropological questions from the Boethian perspective of the person understood as *naturae rationalis individua substantia*: an individual substance of a rational nature.[3] Ratzinger observes how this understanding of person—which became and remains for some a near-canonical feature of anthropology in the Western tradition—"stands entirely on the level of substance."[4] It remains an intracosmic and purely formal definition of person, a bedrock account of identity that strictly speaking need not invoke anything outside of the perspective of nature for its articulation and functional adequacy. Ratzinger's specific lament is that while thinkers such as St. Thomas recognized person as a word for relation at the level of christological and trinitarian description, a way could not also be found to analogously describe *human* persons according to the same fully relational logic by virtue of their new sacramental belonging to Christ. Instead, Christ's unique mode of personal existence was treated as an "ontological exception" that "must remain separate in its box as an exception to the rule and must not be permitted to mix with the rest of human thought."[5]

---

3. Cf. Boethius, "Treatise Against Eutyches and Nestorius."
4. Ratzinger, "Person in Theology," 448.
5. Ratzinger, "Person in Theology," 449.

Thus it is that while the Son himself only makes sense *in relation* (to the Father, and to the Spirit, without whom he is simply indescribable and incomprehensible, i.e., just another created human individual), it was nevertheless asserted that the mark of the *human* person is by contrast to a certain extent adequately described in a purely formal way according to the base level properties that inhere in its individuated rational nature. Relation—to others, to God, if or when we get there—then risks being somewhat unceremoniously and conditionally tacked on after the fact as an "accidental" mode or possibility of substance, strictly speaking not *essential*, at least according to the terms intrinsic to the substantial definition of person.

None of this is to say that substantialist analysis does not capture *something* of what it means to be human. However, it can be questioned whether this perspective can give us much that in fact would mark off anything about the *naturae rationalis individua substantia* that would make possible a unique, incommunicable spiritual subject: a some*one*, a person, one whose greatest "reality" is that which it does not possess as it own. That is, substantialist accounts would not give us a subject who is *more* than just one individual expression of a common species, who bears something *more* than a common nature in individuated form, who transcends the limits and constraint of a definition according to "nature," and who is thus open to the infinite and eternal in a radical way. No mode of description derived from man's natural state can describe or define the *person* of Christ, i.e., his unique subjectivity, his relation to the Father, etc. Similarly, nature cannot describe or define *this* human person *in Christ*, that is, the person who dies and is reborn with Christ in baptism, who awakens to participation in Christ's mission received from the Father. There is here something that goes far beyond the categories of substance and accident, that in fact demands a deep reinterpretation of the human.

This something Ratzinger describes as a "third specific fundamental category between substance and accident,"[6] persons as relations or "pure relatedness"[7] whose fundamental essence or definition belongs to the category of relation. Colin Patterson describes this horizon of "persons-in-relation" (which he calls an "ontological primitive" beyond substance and accidents analysis) as a much fuller description of reality, one unavailable to substantialist modes of description. He says that

> What 'persons-in-relation' communicates is that the model of 'looking at something' is not the only one suitable for ontological analysis. It works well if we are abstracting from subsisting

---

6. Ratzinger, "Person in Theology," 444–45.
7. Ratzinger, "Person in Theology," 447.

things or qualities, quantities, position, time, and so on, to arrive at the categories of 'substance' and 'accident.' Trinitarian doctrine, however, proposes the necessity of moving beyond that simple 'looking' model and indicating that there is much more to reality than what substantialist thinking suggests. 'Persons-in-relation' opens the door to exploring that further reality. Theologically, it leads us not so much to activities such as interest or analysis, but to worship.[8]

His last point in particular bears repeating. It is only within the dramatic matrix of sacramental and liturgical action, we might say, that the full reality of the person can present itself with any degree of fullness. The person only becomes comprehensible and describable as such, within the dialogical I-Thou weighted by the Thou who is the living God, the Thou who calls and names us as one of his own.

Balthasar on Person

In large part complementing Ratzinger, Balthasar accentuates this insight with his claim that person is a term that exclusively names our relation to the person of Christ. For Balthasar thinks it impossible that any other strategy or perspective for articulating the uniqueness and value of *this* human vis-à-vis the many other individual instantiations of the same rational nature could in fact achieve a description thick enough to argue that there is something in the individual that transcends the intracosmic dimension. He begins his analysis by asserting that "we can do without the concept of 'person' much longer than we think."[9] In other words, you may think that by various naturalistic strategies you are describing "person" (the intangible that sets me apart from other members of the same species, which makes me *more* than nature) when in fact you are only describing multiple layers of potential of the nature that we share with other beings of the same nature, albeit in diverse ways.

Foremost among these, says Balthasar, is the sense that I am "unique and incommunicable."[10] That is, there is no other being like me. No one can become me or replace me. In this, I might think that what makes me a "person" are all of the unique accidental characteristics I have amassed that have qualified the substance of my existence in a unique way, thus differen-

---

8. Patterson, *Chalcedonian Personalism*, 111. I am grateful to Patterson for many rewarding discussions on themes related to the topic of person.

9. Balthasar, *Person in Christ*, 203.

10. Balthasar, *Person in Christ*, 204.

tiating myself from other. But, says Balthasar, this is no indication of some *essentially* unique property or quality that inheres in you, as here "we do not get farther than an accumulation of chance details. This individual, under different circumstances, could have become quite a different subject."[11] After all, beings such as animals are unique and incommunicable in their own way, and yet we do not ascribe personhood to them. One might reply that they are not persons because *they are not rational*, but even if you say that the mark of personhood is rationality, one would still need to account for the fact that rationality is not a quality unique to any one individual, but rather belongs to the *genus proximum* of humanity: each member of the species has the capacity for rationality. As such, it does not differentiate me from others as an individual.

As a consequence, Balthasar does not even mention rationality *qua* rationality as a fact that could shed any light on the question of personhood, if by personhood we mean *this particular person* as displaying something more than an accumulation of certain natural features, no matter how developed or customized. The point is that we are still dealing here with merely *accidental* potential and changes to the substance of the individual, not to *essential* determinants which could be claimed as marking off an absolute personal identity as such, beyond the various elements and conditions of circumstantial historical "whatness" that define our existence in nature and history.

Balthasar next asks whether it might be the case however that some kind of trans-material guarantee of personhood could be given *by other human beings*; in other words, within a temporal matrix of relationality not reducible to the autonomous self. Here he points to the "interpersonal path," suggesting that perhaps when a child receives its identity from its mother as one loved and treasured in a unique way, it receives something that transcends its "whatness" with a "who-ness." But here, again, he does not think that this suffices for saying that the individual is a person in some way that transcends nature. For, as he puts it, "the mother's affirmation could be withdrawn." One temporal and contingent conscious subject cannot say *who* another temporal and contingent conscious subject is.[12] It may grant a new richness and *sense* of unique value, but in the end it cannot give an *absolute* affirmation of personal identity, one that transcends the caprice and relativity of finitude and temporality. "The most emphatic affirmation

---

11. Balthasar, *Person in Christ*, 205.
12. Cf. Sweeney, *Abiding the Long Defeat*, 121–27.

can only tell him who he is for the one who values him or loves him,"[13] a *subjective*, contingent, and relative valuation.

And so none of this convinces Balthasar that we have yet discovered anything unique or distinctive about individual conscious beings that could justify calling them "persons" in a sense that transcends nature: "so far we have had no need, in this complementarity of the generic and the individual in man's conscious nature, to introduce the concept of 'person.' No distinction can or need be made between it and the conscious subject." In this, it is clear that Balthasar will require very strict (ultimately katological) conditions for calling an individual a person, as possessing a value and distinction that makes them distinct from and not reducible to the historically mediated aggregate of properties that belong to their nature.

John Paul II on Person

In contrast to Ratzinger and Balthasar, we can next consider the approach of John Paul II whose metaphysical and phenomenological approach[14] to the question arrives at something of an alternative conclusion. He thinks that man's unique personal subjectivity *can* in a certain respect be discovered and ascertained within a certain process of self-reflexive discernment and knowledge on the part of the conscious subject. "Humanness or human nature," he says, "is equipped with the properties that enable a concrete human being to be a person: to be and to act as a person"[15]; "Who the human being essentially is derives primarily from within that being."[16]

In the simplest terms, John Paul II submits that "person," as distinct from merely denoting an individual member of a species, indicates "that there is something more to him, a particular richness and perfection in the manner of his being, which can only be brought out by the use of the word 'person.'"[17] In very classical terms, the reason given for this indication is that "man has the ability to reason, he is a rational being, which cannot be said of any other entity in the visible world, for in none of them do we find

13. Balthasar, *Person in Christ*, 205.
14. Cf. the excellent account of Wojtyla's thinking in Taylor, "Beyond Nature."
15. Wojtyla, *Acting Person*, 84.
16. Wojtyla, "Dignity of the Person," 178.
17. Wojtyla, *Love and Responsibility*, 22. Elsewhere, John Paul II explains that this invocation of "person" has to do with the intuited sense that there is an intangibly unique quality about each individual that demands the invocation of something more than the natural or ontological: "it seems clear that neither the concept of the 'rational nature' nor that of its individualization seems to express fully the specific completeness expressed by the concept of the person" (Wojtyla, *Acting Person*, 73–74).

any trace of conceptual thinking."[18] John Paul II goes on to express his basic initial satisfaction with the Boethian notion of person, which is thought to "differentiate a person from the whole world of objective entities," thus determining "the distinctive character of the person."

In other places, John Paul II speaks more specifically of how self-determination (or what we might also call "agency") plays a central role in intuiting that an individual subject is in fact a person; that is, that an individual exhibits a "something more" that demarcates them as unique and distinct from the rest of the entities in and conditions of the visible world. He invokes St. Thomas's teaching that the person is *sui iuris et alteri incommunicabilis*, arguing that the subject's actualized capacity for self-determination, self-possession, or self-governance is constitutive in terms of the discovery of the subject as more than an individual.[19] Within *experience*—i.e., in the horizon of action—of oneself as possessing and determining oneself, the individual becomes aware of his unique and irreducible identity, which John Paul II names "personal." In this, "Through self-determination, the human being becomes increasingly more 'someone' in the ethical sense, although in the ontological sense the human being is a 'someone' from the very beginning."[20] Here we see *both* the notion that the individual, as already human, in possessing the metaphysical "form" of consciousness, reason, and freedom, is always already a "someone," a *who*, a person possessing an inalienable dignity and value as such, *and* the notion that in subjectively appropriating and cultivating this potential in and through the reflexive and conscious perspective of action and experience (the "acting person," *pace* Cartesian subjectivity), interiorly discovers and deepens personhood *for him or herself*.[21]

But John Paul II also gives a certain theological depth and perspective to what is above essentially still a metaphysical and phenomenological notion of person, through his *Scriptural* phenomenology of the original experience of Adam in Genesis. Here, in Adam's discovery of himself in the

18. Wojtyla, *Love and Responsibility*, 22.
19. Wojtyla, "Personal Structure," 192.
20. Wojtyla, "Personal Structure," 192.

21. John Paul II is clear that it is not enough to remain in a strictly metaphysical perspective, e.g., the perspective of the *humanum* as an ontological type of rationality, consciousness, and freedom. The dimension of action and experience is essential in uncovering *this individual* as a person, as unveiling the person in their full agency and self-determination—their full *subjectivity*. And so, "viewing subjectivity solely from the metaphysical standpoint, and stating that man as a type of being constitutes the true subject of existing and acting, autonomous individual being, we abstract, to a large extent from what is the source of our visualizations, the source of experience" (Wojtyla, *Acting Person*, 57).

context of what John Paul II calls "original solitude," we see emerge again the notions of knowledge, consciousness, freedom, and self-determination as key to the discovery of personhood, but this time intrinsically relative *to dialogue with the Creator*. Adam, in discovering himself "alone" in the horizon of creation, a being unlike all of the other creatures, thus "finds himself from the first moment of his existence *before God* in search of his own being, as it were; one could say, in search of his own 'identity.'"[22] An important dimension of the way in which this identity is discovered is in and through his ability to consciously reflect on his situation:

> When we analyse the text of Genesis, we are in some way witness to how man, with the first act of self-consciousness, 'distinguishes himself' before God-Yahweh from the whole world of living beings (*animalia*), how he consequently reveals himself to himself and at the same time affirms himself in the visible world as a person.'[23]

The pope is clear that as a consequence of this process of rational discernment, man discovers not just that he belongs to a certain class of beings (*genus proximum*), but that he also discovers that intangible "something more" that demarcates the *subjectivity* of a human being: "This process leads also to *the first delineation* of the human being *as* a human *person*, with the proper subjectivity that characterizes the person."

Now, what is here added to John Paul II's earlier philosophical analysis is an account of the way that the discovery of personhood is also deeply framed and punctuated by the divine dimension. Adam does not exist in a neutral or merely natural setting, but is "before God." The stage of this dramatic and existential discovery of self is that of pre-lapsarian integration, harmony, and communication with God. In this theological register, the pope seems to indicate that man's discovery of himself as a person is thus always already irradiated by a supernatural and personal framing, by a dimension beyond the strict boundaries of rational subjectivity: "Already this divine act underlines man's subjectivity."[24]

And so, the very fact that the process of self-discovery takes place *here* suggests that it cannot be so easily bracketed off from its divine source in subsequent contexts without introducing rather severe limitations. The pope goes on to add that subjectivity is also presupposed in the fact that God gives to the man the test of naming the animals (Gen 2:19). All of this is to say, at least in a creational context, that the personhood being discovered

---

22. John Paul II, *Theology of the Body*, 149 (5.5).
23. John Paul II, *Theology of the Body*, 150 (5.6).
24. John Paul II, *Theology of the Body*, 148 (5.5).

by Adam is something in which God is intrinsically involved; it is by no means a closed, Cartesian discovery of self.

Thus, the discovery of self here leads inexorably into the *category of relation* as in some sense deeply fundamental to his personhood. That is, the discovery of subjectivity does not at any point close the man in on himself. For the man's search is by no means completed once he makes the initial discovery that *he* is a person. Indeed, here his existence becomes even more of a problem, inasmuch as the discovery of his personhood only deepens his sense that he is alone in the visible world. He must discover *other persons* to be fulfilled. From this, John Paul II's analysis cascades into a robust theological notion of the person as interiorly constituted in relation to both God and to the sexually differentiated other. The latter archetype—the nuptial structure of the man-woman relationship, consummated in their "one flesh" union—is the sacramental visibility of the former, and communicates to the man that only in the kenotic intimacy of being-with and being-for the *other* person can he realize the potential of his personhood. This peaks in John Paul II's statement that

> man becomes the image of God not only through his own humanity [his subjectivity], but also through the communion of persons, which man and woman form from the very beginning ... man becomes an image of God not so much in the moment of solitude as in the moment of communion.[25]

Still further, there is great significance in the fact that all of the potential of Adam's subjectivity is placed within the context of an existential relationship with its divine source. His subjectivity comes with the imperative to freely choose either good or evil: "You may eat of every tree of the garden, but of the tree of the knowledge of good and evil you shall not eat, when you eat of it you shall certainly die" (Gen 2:16–17). To *realize*

---

25. John Paul II, *Theology of the Body*, 163 (9.3). This relational dimension was certainly already a key motivation in his philosophical writings. For example, in "Structure of Self-Determination," written in 1964, he is already invoking the perspective of *Gaudium et Spes* as an important deepening of the Aristotelian, Boethian, and Thomistic notion of person. After mentioning this perspective, he suggests that "in the experience of self-determination the human person stands revealed before us as a distinctive structure of self-possession and self-governance. Neither the one nor the other, however, implies being closed in on oneself. On the contrary, both self-possession and self-governance imply a special disposition to make a 'gift of oneself,' and this a 'disinterested' gift" (John Paul II, "Structure of Self-Determination," 194). However, the theological dimension introduced by *Gaudium et Spes* is not yet fully integrated into his still largely philosophical approach to the question. It is not until the theology of the body that this perspective is explicitly linked to the image of God within a theological phenomenology of the "Beginning."

himself as a person, as the recipient of a divine gift that demands a response, Adam must *engage* his subjectivity within the sphere of freedom and action, in dialogue with the living God. *To be*, is to be faced with the existential imperative to act and to choose, to form oneself in and through one's acts, all against the backdrop of existence as test and choice. This existential imperative forms the structure of the arena of action within which man's subjectivity will be engaged.

All of this qualifies theologically the conditions of what still seem to remain for John Paul II the fundamental determinants of the first discovery of personhood, namely rationality, consciousness, self-knowledge, and self-determination, even if all are in the end inflected or "existentialized" by the perspectives of action and relation in an original way. In the Theology of the Body, these emerge and play out within the sacramental world of the original experiences, thus fleshing out in much more explicit detail the non-Cartesian nature of the whole process, and a much more dynamic and relational notion of person.[26]

Becoming a Person in Christ

However, *in substance*, it still remains the case that for John Paul II the first and key determinant in the process of discovering personhood continues to rest within the immanent, natural structure of human consciousness and rationality, *a la* the Aristotelian-Boethian-Thomistic tradition of substantialism. In the philosophical mode, John Paul II still seems happy to say that "person" can be discovered by the process of rational reflection and action.

However, even considering the theological register of the beginning of Genesis, can it be said that the man has in fact on his own powers discovered some essential property or quality unique to him and to him alone by which he could say that there was a deeper significance attached specifically *to him*? Has he discovered himself as *more* than *a kind of being* who can talk to God, who can think and reason, who is called to exercise his freedom in a certain way, who is called to live in communion with God and with woman? Does he yet truly know *who* he is, on this basis, i.e., prior to the personal address of Christ? More to the point: if he *does* know that he is a person (in a sense beyond his nature), has it *first* arisen from out of the powers of his own cognition or has it been given to him in a way that first arrests and transforms the structure of cognition itself? And then, what would be the significance of answering this question one way or the other?

---

26. For a similar account, see Clarke, *Person and Being*.

While perhaps having certain quibbles (I will get to these in a moment) with John Paul II's approach, Balthasar would no doubt be in fundamental agreement with the pope in terms of the question of *the nature* of the human individual, his or her whatness or *haecceitas*. He would agree that it belongs to the *nature* of individuals who belong to the human species to have the capacity for rationality, self-determination, consciousness and the like and to discover these within the perspective of dramatic action. He would no doubt be happy to say that this automatically marks off the *humanum* in general as possessing a fundamental dignity and inviolability, and he would recognize that when circumscribed within the absolute horizon of person properly speaking, these features will remain of fundamental, if adjusted, importance.[27] What is *not* in question in this discussion is the fact that human individuals, *as possessing human nature*, possess a value and dignity *as such*, in virtue of simply belonging to the species. From my own point of view, I am quite happy in theory and up to a point to hold on to the insights of this hermeneutical approach (although we also need to recognize that such a notion of universality is paradoxically dependent on the *particular* revelation of Jesus Christ). What Balthasar might be most happy with here is the way in which John Paul II has at the very least shown how "nature" contains within itself the dynamics that reveal relationality to be constitutive of the *humanum*, and as such points "sacramentally" to their re-inscription and consummation in what will become the hermeneutics of personhood proper as revealed and starting in Christ. That is, John Paul II's ontology reveals the extent to which love is in the end the only appropriate measure for determining the essence of what it means to be human.

But we can again ask the question: has the man in fact *himself* discovered his own personhood here within the conditions laid out? Perhaps he has personhood, but perhaps it has *not* been discovered on his own terms, by his own powers, but is rather a pure divine gift, the fruit of an addressing and naming that establishes *an immediate relation* to the God who is more internal to the person than that person is to himself; that reorders the person's internal powers. Perhaps then it is not *personhood* that Adam discovers in any act of self-knowledge and self-determination, but rather existential

27. Having experienced first-hand many of the dehumanizing ideologies of the twentieth century, John Paul II was always particularly motivated by defending the intrinsic dignity of the person on universal grounds. Referring to the importance of establishing the dignity of the person "from below" he refers to its necessity "for those who do not acknowledge a religious reality and do not find the fullest confirmation of the dignity of the human person in such a reality, those for whom the human being is confirmed only from below: in relation to the visible world, in the economy, technology, and civilization" (Wojtyla, "Dignity of the Person," 180). John Paul II's confidence in human rights illustrates his commitment to the definition of personhood from below.

perception of a lack peculiar to himself as a being in the world. That is, what he discovers by his reflexive capacity is something more akin to a disturbing awareness of possessing a nature that requires an "other" to be itself. Fast-forward to a post-lapsarian context, and this awareness becomes the horror of possessing a nature that no "other" and which nature itself cannot satisfy. If all of this is the case, then, it would mean that we would have to readjust just how important the question of consciousness and self-determination are as regards their being the stuff of personhood per se. And we would thereby also have to readjust the extent to which the gift of personhood in Christ is understood as a qualification rather than a much more radical re-creation of the self and its powers.

In the end, both a philosophical phenomenology and a theological phenomenology based on pre-lapsarian Genesis cannot on their own be enough for adducing or supporting a theory of personhood in the strict sense for *historical* man and the man of the redemption; the man now *in Christ*, the man shaken to the core by the earth-shattering and ultimately apocalyptic event of the incarnation and resurrection that meets him in the depths of his insecurity and existential alienation from the Father.[28] In the experience of Edenic bliss I think that it is obvious that man and woman are "persons" inasmuch as they are "with God" in a condition of unimaginable intimacy (how could they be otherwise?), but given the specific constraints on reading this unique text from a *philosophical* point of view, I doubt whether there is in the end much to be gained from inferring *a specific and constitutive moment, process, faculty, or condition* whereby this is indicated or made clear from the point of consciousness, especially one anything like personhood ostensibly discovered from the side of the human self through rational reflexivity. An analysis of the possibilities of personhood within the constraints of a *post-lapsarian* perspective via the framing of metaphysical and phenomenological analysis—one necessarily shaped by a certain caesura between God and man typical of our fallen condition—seems to me incapable *ipso facto* of producing personhood in and through a process of rational self-determination and self-knowledge. *To be*, in a *fallen* existence, *is to be separated from God*—it is to lack *the existential relation* without which death is the inevitable end. No rational process or intuition can overcome this condition, save to make it appear all the more unsolvable and that much more horrifying. Personhood can thus be here only a speculative intuition, a faint hope that can in no concrete, demonstrable, or fruitful way ever really be realized.

28. For perspectives on how the event of Christ shatters the trajectory of human history and thought, and in specifically apocalyptic directions, see Hart, "God or Nothingness"; Girard, *Battling to the End;* Illich and Cayley, *Rivers North of the Future.*

And so, with Ratzinger and Balthasar, if we can find a way to call an individual a person, it will only be as a consequence of a *new* "unnatural" relation—being in, with, for, and from the *eternal* other—that goes all the way down, as it were, that truly brings the individual into contact with something—or *someone*—who can reset the foundations of the self, who can resolve the aporia of an existence that ends in death, a death that in the end denies to the individual every hope that *I* might be special, that *I* might be an exception to the law of mortality, that *I* might be more than a collective or some cosmic process within which individuality is chimerical.

Thus, notwithstanding certain important qualifications that John Paul II adds to the classical substantialist notion of person, I remain unconvinced that it is in fact possible for a thick enough notion of person (in a meaningful enough sense) to be deduced from *any* resource internal to the capacities or properties of the human individual qua individual outside of the historical drama of election and adoption. I do not think that John Paul II in fact *demonstrates* that consciousness could in fact perceive or produce person, i.e., something more than nature, some properly unique and transcendent element. Indeed, one is struck by the fact that in trying to describe what this might be and where it comes from, he is limited by phrases such as "something more" or "particular richness," both somewhat ambiguous notions, aesthetic judgments perhaps. It seems that the act of positing and actually *describing* persons cannot in the end go very far beyond the intangible and indescribable, a problem that is in the end only overcome by a kind of jump that relies on smuggling in "spiritual" data from elsewhere, which is then appealed to as the contents of man's discovery of himself as a person. Even invocations of soul, spirit, or a unique immaterial self are small, near-incomprehensible solace to an individual who faces the inevitable prospect of phenomenological death. And short of theological specification about what might happen to said souls or spirits after death, they again are decidedly thin as regards to what they can say and offer on their own terms.[29]

Returning to Balthasar, we see him argue that in the end it is impossible to generate person on the basis of reflection on *any* of the natural properties that inhere in the individual subject. He says that

---

29. Moreover, as Patterson points out, any positing of an immaterial dimension, "because it still inhabits the world of thought as form and process is vulnerable to the implications that might reasonably be drawn from recent psychological/neurological work on the brain, i.e., that there is no need to postulate any such reality as a transcendental cogito" (Patterson, *Chalcedonian Personalism*, 231). He further argues that "Deeper than notions of the soul or the mind is that of the human heart or spirit which stands exposed in the presence of God, in other words the believing self-within-conscience" (Patterson, *Chalcedonian Personalism*, 250).

> Philosophy [and we might add, even a philosophy with a theological veneer] can develop only a general anthropology, with a general psychology (a theory of individual conduct) and a general sociology (a theory of collective conduct), both of which can be dissolved all too easily into so-called scientific statistics in which the criterion and the goal are, on the one hand, the anonymous average and, on the other hand, the capacity to be directed from below (chemical means, suggestion, propaganda, etc.).[30]

Practically speaking, this Balthasar regards as a fundamentally unstable arrangement: "in the absence of any further guarantee, this *who* [the one generated by philosophy] is always in danger of being sacrificed, as an allegedly limited individual, for the sake of some larger totality or other." One should note that this instability is not limited merely to the *loss* of individuality *a la* totalitarian regimes, but it seems to also make possible the *idolization* of individuality in the Cartesian, Kantian, Lockean, and ultimately Nietzschean or Sartrean sense, inasmuch as the discovery of selfhood is premised on a power that inheres within the individual qua individual that, while grounded in nature, also incorrigibly seeks to go beyond it. In this, it is but a short step from conceiving oneself as generated *from* nature to thinking of oneself *beyond* nature in a dualistic or transgressive sense. Nature very easily comes to be seen as *restrictive* of personal identity, while personhood understood *beyond* nature seems to come with unlimited imaginative possibilities for the expression of the self's perceived infinite freedom.

Thus it is today that *our* problem within a social and cultural context that ritually celebrates the death of God is the *idolization* of the individual and its freedom, *viz.* "identity politics"; the individual conceived in absolute terms as a being who wields a formalistic subjectivity and freedom over against God, nature, and others[31] who and which become mere accidents in a *new* "substantialist" definition of the "essence" of person as pure freedom and will, an essence now made possible by technology in what would have not long ago been regarded as unthinkable ways.[32] My argument is that the same approach that seemed to guarantee the substantial definition of the individual as *both* nature and person in an integrated whole, has at the same time not so paradoxically or surprisingly fostered the notion of the individual ("person") as a free-standing entity in no way bound to the natural elements that ostensibly ground it. I say this

---

30. Balthasar, *Creator Spirit*, 309.

31. Cf. David L. Schindler's discussion of the liberal notion of self, *a la* John Locke. Schindler, "Repressive Logic."

32. Cf. Hanby, "More Perfect Absolutism."

should not be thought of as a paradox or contradiction in that it is the shared premise of both accounts that the individual has a least a *relative* autonomy vis-à-vis others according to which they can bracket themselves out as distinct from and to a certain extent sovereign over the common existence within which they participate. When this reflexive capacity of the individual is thought of as the determinant for what constitutes identity and reality, then it is but a short and in many respects logical step from this to the nihilistic completion of the person.

The problem is that the moment the individual thinks they have discovered some elemental property within them that indicates something more than nature, they feel—quite rightly—the need to press out beyond the constraints of nature *qua* nature, which appears increasingly restrictive and depersonalizing. If what ultimately defines you is that intangible "something" that might be discovered on the basis of nature but which is ultimately *beyond* it, then the horizon of natures, essences, and substances must soon become a plain and unsatisfying condition of thinking more preferable to do away with completely. This person will no longer be satisfied with being part of a collective (just another worker ant subordinated to the much bigger aim of the good of the colony), but will wish to define himself according to this mysterious intangible that they allegedly bear in their self and manifest in their freedom. But if this "something more" of unique subjectivity is ultimately indescribable and obscure, grounded in little more than the aspirations (and often delusions) of the self and not ultimately fed by anything concrete *outside* the self, then it should be no surprise when this perspective increasingly leads us to a nominalist and nihilistic notion of the self as pure freedom and pure will.

This is to say that the Nietzsches, Sartres, and Camuses, etc. belong just as comfortably to the history and genealogy of the West as the Boethiuses, the Thomases, and the Wojtylas. Sure, the former and the latter end up in two fundamentally different places, but one could venture to say that the only *essential* thing separating them from each other is that whereas for Boethius, Thomas, and Wojtyla the "leap" into personhood is consolidated by their concomitant confession of faith (which, as it were "saves" personhood by fleshing it out and giving it genuine content beyond the ambiguous, subject-centered "something more"), our existentialists see no necessary reason—rightly or wrongly—for retaining this illicit (that is, theological) legitimating premise. In fact, one could argue that someone like Nietzsche is in a sense *more* "rational" in terms of pursuing Boethian subjectivity through to its nihilistic completion. Ultimately, the only way that substantialists save subjectivity from terminating in nothingness is by attaching it to Christ. Religious commitment may slow the process, but there nevertheless seems to be an irrepressible dynamic within an intellectualist and substantialist understanding of the person that heads in just such a direction. Inasmuch as this attachment happens "after the fact," as an accidental mode not intrinsic to the first movement of self-discovery, then there will always be a tension here, a nihilistic seed that need only wait for faith's disturbance and eradication.

And so perhaps it is not so surprising that nihilism could arise so decisively from the heart of the very same tradition that showed us the face of God. This fact should never fail to trouble and provoke us. The very best can more readily become the worst.[33] And if we do not perceive how deeply this is aided by our own failure to accept the first movement of the mystery of divine adoption according to the terms of its givenness, we ourselves risk becoming accomplices in the death of God. The dream of personal subjectivity that divine adoption made possible was ultimately strangled by a hermeneutical strategy that wished to have sonship on its own terms; that came to believe that it could by its own powers establish and justify itself and peer into the very living essences of things and name and control them. In this, as Heidegger pointed out, the history of the West is punctuated by the mistaking of the sign for the signified. What he called "onto-theological" thinking believes that it can penetrate into the absolute essence of things, and as a consequence, this kind of thinking "forgets" that the true ground of man's being remains an impenetrable mystery and enigma of which he remains incapable of generating deep knowledge of on his own.[34] This forgetfulness eventually produces the hubris of the being who thinks that that he has discovered and knows himself, when in fact all he knows with any certitude on this basis is that he is one of a kind of beings who can think, reason, and reflect. This does little to solve the riddle of existence, and in fact potentially obfuscates it further, inasmuch as the man who *thinks* he has discovered himself thus closes himself off to the radicality of a horizon that *might* in fact break open his existence for him in a *genuinely* personal, infinite, and eternal way.

It is probably true that the paradigm of John Paul II offers us the best possible integration and synthesis of person and nature "from below," as

---

33. I have found much food for thought in the reflections of Ivan Illich on two enigmatic sayings (see Illich and Cayley, *Rivers North of the Future*). The first is the ancient Latin maxim, *corruptio optima quae est pessima*—the corruption of the best is the worst. The second is from 2 Thessalonians 2:7, the *mysterium iniquitatis*—the mystery of evil. Both draw our attention to a mystery of self-created evil and apocalypse gestated and born in the very heart of the bosom of the Church and faith. Illich is not, of course, the only one who has probed the mystery of this phenomenon. See, for example, Girard, *I See Satan Fall*.

34. Cf. Heidegger, *Identity and Difference*; Westphal, *Overcoming Onto-Theology*.

it were. However, it might *today* be questioned as to *whether it is enough*; whether it gives us a post-nihilistic vision of man so thoroughly penetrated by the relation established by his filial adoption that *any* thought of an existence outside the Father could only be a prelude, however unintentional, to the separation of Hell. Perhaps it can only be after the "second fall," as it were, that is the nihilistic rejection of the Face of Christ nurtured and consummated in none other than the very tradition which stretched towards and peaked in Christ, that we could rediscover the true depth, originality, and radicality of this new relation—this relation that makes us persons, children of God the Father in the Son. If ever there was a time to think the human more deeply, *it is now*.

It was the unflinching conclusion of Balthasar that the only salvation for personhood in the strict sense is Christ. The guarantee needed for the discovery and sustaining of the individual as person "can be provided neither by the nonpersonal, empirical world nor by our fellow man—each of whom can only give questionable and precarious assurances to the other."[35] Similarly,

> There exists absolutely no philosophical substructure for what is *decisively* Christian, and it matters little whether one constructs the philosophical anthropology in the mode of Plotinus, of Thomas, of Nicholas of Cusa or of Fichte (like Maréchal and those who follow him): 'for the pagans, too, do all this.'"[36]

Balthasar simply accepts that philosophy cannot answer the only question that really matters: *who* am I? This question can only be answered by Christ.[37] Indeed, the very possibility of even imagining "person" in the first place could only ever be *posed* because of Christ, the concrete universal, the one whose personhood is only explicable in relation to the Father and the Spirit, to an object and an order *beyond nature*. Christ is thus for us the unavoidable horizon and premise, always already present in *any* post-incarnation formulation of person, either the positive reality that consciously or unconsciously colors the questioner's horizon of meaning, or a negative

---

35. Balthasar, *Person in Christ*, 207.

36. Balthasar, *Creator Spirit*, 310.

37. It is also worth listening to the conclusion of Jean-Yves Lacoste, made in relation to Heidegger's refusal to countenance the possibility of the absolute manifesting itself in time: "Neither the world, such as *Sein und Zeit* thinks it, nor the play of earth and world, nor the 'infinite relation' of earth and sky, offer to Dasein, and subsequently to mortals, the theoretical conditions which would enable them to come face-to-face with God—to the Lord of Being, to an Absolute who is a someone, and who promises a relation with him. This is, with all due respect to him, reason enough to take leave of the philosopher [Heidegger]" (Lacoste, *Experience and the Absolute*, 21).

against which the questioner struggles mightily, but without being able to slough its terms and standards off from their imaginative horizon.

This would seem to be at the heart of Balthasar's simple, but properly *Gospel* recognition that we can "be persons only in virtue of a relationship with him [Christ] and in dependence on him."[38] He says that

> I do not know who 'I' am on the basis of a general *gnothi seauton* and *noverim me*, but precisely as something that redounds from the deed of Christ, which tells me both how valuable I am to God and how far I was from God in my lost state. And the deed of Christ makes known the eternal love of God my Father by the fact that a fellow human being, a 'Thou,' has committed himself to the uttermost for me, has redeemed me vicariously and has brought me back into the state of being a child of God.[39]

It seems to me that all we have here is someone who takes the newness offered by Christ seriously. To embrace the radicality of all of this is to show up all other efforts to ground personhood anywhere else as at best pale, half-life *simulcrae*; and at worst, outright idols. By contrast, to take Christ seriously is to locate oneself within the dramatic, existential world of election and adoption, receiving them as pure gifts. This is to recognize that "Neither religious philosophy nor existence can provide the criterion for the genuineness of Christianity."[40] It is to stake your claim on the fact that "what is distinctively Christian begins and ends with the revelation that the infinite God infinitely loves finite man, and this is made known in the most exact way in the fact that he dies the redemptive death (i.e., the death of a sinner) in human form for his beloved 'Thou.'"[41] It is to accept that

> It is when God addresses a conscious subject, tells him who he is and what he means to the eternal God of truth and shows him the purpose of his existence—that is, imparts a distinctive and divinely authorized mission—that we can say of a conscious subject that he is a 'person.'[42]

---

38. Balthasar, *Person in Christ*, 207.
39. Balthasar, *Creator Spirit*, 310.
40. Balthasar, *Love Alone Is Credible*, 51.
41. Balthasar, *Creator Spirit*, 310.
42. Balthasar, *Person in Christ*, 207.

Sacramental Incorporation and Participation

What has been established so far is the still general principle that to be a person is to be in Christ. That is, we have begun by simply taking it very seriously that Christ is the definitive historical event that shatters the terms and conditions of human thought, that "dramatizes" the very posing of the question of who man is and which gives the only real hope of an answer to that question capable of transcending the condition of temporality and finitude. Now, for us, "the simple 'nature' of the creature stands in relation this decree [God's ennobling of the Creature through election and adoption] as clay in the potter's hand."[43] In Christ, we are wholly the Father's.

What remains to be seen, however, is the precise manner in which the Potter shapes the clay. And it is at this point I submit that to faithfully follow the language of Scripture requires that we give a certain priority of place to a fully-fledged filial and nuptial description of the person. That is, becoming a person takes place within the new liturgical and sacramental framing of existence in the Spirit-fecundated mystical and ecclesial body of Christ. And from the existential point of view of the baptized person, immersed inside this body as a participant, this is what is discovered: God is *Father*. God is *Son*. As *Son*, God is *born*. He is *born for us* and in a certain sense *from us*, not from any intra-trinitarian parthenogenic generation, but from the *"marriage"* of God and man in and through the initiation of the Bridegroom, Christ, and the consent of a fruitful *spouse*, the *woman* Mary who conceives of the Holy Spirit (Luke 1:35), who bears the *Son* of God in her own *body*, who becomes the *Mother* of God. God is *Bridegroom*, *husband*. Christ the *Son* marries the *bridal* Church, figure of Mary, and as *husband* dies for *Her* so that *She* might have life. The death of the *Son* is *life-giving*, made so by the *fruitful* intercession of the Holy Spirit who continues to spiritually *impregnate* and *fecundate* the *Bride* and *Mother* Church with the gift of the *Son's* life-giving sacrifice. The Church, *Bride* and *Mother*, in receiving the self-gift of the *Son* and the *fruitfulness* of the Spirit, then gives *birth* to *children*, to the *sons* and *daughters* of God the *Father*, *children* who receive the gift of a *filial* relationship to God the *Father*. Finally, the *children* of God look forward to the fullness of eternal *sonship* in the world to come in the *wedding feast* of the Lamb.

---

43. Balthasar, *Prayer*, 34.

The Nuptial Trilogy

What we can in shorthand simply call the "nuptial mystery" of faith above is, for the Christian, not just something in a text, not just one trope among many in the deposit of faith. It is not just a nice story or a series of helpful pedagogical ideas or edifying aspirations which can easily be reduced or situated by more fundamental natural or metaphysical categories or contemporary pastoral imperatives, or by whatever passing hermeneutical motivation serves your purpose. Rather, my argument will stress how faith is existentially and dramatically enacted—that is, it leaps out of the text of the Scriptures and becomes embodied in the lives of theological persons— in and through the liturgy and sacraments, particularly in what I call the "nuptial trilogy" of baptism, the eucharistic liturgy, and marriage. In the sacraments, which we might call the *actualized* word of God, the nuptial and filial story of salvation takes on literal flesh: it is here, in the concrete action of liturgy and sacrament, that we become embodied persons; that the textual data of Scripture is organized and literally enfleshed *in us*. In this, holding fast to the integrity and credibility of the liturgical and sacramental rites themselves, we ourselves, in our new sanctified sacramental spiritual and bodily personhood, become the definitive, embodied, anthropological interpretation of the text. The story is definitively "interpreted" by the embodied forms that life in Christ takes in and through the Church, and it is to these forms that the new theological person owes their first and foremost allegiance.

Of our nuptial trilogy of sacraments, it is the eucharistic liturgy,[44] as "source and summit," that is paramount in the sense that what is signified, accomplished, and received here is the very enactment and consummation of the historical unveiling of the Mystery itself, in sacramental form. The eucharistic liturgy is the *anamnesis* of "*the mystery hidden in God from all eternity*"[45] unveiled in its fullness in the Son's spousal, salvific relation-

---

44. The reader should note here my deliberate use of "eucharistic liturgy" rather than simply the "Eucharist." This is done so as to make clear that that Christ's eucharistic presence in the sacrament should not be thought of first and foremost as a static presence (however much it is true that its "reality" persists beyond the liturgical celebration in the sacred species itself) as much as it should be thought of as origin, archetype and, in the fullness of its liturgical context, the dramatic enactment of the believer's baptismal transformation and participation in the events of salvation history. In this, it is in the full drama of the eucharistic liturgy that is expressed the full meaning of eucharistic presence. Otherwise, without awareness that the change of bread and wine into the body and blood of Christ is aimed towards a change *in us*, we risk abstracting and thus "devotionalizing" Christ's eucharistic presence, diminishing its radical anthropological effect and demand on us.

45. John Paul II, *Theology of the Body*, 203 (19.4).

ship to the Church constituted in history, the union from which we are conceived and birthed as children of the Father in and through the Son's spousal relationship with the Church. But if the eucharistic liturgy—the sacrament of the Bridegroom and the Bride—is the source of all possibilities offered to the Christian, it is only in virtue of its *first* gift that the Christian can ascend to the summit.

The first gift of that which the eucharistic liturgy celebrates is baptism,[46] the gate opened by the efficacious sacrifice of the eucharistic Lord through which the self, otherwise "naturally" alienated from God by sin and death, is immersed back into the Mystery, incorporated as an adopted participant—a "person"—in the passion, death, and resurrection of the Bridegroom, the history consummated and poured out sacramentally in the eucharistic liturgy. Without the events celebrated and made present in the eucharistic liturgy, there can be no baptismal adoption of the self into the Father. But without baptism, there can be no access to and participation in the eucharistic feast. A baptismal anthropology, then—that which we are moving towards here—must begin phenomenologically in the experience of the person who comes to be for the first time as a consequence of their generation from the font; the font created from the blood and water that flowed from the side of the eucharistic Lord. Without this, there is and can be nothing: there is for us no access to the mystery of Christ's nuptial, eucharistic love, no access to the Father's filial love.

But before articulating this in more detail, we need to introduce the third pillar in our nuptial trilogy, which is marriage. Sacramental marriage, a vocational sacrament distinct from the sacraments of initiation and healing, is included in this trilogy not because partaking in it as a vocation is necessary per se for full membership in the body of Christ, but rather because in it is impressed in sacro-anthropological form a created, "symbolic" or iconic vision of the eucharistic and baptismal grammar of faith, one present from "the beginning." It is in a concrete sense the "visibility," the microcosmic anthropological instantiation of the full nuptial and filial grammar of the eucharistic liturgy and of baptism.

And it is at this point that the particular contribution of St. Pope John Paul II must be specifically flagged. Even if we expressed certain reservations regarding the *philosophical* infrastructure that still broadly informs his hermeneutics of personhood, there can be no question that this pope made inestimably valuable contributions when it came to describing who

---

46. When I speak of baptism I presuppose that the sacrament of Confirmation belongs also as an intrinsic part of it, as indicated in the restored order of receiving both together prior to the first reception of the eucharistic Lord.

the specifically *sacramental* person is, both in general, and in relation to the spousal vocation in particular.

At the heart of John Paul II's "theology of the body" is a deeply sacramental description of the person within the perspective of the network of personal relations signified and made possible by the filial and nuptial body whose range of *signification* extends far beyond the limits of the horizon of nature, even if the body of *fallen* man can never access and attain this signifying power on its own. In the beginning, Adam is brought to the realization that his body is not like that of the other animals (Gen 2:20). In tandem with his discovery of himself as having subjectivity, as being loved, (as set aside, chosen by God, from and for God) Adam begins to discover further layers of what his being is all about via the symbolic "speech" capacities of his body. John Paul II says that "Man is a subject not only by his self-consciousness and self-determination, but also based on his body. The structure of his body is such that it permits him to be the author of genuinely human activity. In this activity, the body expresses the person."[47] The most genuinely human activity that it permits him to be the author of and participate in—in what we might call the "horizontal" expression of man's capacity for relation to God—, is discovered and expressed in and through the "one flesh" communion of persons formed with woman (Gen 2:24). This capacity for John Paul II constitutes a "primordial sacrament" of the "*mystery hidden in God from all eternity.*"[48] That is, it signifies something about man's first and fundamental capacity to be in relation with God.

Here, we can note how in the creation accounts of Genesis we get very little indication of what man and woman's relationship to their Creator looks like in terms of fine details. Instead, what is "fleshed" out here in this ancient, multi-layered text is man's capacity to be in relation *with woman*, which becomes a kind of sacramental "visibility" of the terms of man's radical capacity for relation *with God*. The (chronologically) pre-christological text preserves a mysterious silence on what it actually means to be in relation to God, for this God, in the Jewish faith, is the totally and ineffably Other. At no point can or does the text directly suggest the full contours of the pre-lapsarian relation of man and woman to God. For the mystery of God's love in Jesus Christ has not yet arrived (i.e., historical event: incarnation, death, resurrection, redemption, salvation). But it is precisely in the second meaning of original solitude, in the "one flesh" relationship of husband and wife that we see the text articulate, in horizontal form, a worldly "incarnation" or concrete "echo" of the vertical relation, so to speak, in the unity

---

47. John Paul II, *Theology of the Body*, 154 (7.2).
48. John Paul II, *Theology of the Body*, 203 (19.4).

and communion that takes visible shape here. The *original unity* of man and woman seen here is in some way the visibility and foretaste of the relation to God that the Incarnation will open to the person.

The point of the above is that from the very beginning the Mystery offers itself to be interpreted according to its archetypal sacramental figures. As a consequence, it does not "hang" above us as an abstract reality to which we only ever have discrete and disconnected glimpses. Rather, it is present via the very bodiliness of existence, via incarnate relationships taken up in real time and space between real human persons. The "body," then, in both a literal sense (the human body) and as a symbolic marker for history and context as the worldly theater of revelation, is the lynchpin, the "hinge" (Tertullian) of the relationship between God and man. It is the *place*, the *context*, the *history*, the *mediation* of and through which our relationship to God is made real and concrete, through which he becomes something much more than an idea or an abstraction "out there." Through the drama that takes place within bodiliness God himself in his fullness proclaims himself. And it is only on this basis that we can understand properly one of the more well-known phrases from the Theology of the Body: "The body, in fact, and only the body, is capable of making visible what is invisible: the spiritual and the divine. It has been created to transfer into the visible world the mystery hidden from eternity in God, and thus to be a sign of it."[49]

It is here that the Mystery first begins to be revealed. The entire theater of salvation history is the bodily space *par excellence* where the Mystery is unfolded amidst the ever-increasing dialogue of God with man. And the nuptial relationship is central to this story. Here, from the very beginning, the man-woman relationship is the typological and sacramental visibility or human incarnation of the God-man relationship as it will be revealed in Christ, and further, hints the pope, of the very trinitarian Mystery of God himself:

> we can deduce that *man became the image of God not only through his own humanity, but also through the communion of persons*, which man and woman form from the very beginning. The function of the image is that of mirroring the one who is the model, of reproducing its own prototype. Man becomes an image of God not so much in the moment of solitude as in the moment of communion. He is, in fact, 'from the beginning' not only an image in which the solitude of one Person, who rules the world, mirrors itself, but also and essentially the image of an inscrutable divine communion of Persons.[50]

---

49. John Paul II, *Theology of the Body*, 203 (19.4).
50. John Paul II, *Theology of the Body*, 163 (9.3).

Relationality—specifically, a nuptial relationality—lies at the heart of the original revelation of the Mystery in the opening pages of Scripture, is progressively revealed in the nuptial metaphors of the Old Testament prophets (e.g., Isaiah, Hosea), is explicitly and authoritatively referred to by Christ himself in his three words ("beginning," "heart," and "resurrection"), and is brought to its theological fulfilment in the theology of St. Paul (Eph 5). The significance of this is that this "visible sign of marriage in the beginning, inasmuch as it [will be] linked to the visible sign of Christ and the Church on the summit of God's saving economy, *transposes* the eternal plan of love *into the historical dimension* and makes it *the foundation of the whole sacramental order*."[51]

And this is why the sacrament of marriage is so important, worthy to be included in the same breath with the eucharistic liturgy and baptism, our other two sovereign sources of Christian identity. For we see replayed or rehearsed in the fundamental created constituents of marriage, in microcosmic form, even from the beginning by way of primordial sacramentality, the baptismal drama of begetting, origin, creation, and filial belonging, and the eucharistic drama of consummation, gift, sacrifice, and conjugal fidelity. Marriage is the original *anthropological enactment* of what is existentially and historically accomplished in the eucharistic liturgy and baptism, the articulation of their fundamental logic, the stuff with which they are made, the rhythm upon which they are based. Though the body after sin and before the Incarnation cannot deliver on the signifying range of possibility that it proclaims, it nevertheless bears within itself the vision of the deepest sacramental fulfilment of the person which will emerge in the history of Jesus Christ.

The Eucharist and Baptism as Nuptial Mysteries

With the Incarnation, passion, death, and resurrection of Jesus Christ, the full signifying range of the body is finally activated. The primordial sacramentality of the beginning is definitively fulfilled by its archetypal source and expression in the nuptial union of Christ with the Church. According to the logic of what we might call the great Johannine and Pauline "reversal" (cf. John 1:1–3; Eph 1:3–6), Christ and the Church are revealed as the *definitive* source and archetype of the man-woman pair—not just some optional, merely extrinsic and instrumental add-on due to unforeseen circumstances, i.e., sin—according to a plan of election made by the Father from before the foundation of the world. The Genesis "beginning," then, is only a chronological beginning,

---

51. John Paul II, *Theology of the Body*, 503 (95.7).

not an ontological one. The big surprise is that the *real* story, the real form is and always was the christological and trinitarian story and form, as they are expressed in their anthropological fullness in baptism, the eucharistic liturgy, and in full *sacramental* marriage in the Lord.

To take this seriously would mean that at no point was the manwoman relationship—in everything, including its *bodiliness*—ever *anything but a proto-sacramental reality*, an anthropological impress and icon of the God who is Love. From this absolute perspective, then, there is therefore no mediating, purely "natural," substantial body that would signify merely the capacity for union, human flourishing, social stability, and the place for raising children that is then only merely extrinsically and conditionally raised or elevated to the status of a sacrament.

This more naturalistic approach—which Ouellet describes as the "imitation model"[52]—, as we can recall, has been the dominant motif in the tradition when it comes to the hermeneutics of marriage. I have already referred to Ouellet and Scola's belief that the tradition has struggled to reconcile the natural and sacramental hermeneutics of anthropology in relation to what it means to be married *in Christ*. We have already seen the elements of this struggle in chapter 1. Here, a still essentially naturalistic hermeneutics which exhibited many of the substantialist presuppositions and characteristics just outlined above has made it difficult to describe the sacramental dimension of marriage as a *structural* ontological component of a couple's relationship according to the kind of sacramental rewriting of the laws of nature and grace that might become possible on the basis of a properly baptismal, eucharistic, and nuptial existence. Recalling Ouellet's words, marriage has in the past been understood "almost exclusively from the point of view of 'nature,' even if one affirmed that this nature was 'elevated' by Christ to the dignity of a sacrament."[53] Within this hermeneutic it has proven difficult to bridge the gap between a naturalistically conceived substantialist notion of person (with all of its attendant ambiguities regarding how to read the sexually differentiated person) and an adequately radical view of the person as a new sacramental creation in Christ by virtue of the eucharistic liturgy and its baptismal consequences. The tendency has always been a ground-up approach from nature to which the sacramental dimension has been added as a rather uncomfortable and disjointed moral and medicinal afterthought.

For the purpose of greater clarity regarding just what our baptismal and eucharistic alternative implies, it is worth returning first to crystallize

---

52. Ouellet, *Mystery and Sacrament*, 83–84.
53. Ouellet, *Divine Likeness*, 214.

how the classic account of what we might call "theological naturalism" dealt with the question of marriage as a sacrament, and thus lost out on its truly theological and anthropological significance. In its first utterance, marriage is in this hermeneutical tradition stressed as a natural reality of the world to which the sacrament is then added (note the similarity here to our preceding discussion of the nihilistic fate of person understood according to the conditions of a substantialist ontology—should we be surprised that now many Catholics themselves think of the sacramental dimension of their marriage as, at best, a mere ornament?). The classic expression "Christ raised marriage to the dignity of a sacrament," a staple in the Tridentine approach to marriage[54] and a formulation still commonplace today,[55] was employed with the presumption of a clear delineation between nature and grace in this context where the former was thought of as the bedrock to which the sacrament is added by the language of elevation or addition.

Now it well may be that very elevated sacramental things are in the last analysis said about marriage that deeply qualify the natural bedrock of the sacrament, but as long as the controlling hermeneutic is one that suggests that man and woman *first* constitute a self-contained *natural* unit which is then "raised" more or less intact only after the fact, as it were, to the status of some special extra dignity, then the element of a deeply dramatic, historical, and infrastructural re-qualification or re-signification will always be missing or only tenuously and partially "added."[56] And marriage will therefore present as a reality more deeply or structurally controlled by principles and perspectives internal to nature, with the added qualification of course that this nature embodies the wisdom and laws of the Creator.[57]

---

54. Cf. Leo XIII, *Arcanum Divinae*, 9, 39; Pius XI, *Casti Cannubi*, 1, 12, 34, 49.

55. Cf. Second Vatican Council, *Gaudium et spes*, 48; *Familiaris consortio*, 13; *Catechism*, 1601; *Order of Celebrating Matrimony*, §1; *Compendium of the Social Doctrine*, §220. I am indebted to Reina Kido for tracking down many of these references.

56. Scola suggests that the problem with the category of elevation is that it risks fostering extrinsicist analysis of the married state, "that is to say, the view of marriage as an institution fulfilled in itself, to which the grace of the sacrament is added only in the second instance" (Scola, *Nuptial Mystery*, 205). In the footnote to this claim, Scola adds the important observation that "This perspective has not entirely disappeared from current theological discussion." In fact, it appears today to have reasserted itself under the auspices of a kind of *pastoral* extrinsicism of reduction, where the concrete and living dimension of married life is thought of as imposing its imperatives and necessities on the possibilities of the sacramental norm, now conceived of as an abstract "ideal." Cf. Francis, *Amoris Laetitia*, 121–22; Kasper, *Gospel of the Family*, 12.

57. A classic example of this is Paul VI's encyclical *Humanae Vitae*, where the structural language of articulation regarding the ethical status of the conjugal act is one still based strongly on "nature" and the "moral law." It can be noted that while the words "sacrament" and "sacramental" appear only 6 and 2 times respectively, "nature" appears

Once marriage is conceived from below thus, its sacramental dimension can then be thought to involve divine grace understood as a supernatural gift of spiritual "energy" or "animation" layered overtop of our merely "human" nature, offering the carrot of eschatological fulfillment and added possibilities to attain the holiness needed to get there. Sacramental grace in such a marriage, then, would not entail a real "structural" or "bodily" change to the spouses in a marriage which would re-signify and reanimate the classical "ends" and "duties" of marriage, but would only give them the strength to be more "natural," more as God intended them to be from creation as a *natural* ordinance and according to universal moral laws: "Be fruitful and multiply" (Gen 1:22). And sacramental grace would accomplish this from the outside, as it were, medicinally: through a "moral depositing" of the power (grace) that flows from the relationship of Christ and the Church into the heart of each individual spouse, giving the spouses spiritual *viaticum* to fulfil their marital duties and obligations to one another (cf. 1 Cor 7:3–5; Eph 5:21–24; 1 Pet 3:1–7), to respect the dictates of the natural moral law, and to raise up children in the Lord (cf. Eph 6:4). Included in this would be the "politics" of the conjugal relationship, whose hermeneutics is largely derived from perceived universal truths of human nature which, as we have seen, has among other things always tended to presuppose that the position of receptive femininity cannot be called a full perfection of existence.

A marriage so functioning—firing on all of its "natural" cylinders, if you will—will then have fulfilled its mandate to be a "sign" (extrinsically, of course) of the new covenantal love of Christ for his Church and will have accomplished it analogously in the married couple. The couple will have adequately "imitated" this archetype, but they will have done so first and foremost by obediently conforming themselves to "structural" truths about their union *a la* nature.

But something critical is lost in this approach. To refuse *marriage* a deeper signification is to refuse also the deepest possibilities of the eucharistic liturgy and baptism. What is critically important about the *theology* of the nuptial and filial body as articulated by John Paul II is that it provides a deepened sacramental infrastructure within which to more radically appreciate the depth and significance of the Johannine and Pauline reversal

---

17 times, "natural" 21 times, and "law" a grand total of 52 times. The latter three are clearly the fundamental hermeneutics through which the question is explored, even if Pope Paul's understanding of them is always deeply informed by recognition that nature and law are expressions of God's command and wisdom, and even if an incipient personalist conjugal spirituality is also present. The point, however, is that the governing principle is of nature and law as immanent expressions of God's will which, as such, are easily detached from Him. As we have discovered, it is a shorter step from nature to nihilism than we have perhaps recognized.

and the sacramental economy therein; specifically, the way that it challenges the more segregated approach to anthropology according to a substantialist hermeneutics. To treat the body (nature) theologically and sacramentally (on the authority of Christ), as *already signifying* (even if not able to attain its aspirations on its own) *something of the possibilities of personhood* (a fact that only becomes fully apparent in the Incarnation) is to prevent the transition from natural individual to theological person from being reductively and dualistically understood. A theology of the body points *both* to a sacramentally constructed body that is always already more than merely natural, *and* to the ultimate sacramental principle of fulfilment and integration in the theology of *Christ's* body.

Thus, it is on these grounds that when we say that the individual becomes a person in Christ, this does *not* mean either 1) that Johannine and Pauline theology (particularly in their eucharistic and baptismal import) only every merely conditionally "hovers" over a still essentially naturalistic anthropological superstructure (as in the dominant anthropological approach in the tradition, i.e., the imitation model); or 2) that the nature which the individual bore previously is simply sloughed off as a consequence of the Johannine and Pauline reversal so that the subject who is produced bears no intrinsic relation to the capacities and signification of his native, pre-baptismal being.[58] Instead, the person produced by baptism is a radiant *sacramental* person, *first* a "hylomorphic" unity, not of body and soul (i.e., not according to a intracosmic standard), but of the union of sacramental humanity and the divinity received by inhabiting the Son's perfect hypostatic personhood. For the baptized, this *new* "hylomorphic" unity, which *now* takes precedence over any principle of unity internal to the natural individual, is the unity established *on the basis of relation*—hylomorphic unity thus becomes *"hypostatic"* unity. More precisely, hylomorphic unity (i.e., body and soul) is placed within hypostatic unity, inside the relation of the son in the Son. This places the principle of internal unity of the individual "inside" the now prior and constitutive Johannine and Pauline reality of the individual elected, named, redeemed, and adopted in and from the nuptial work of Christ, releasing its deeper symbolic or signifying capacity from both the horizon of death and from the substantialist prison of Greek anthropology and metaphysics. In this way, we can thus begin to see hints of how interpreting marriage from within *this* hermeneutical strategy will bear fruit when it comes time to examine the conjugal politics of the couple whose marriage is so placed "inside" the mystery itself.

---

58. We will see the details of this second point in the next chapter.

For now, my cumulative point is thus that taken together, the nuptial trilogy of the eucharistic liturgy, baptism, and marriage have the potential to release us from inadequate anthropological hermeneutics and strategies that end up truncating not only the anthropological possibilities of faith but also its deepest theological reality. To read these sacramental mysteries as *the* hermeneutical figures of faith (as opposed to offering mere modifications and grace in the abstract) is to have the broader text of faith deeply incarnated within the living visibility of the sacramental acting person. Of these three, I wish argue that it is baptism which is the most *epistemologically and hermeneutically* important inasmuch as it is the fundamental and constitutive experiential condition which places *this* person inside faith, which makes them the literal signifying bearer of the mystery, and is thus the condition of the capacity to perceive and integrate the form signified by the nuptial trilogy as a whole, i.e., the Christ-Church form in both its theological and anthropological expression in the sacraments of the Eucharist and marriage. It is thus from this point—from the point of view of what we might call the perspective of a theology of the *baptized* body, or as we have previously said, from the perspective of a baptismal theology of relation or simply from the perspective of the baptized person—that we propose to construct a baptismally supercharged version of the cumulative perspectives embodied in the key theological insights of Ratzinger, Balthasar, John Paul II, and Ouellet.

We have already suggested the broad lines of what this project might look like, and hopefully we now have the perspective to begin to more deeply appreciate its shape and significance. At its heart it involves the unflinching determination to think all substances and all relations from within the dramatic heart of our adoption by the Father in Christ. To think, is to think as a child. It is to think as one for whom the borders of nature and grace have been collapsed and rebuilt with the new synthesis generated from the fruitful marriage of Christ and the Church wherein and whereby the hypostatic gift of Christ's own personhood can be extended *even to us*. In the context of the baptized person, this synthesis is absolute. Grace does not just hover above the nature of one who receives it, perhaps making conditional incursions from time to time therein; rather it *marries* it. The radicality of baptism is such that it brings to its recipient the concrete ontological realization of the union of nature and grace which is archetypally united in the hypostatic being of Christ, and which is poured out for us his spouse, the Church. Inasmuch as Christ's fundamental mode of being (here, his relation to the Father) is made available by the baptismal death, immersion, and resurrection of the individual in this sacrament, it can be asserted that what is produced is a form of personal existence that radically deconstructs any binary notion of a being who, as it were, merely straddles the dual reality of nature and grace.

What we have here, then, is a baptismal metaphysics of the acting person—e.g., the *concretized* concrete universal that is the *analogia baptismi*—where for this person the very fabric of the space and time which had formerly supported and mediated their existence is in fact shattered, replaced by a new sacramental subsistence in the filial relation to the Father, taken up in and through the Son's own Spirit-filled filiality, existentially expressed and communicated in the sacramental forms of the ecclesial body of the Bride. It is this existence which is definitive for the baptized person.

It is of course true that everything "rational" or "realistic" about us resists the radicality of this claim. For empirically speaking, the concrete experience of grace might most of the time be felt only as a kind of feeble moral or eschatological qualification rather than a deep ontological one. This pull of realism or what Jean-Luc Marion, following Husserl, calls the "natural attitude"[59] can perhaps be thought of as the persistent bane of anthropology, one that has prevented and continues to prevent full appreciation of the Johannine and Pauline christological reversal in its properly *sacramental* cast. Today, particularly, the realist in us refuses to believe that Christ's work in the world could be very much more than a moral, cognitive, and intentional gift of inspiration to which we are obligated to try to approximate, albeit with a very generous principle of critical freedom regarding just how far I can be expected to do so given any number of life circumstances, which may thus absolve me of the prerogative to actually seek holiness or become a saint. We continue to make false alliances with the old, to absolve ourselves of the responsibility to give of ourselves ever more fully to the new.

But my argument is that we are called to embrace the paradox that in fact everywhere permeates the New Testament text, which we might better perceive once we have relativized the notion of a bedrock anthropology thick enough to give us personhood. For the baptized, it must be the case that the "real me" is the sacramental me, the me made by the genealogy of faith. This is despite the fact that empirically, according to my "substantial" mode of being, I remain the same individual I was before. I possess the same visible nature, I inhabit the same visible time and space. But here the hypostatic logic of Christ's existence shows us the expanded possibilities for our own. It will not be the case that our possession of "divinity" is absolute as it is for Christ (there is only one eternal Son), but it must be thought of as no less real, *for we are really joined to Christ in a one-flesh union.* Christ's humanity has bridged the gap between our humanity and the divinity. In Christ, the

---

59. Cf. Marion, *Erotic Phenomenon*, 29.

Father has adopted us. He has inconceivably allowed us to inhabit the relation which, rightfully speaking, belongs only to his Son.

And the way we are permitted to inhabit it is through the body; specifically, through the *baptized* body, the fully realized body. Because we are from the Father, inasmuch as creation is formed in the Son, an outpouring of this Father-Son relation *ad extra*, the body—the same body inscribed with the nuptial and filial attributes—has always spoken of our capacity for full adoption, even during its long self-imposed exile in sin. Now, in Christ, its signifying potential, its memory of its origins, has been fulfilled. It has met the relation which constituted it. Its immersion in the font has now made it that much more than a signifying reality that could only ever hope to one-day reach the signified. The relation has been fulfilled in the new, radiant sacramental person who arrives to the reality of which their body continued to speak of and hope for, in an embodied and fully conscious living presence-to-divinity via the mode of a child. All bodies speak of this hope: for the baptized, this hope has become real.

It is because of the specifically *baptismal* person that that we can also speak of a properly eucharistic and nuptial person. That is, the baptismal person, born from the nuptial and eucharistic font can now inhabit the broader sacramental and liturgical forms of Christian existence from which he has been generated. Thus it is that the baptismal person is more broadly the *sacramental* person, the person whose being occupies and is occupied by the full mystery made possible by Christ's hypostatic, filial, and nuptial accomplishing of our salvation. And as we will see in our next chapter, it is this person who will take up the vocation of sacramental marriage in an entirely original way. To more deeply and adequately clarify the conditions of the person's baptismal and sacramental participation in the mystery, is to open a more radical path to the "corporate" resignification of the person that happens in sacramental marriage.

Trinitarian Incorporation and Participation

But before we move to this task, there is one final thing to be done. We can now say with a certain confidence, with the necessary conditions in place, that the baptismal and sacramental person is also by extension the *trinitarian* person. As the general introduction to the rites of Christian initiation puts it, "The Blessed Trinity is invoked over those who are to be baptized, so that all who are signed in this name are consecrated to the Trinity and enter into communion with the Father, the Son, and the Holy Spirit." The theological person who has received the Father, Son, and Holy Spirit *sacramentally* in and through the sacramental forms of the Church, is a person whose flesh has been stamped with a trinitarian impress, and who has been invited into and is already participating in its *communio*.

But what we have hopefully clarified more precisely is that at no point can this gift of trinitarian identity be thought of as something for the human person that is *anything else but the baptismal and sacramental reality that mediates it*. That is, for the person whose existence is enveloped by the folds of his or her adoption, lived and experienced here and now in liturgical and ecclesial time and space, the trinitarian dimension will not appear for us as anything but a lived, enfleshed, concrete, personal, and *mediated* reality of the Father, Son, and Holy Spirit active and present in our midst in our baptism and in the ecclesial forms of faith. That is, the Trinity *for us*, will be the same Trinity as received in and through the action of baptismal existence. If there is certain "doctrine" associated with the immanent Trinity in the abstract, it can only become anthropologically significant within the hermeneutics of baptism.

In this regard, it is my contention that it will not be enough to conceive of the relation between Trinity and anthropology from any point other than that of a radical baptismal actualism, any point other than the sacramental middle. One may of course be able to generate valid general or systematic claims, perhaps general statements about the affinity between human *communio* and divine *communio*,[60] about sexuality being part of the *imago Dei*,[61] of marriage and family being the privileged *imago Trinitatis*,[62] perhaps even an affinity of human sexuality with the immanent Trinity.[63] But unless these links between the Trinity and anthropology are first and throughout framed by a more dynamic notion of Trinity active in the body of Christ and communicated to the person in the sacramental forms of life in Christ, it will not be possible to "marry" the two realities in a genuinely integrated *hypostatic* union.

In this, a baptismal theology of relation will provide an essential deepening of the two modes of thinking that have to date generated the most fruitful possibilities for trinitarian transpositions: analogy and katology. Ouellet has stressed the need to balance and supplement the traditional analogical approach to the creature's relation to God (an ascending method that

---

60. John Paul II, "Letter to Families," 6; *Mulieris dignitatum*, 7; *Theology of the Body*, 163 (9.3).

61. Scola, *Nuptial Mystery*, 32–50; Ouellet, *Divine Likeness*, 20–37.

62. See Balthasar, *Truth of God*, 62; Ouellet, *Divine Likeness*, 20–37.

63. Cf. Schindler, "Catholic Theology." Schindler gives an account here of Balthasar's (somewhat controversial) "suprasexual" reading of the relation of the trinitarian persons. See also Scola's discussion in Scola, *Nuptial Mystery*, 117–18.

balances "affirmation and negation in expressing the resemblance and difference between creature and Creator"[64]) with what he describes as the "katological" method espoused particularly by Balthasar. Katology, as distinct from analogy, "reverses the perspective and starts from on high to enlighten created realities."[65] This change of perspective relies heavily on Balthasar's dramatic re-framing of anthropology wherein the starting point and animating center is not "the *a priori* structure of the spiritual creature" (i.e., "nature"), but rather the "*a posteriori* determination that is given in Christ."[66] More generally, Balthasar's Barthian-clarified insistence that the *analogia entis* must be interpreted according to its christological center made it possible to shift from an abstract metaphysical approach to analogy to a dramatic and historical one. Balthasar's approach could be described as "kata-analogical."[67] In this, while Balthasar retains the notion of an analogical impulse that ascends from below (*eros*)—a genuinely creaturely longing and yearning that seeks union with the infinite and eternal from which it originates—it is only in Christ (*agape*) that any claim of human thought or experience could become truly meaningful. Without this original and perspective-altering experience whereby God "interprets Himself," so to speak, through his Word, Jesus Christ, any "analogical linking remains inchoate, the stuff of images and traces, confused experience, dead-ends. Only through the revelation of the absolute—through Christ as absolute form—can the images and traces of *Dasein* finally be perceived in their fullness."[68]

Peter Henrici observes how Balthasar's approach is thus able to "take analogy more deeply into the event of revelation, so that it turns for him more and more into a 'cata-logy' inasmuch as the ontological difference(s) become increasingly evident in the light of, and are increasingly grounded in, the trinitarian and Christological difference."[69] Wolfgang Treitler argues that Balthasar's katological approach both provides safeguards against the tendency of analogy to set the terms of Christ's engagement with the world and saves the genuine content signified by the world.[70] The descending movement of God's love, given sacramental form and occupancy in the

---

64. Ouellet, *Divine Likeness*, 14.

65. Ouellet, *Divine Likeness*, 14–15.

66. Ouellet, "Foundations of Christian Ethics," 237.

67. In *Divine Likeness*, Ouellet suggests that a "harmonious integration of the two methods should allow us to go beyond the limits present in the tradition of the familial analogy of the Trinity, a tradition that restricts itself to a rather essentialist approach to resemblances and differences between Trinity and family" (Ouellet, *Divine Likeness*, 15).

68. Sweeney, *Sacramental Presence after Heidegger*, 215.

69. Henrici, "Philosophy of Balthasar," 165–66.

70. Treitler, "True Foundations," 174.

world in Christ, is the fundamental hermeneutics which exposes and fulfils all of the genuine patterns and longings in nature: "in Jesus Christ the mystery of the ground of the world burns out more brightly than anywhere."[71] A katalogical starting point in the descending movement of incarnate christological love is thus at the center of all analogical consideration. Jesus Christ, for Balthasar, is the "concrete analogy of Being."[72] And we become persons inasmuch as we are incorporated into participation in his mission given to him by the Father.

Ouellet has put all of this to good use in his own approach to anthropology, particularly his development of a *trinitarian* anthropology. His 2006 book *Divine Likeness* delineates an explicitly trinitarian anthropology of the family, a task he thinks is incumbent on the personalist and christocentric framing of anthropology in the teaching of the Second Vatican Council and in the contributions of John Paul II, in this case, particularly *Familiaris consortio*, which he regards as typifying an approach which tries to take "God's view on marriage and the family."[73] At the heart of Ouellet's project is thus his determination to think the reality of marriage and family from the point of view of a "trinitarian theocentrism" which has become native to the person through the work of grace. It is this perspective which thus liberates one from having to proceed "exclusively from the family to the Trinity (analogy)," and also invites one to "proceed also from the Trinity to the family" (katology)."[74]

Methodologically speaking, Ouellet begins with the question, not of what light the family might (or might not) be able to shed on the communion of the Trinity, but rather: "What does the Trinity wish to express through the family in a global context of covenant?" He goes on to say that this

> should lead us to rethink the familial analogy of the Trinity in a descending perspective, dynamic and existential, which opens naturally into the mystery of the Church as communion, concretized in the 'domestic church.' Such a 'katological' approach should allow us to deepen theological understanding of the covenant between the Trinity and the family, and the significance of this covenant as a missionary reality and as service for the glory of God.

---

71. Balthasar, "Unknown God," 42.

72. Balthasar, *Theology of History*, 74. Cf. also Balthasar, *Epilogue*, 69, where he calls Christ "the analogy of being in person." Nicholas J. Healy argues that this understanding of Christ as the concrete analogy of being is the "most original aspect of Balthasar's understanding of analogy" (Healy, *Eschatology of Balthasar*, 21).

73. Ouellet, *Divine Likeness*, 16.

74. Ouellet, *Divine Likeness*, 15.

As part of his trinitarian theocentrism, Ouellet appeals to Balthasar's view of "the divine work *ad extra* as the prolongation of the intra-Trinitarian processions," in particular, the Swiss theologian's determination that "all work *ad extra* is integrated in the exchange of love between the divine Persons."[75]

Key for Ouellet are the christological and pneumatological elements that mediate the trinitarian exchange of the persons economically. First, the hinge upon which access to the Trinity depends is Christ, the concrete analogy of being. Access to the inner life of the Trinity comes from the possibilities of "the universal mediation of the hypostatic union, which places Christ the Lord at the summit of creation as mediator of the participation of creatures in the divine life."[76] As we have suggested, the Christ who occupies space and time hypostatically and sacramentally and who shares this with his creatures by immersing them in his relation to the Father through baptismal adoption means that the dimension of divine life becomes native—*really* native—to them in Him. Second, Ouellet stresses how the capacity for the christological dimension of marriage to be more than a merely imitative or exemplary dimension becomes actualized through the dynamic mediation and intercession of the Holy Spirit, by and through whom the person is "caught up in the very reciprocity of the Father and Son."[77] The Spirit is the seal of trinitarian love itself, of the covenant between God and humanity, and of the conjugal covenant.[78] The Spirit is, so to speak, the active principle of the present Christ. The Spirit mediates and seals the Son's salvific work in the "real time" of the person or couple who have received adoption and been joined in holy matrimony. And in sealing the relation of the person to the Father in Christ, the Spirit thus seals the relation of the believer(s) with the Trinity itself.

Ouellet explains that

> After having collaborated with the Creator Father in forming man and woman in the image of God; after having collaborated with the Redeemer Son in redeeming fallen love in need of healing, the Holy Spirit lets himself be given to the couple and the family as a royal seal of Trinitarian Love imprinted in the 'one flesh' of the *imago Dei*.[79]

---

75. Ouellet, *Divine Likeness*, 17. Cf. Balthasar, *Seeing the Form*, 506.
76. Ouellet, *Divine Likeness*, 17.
77. Ouellet, *Divine Likeness*, 17.
78. Ouellet, *Divine Likeness*, 79.
79. Ouellet, *Divine Likeness*, 94.

In all of this, then, the dramatic and dynamic christological-ecclesial and pneumatological dimensions of faith constitute the "form" of the trinitarian *imago* in the creature. This would be to say that the trinitarian *imago* is always interiorly constituted by a sacramental principle of mediation, accessible only *dramatically*, by a person sacramentally animated and transformed by the living presence of Christ and the Spirit. The link between Trinity and anthropology can only ever be perceived *in the action*, in the sacramental forms of the drama of *election and adoption*.

What Ouellet wants to avoid is anything static, imitative, or exemplary wherein trinitarian transpositions could come to be conducted in a purely formal manner above or outside the concrete conditions of adoption in the Son. In this regard, it is instructive to note his subtle criticism of Alain Mattheeuws approach in the latter's *Les 'dons' du marriage*,[80] a work that Ouellet otherwise praises. Ouellet's complaint is that Mattheeuws does not sufficiently incorporate the perspective of grace into the conjugal relationship. He thinks that Mattheeuws "remains conditioned by a philosophical starting point which imposes certain limits on the gift analogy. The image and Archetype remain at a prudent distance from one another."[81] Ouellet suggests that Mattheeuws's perspective is still too formalistically centered on the couple imaging the Trinity, rather than the couple *being indwelt by the Trinity itself in and through the dynamic sacramental action of Christ and the Spirit*. "In a word, the absence of a more intimate co-penetration of the Archetype and the image confines certain sacramental riches of marriage to the background."[82]

Another example of Ouellet's concern with an insufficiently christologically and pneumatologically inflected exemplarism is found in a 2013 address where, in reiterating the importance of a trinitarian logic, he stressed the importance of an "existential" *analogia amoris* for our contemporary self-understanding. His point here, following Balthasar, is that the medieval notion of exemplarity must be strengthened by an acute sense that the *analogia entis* is in fact rooted in and nurtured by "a living participation in the synergy of human love and divine love in Christ."[83] The point of all of this is to show how one of Ouellet's primary concerns has to do with enriching the sacramental staging of the theater that mediates the communication of trinitarian love, so that it does not constrict the capacity

---

80. Mattheeuws, *Les 'dons' du mariage*.
81. Ouellet, *Divine Likeness*, 232–33.
82. Ouellet, *Divine Likeness*, 233.
83. Ouellet, "Co-operators of Truth," 223.

of the creature for a much fuller and dynamic incorporation and participation in the triune life of the divinity.

To so enrich the sacramental dimension is to prevent a merely formal perspective from causing the eclipse of the *maior dissimilitudo* from both directions. To "fix the middle," so to speak, is to prevent both a sacramentally uninflected analogical approach from below that imposes an anthropological form on the Trinity and a sacramentally uninflected katological approach from above that imposes a univocal trinitarian form overtop of anthropology. To clarify the sacramental middle is to place all questions of similarity and difference within the context of the incarnate coordinates of the Love that has truly entered into our horizon.

My own baptismal theology of relation and baptismal anthropology—and my conjugal politics—finds its point of departure here. The *trinitarian* person is such only according to the limits of the ecclesial shape of a baptismal, eucharistic, and spousal frame of existence paradigmatically enacted in the nuptial trilogy of baptism, the eucharistic liturgy, and marriage, the logic of which we have already seen. The Father, Son, and Holy Spirit *pro nobis* live here. This is our only real *anthropological* access to any of the doctrinal truths that we might ascribe to the Trinity, especially as they might relate to us. What I propose to do beyond the approaches of the range of commentators we have seen thus far is to attempt to speak of the baptized trinitarian person from even more deeply "inside" their baptismal subjectivity. That is, I begin with the somewhat more radical premise that for the baptized person, there is no longer an above or a below, *strictly speaking*. Above and below—the *kata* and the *ana*—have been exceeded, drowned in the waters of baptism, reincarnated in the new living, immanent synthesis of the sacramental "now," enfleshed in the *analogia baptismi* that is the baptized person who now shares in Christ's hypostatic personhood and filial relation to the Father. Within the *analogia baptismi*, the person will live the gift of a trinitarian identity received from the eternal Trinity within and according to the actualized "now" of baptismal existence. There is no jumping out of one's skin to live according to any law except the one given to us in history. For this person, there is no Trinity except the Trinity poured out in baptism and active in their being through the sacraments. From the point of view of our sacramental "now," there is nothing that can remain untouched and unshaped by the baptismal text. It is from this dynamic, actualized point that the person inhabits the mystery and confronts the complexity of existence. The person will read the mystery and themselves within the transformative *now* of adoption, the most fundamental beginning, the most fundamental hermeneutic.

All of this would mean that to explore the question of conjugal politics will not for me involve an objective or formal approach which would approach the issue from the point of view of any abstract principles (whether naturalistic, historical-critical, or theological in the abstract, say) which could be nakedly or systematically applied to the theme in question outside the perspective of a living human person who "inhabits" the realities in question first-hand. For example, I will not treat the paradigmatic Christ-Church relationship except explicitly through the experience of the one for whom this relationship has become a living presence in and through adoption. I will not treat any creational foundation for Christology except through the experience of one who has had this foundation redimensioned according to the living christological participation they have received. And I will not treat any trinitarian dimension except through its communication in the actualized christological and creational dimension of the baptized person.

My point of departure and my fundamental hermeneutics, rather, is the person who has been grasped and existentially awakened by the mystery, the person who bursts from the font gasping for air, and who then looks around in amazement at the new world of meaning he has been born into. It is the person whose reality is pregnant with a theological meaning that can be seen, tasted, and touched here and now. It is a person for whom the events of the story of salvation have become living, immanent and actualized events right here, right now in my flesh and in the liturgy. It is the person who is already "inside" the Son's relation to the Father, already internally fecundated by this relation of relations in and through the sacramental and liturgical forms and figures of the Church.

In the next chapter, I will attempt to express more deeply the way in which this perspective of the baptized person is realized in its definitive male-female iteration.

4

Sexual Difference in the Baptismal Relation

The previous chapter sought to develop the broad infrastructure of the baptized, acting person, the new reality to which we are all called as persons in Christ. It showed how the hermeneutical norm for anthropology lies first and foremost within the perspective of the person's hypostatic participation in Christ's filial relationship to the Father as son by baptism. This norm is communicated above all in the archetypal sacramental forms of baptism, the eucharistic liturgy, and marriage which together constitute the key parameters of a fundamental theological anthropology. Of these, baptism was argued to have pride of place as the existential point through which the mystery is entered, perceived, and existentially realized in and through the sacramental coming-to-be and progressive conversion of the baptismal person crucified and raised with Christ. It is from this point that the grammar of the eucharistic liturgy and marriage can then be made an effective, living reality in a person's life. This baptismal person here receives the sacramental impress of and participation in the form of Christ's relation to the Church. And they further receive a sacramentally mediated trinitarian identity as one adopted into the Son's relation to the Father.

I have suggested that a robustly *baptismal* anthropology may help us to more adequately interpret the variables associated with the question of conjugal politics. As we saw in chapter 1, the predominant presupposition that has governed treatment of the male-female polarity in the tradition was that it belonged ontologically to an order of nature within which, for a variety of hermeneutical reasons, the male was perceived to be the superior "first" to the female, who was in turn the inferior "second." This was claimed to be theologically underwritten and legitimated by a revealed structure of theological archetypes (christological, ecclesial, mariological). As a consequence of a methodological naturalism in the former, along with the subsequent tendency to extrinsically juxtapose the two orders, the theological archetypes were easily construed as "imitative" ideals—not intrinsic sacramental norms anthropologically native to the person via the theology of the baptized body—crowned extrinsically in the perspective of the redemption of the body (cf. Rom 8). The interpretation of St. Paul's specific teaching on headship and submission as merely a theologically inflected or repristinated affirmation of the ontological norms of human nature qua nature is located here.

The logical flipside of this more essentialist-naturalistic framing of the anthropology of conjugal politics is today's now-dominant historical-critical set of hermeneutical tools which tend to strip anthropology of *any* determinative ontological content, instead privileging an historicist mode of cultural theory (more often than not, atheistic in basic presupposition) wherein both anthropology and the theology that grounds and informs it come to be regarded as equally culturally generated realities, and therefore fluid, time-bound, and provisional. In this case, any textual realism regarding Paul's teaching can be easily abandoned or re-symbolized in an androgynous and egalitarian manner.

In each instance, my argument is that we are dealing with insufficient accounts of the historical-sacramental "now" that is in fact constituted by the hypostatic union of divinity and humanity in Christ, and shared with the believer by baptism, one that must now impact how one approaches the textual foundation for conjugal politics. We see above two variations of the same tendency to compartmentalize and "substantialize" that which belongs to the created sphere, whether this takes form as the absolutizing of nature or history, or whether it takes form as hybrids of nature-plus or history-plus (which more or less each amount to the same thing).

In a *baptismal* anthropology, by contrast, there can be no construction of personal identity that begins in either a purely natural or a purely historical-cultural hermeneutics. There can be, for the baptized person, only a *dramatic* identity where the natural and historical determinants of identity are brought into a higher synthesis. That is, according to a hypostatic understanding, there is only *one* baptismal person and identity: there is no longer both person *and* nature, properly—that is baptismally—speaking. Nature and history have been reforged in the personal identity of the one elected, redeemed, and named by the Father as son in the Son. Now your true nature and history is this relation to the Father that makes you a "person," which is to say that *what* you are has been dramatized, brought into the hermeneutics of *who* you are. In the baptismal identity of the self, temporal and finite "whatness" have met eternal and infinite "who-ness." Thus it is that when we search for an answer to the text's apparent teaching that the husband is the head of his wife, and that the wife is to be subordinate to her husband, we must presuppose at all times the *"living forms of the 'new man'"*[1] as the existential lynchpin of all anthropological analysis from the point of view of faith; the new baptismal and personal flesh of the adopted son of God the Father first and foremost according to the intrinsic criteria of the baptismal "now" of the sacramental middle.

Thus it will be that sexual difference—with all of its questions of rank, authority, obedience, order, and the like—must be pursued within the new filial missions that each man and woman receive by being crucified and raised with Christ, by having their masculinity or femininity "remodelled" according to the norms of their new identity as radiant sacramental persons; according to their inhabitation of the filial and nuptial archetypes of faith in more than a merely exemplary or imitative manner. Here, I will contend that fundamental anthropological questions that belong to being male or female (sexual identity, sexual difference, or "gender"—namely, all of those features which will underwrite sexual and conjugal politics in essential ways) can only be properly explicated in the eschatological identity framed by a specifically *sacramental* logic of faith. On my account, the baptismal man/husband and the baptismal woman/wife will emerge from the heart of a baptismal logic enriched with something more than the accounts given by both teleo-substantialist and historico-cultural accounts. I will assume that all of the designations of what for lack of a better word we can cumulatively call the "gendered discourse" intrinsic to faith—whether said discourse takes place in relation to human persons or divine persons therein—derive from the *sacramental middle*, and are read most fundamentally within the hermeneutics of adoption. And I will contend that to begin in the dramatic, historical perspective of adoption will release the gendered discourse of faith (including its sharper edges) from captivity to non-personal, non-baptismal modes of description that limit the contents of said discourse to either the partial or illicit strategies of nature or history. The signification of the sexually differentiated body (with all that it portends for both human persons and divine persons) will here appear within the measure and constraints of the givenness of becoming a son of God, of inhabiting Christ's own relation to the Father as Son.

In simply taking it for granted that the central archetypal nuptial and filial designations received here—God is Father, that Church is Mother and Bride, that Christ is Son and Bridegroom, the reality to which the person enters as adopted son and daughter—belong "literally" to the revealed deposit, I will therefore be assuming that approaches that begin from fundamental

---

1. John Paul II, *Theology of the Body*, 323 (49.4).

disagreement that such designations could bear a "literal" meaning (such as radical feminist approaches or the approach of "queer" theology) are, in terms of hermeneutical foundations, based on fundamentally flawed anthropological presuppositions, as are (albeit, to far lesser extent) approaches that begin from the premise that such designations belong to merely substantialist and teleological premises that faith will then prop up extrinsically. Rather than doing violence to the givenness of the text in its "literal" presentation of itself, I will thus be committed to more adequately expositing *what is already there, according to the possibility of its deeper givenness*, hopefully releasing it from hermeneutical strategies which have served to mask its truly "excessive" and theologically "saturated" character.

In this, on the one hand, the "literal" meaning that I assume will from the start be "traditional" in the sense that I will remain within basic doctrinal limits when it comes to many historical conclusions generated from taking the gendered discourse of faith seriously. For example, on the basis of the baptismal discovery of Fatherhood, I will assume that when Scripture calls God "Father" it refers, not to a culturally generated conception of fatherhood then mapped blindly or naively onto divinity, but rather to *the highest and purest form of Fatherhood* which then in and through the baptismal-sacramental dimension of personhood is given to the male person in an eminent and perfective way, clarifying, critiquing, or consummating every element of created human fatherhood.

On the other hand, where I will depart from the substantialist interpretation of this gendered structure of the faith is in my willingness to see in this structure per se and a priori the grammar of a much fuller eschatological and ontological meaning of the person. In other words, I assume that "body" belongs to faith *from the theological "beginning."* What is accounted for here is everything that unbaptized nature wants and desires in its fullness, that to which both its existential and bodily pattern of signification irrepressibly tends. The terms and structure of the gendered discourse of faith are "real" in the most eminently possible sense. But only in the sacramental middle can we discover what this might truly look like, beyond the frames of both substantialism and hermeneutical suspicion. This will set us on the road to the question of conjugal politics.

In this chapter, then, I will sketch what can only still be a rather halting and imperfect theological portrait of the man and woman who, as it were, descend together back into the baptismal font which birthed them as individual persons to emerge from it as *a couple*, no longer as individuals properly speaking: a one-flesh, sacramental communion of persons remade in a new creation of personhood in Christ. I will seek to articulate the terms of their deeply dramatic and sacramental origin in Christ and try to reach a deeper account of what their relating to each other as man and woman in the context of this origin might hint toward when thought more radically according to a baptismal ontology and anthropology. I will then conclude by considering anew, in light of the hermeneutics generated herein, how one might then negotiate the textual foundation of conjugal politics, focusing on the specific difference implied in the Eph 5:21–33 *Haustefel*.

Becoming a Man and Woman in Christ

We have already seen the basic logic of the (still generically conceived) self's transition from natural individual to theological (baptismal) person, adopted child. In terms of the basic elements of the rite of baptism, we know that in descending into the font, the *individual* catechumen—man or woman,—descends to crucified incorporation into the mystery of Christ's passion and death and in this baptismal "mini-passion" rises again with Christ as a Spirit-filled adopted child of the Father, sharing in Christ's relation to the Father as beloved Son. This individual's old "nature" is put to death, so that the new person who is generated can, by adoption, therefore really and truly inhabit Christ's own filial relation to the Father. In the death-for-life of baptism, this inconceivable grace is offered to *us*. We become persons in Christ, sons in the Son. In all of this, we become something much more than "nature"—we become persons, in the fullest sense, through the mystery of election and adoption enacted in the baptismal font.

To read this from a different angle, we can say that baptism represents the consummating re-signification of the same body, male or female, that from the beginning proclaimed the original sacramental gospel of filial and nuptial existence. Baptism, we might posit, is *the* moment, *the* historical *event* that definitively *fulfils* the first meaning of original solitude, the meaning that John Paul explained in terms of the first man's realization that he is "from the first moment of his existence *before God* in search of his own being."[2] Everything about his being from the first searched for communion with his Maker; he is incomplete and ultimately meaningless without it. In the offer of baptismal adoption, this search finds its eminent fulfilment in redemptive filial union, *real, dynamic, historical union* with a God revealed and discovered as Father in and through the event of the Son.

In this sense, baptism offers the definitive answer to original man's primordial recognition of himself as created for "*unique, exclusive, and unrepeatable relationship with God himself.*"[3] It reveals man's ontological,

---

2. John Paul II, *Theology of the Body*, 149 (5.5).
3. John Paul II, *Theology of the Body*, 151 (6.2).

existential, and historical status as a child of God, in relationship with God *in time* through the mediation of the ecclesial-Marian body of the Church. It definitively fulfils the sacramental watermark of the event of Christ carried in his body from the beginning. Baptism is thus the historical consummation of original solitude that places man in a situation of *definitive* unity with his Creator. Existential filiality, therefore, is *the* mark of the relation of the creature to Creator: to be a person, is to be a child.

But we also know that the baptismal font has more than a filial significance. For to be filial, it must also be nuptial. It must belong to and be generated by a deeper drama of a prior love. Children do not come from nothing. Children are generated, brought to being from *a prior reciprocal relation*. To be a father or mother requires the union of husband and wife; hence the centrality of sexual difference. The origin of *theological* persons, theological children, is no different. For to trace the steps of our filiation is to discover that along with the Father, there is the Son, the Bridegroom in his spousal relationship with the Church, who is called Bride and Mother. It is to discover that our new existence as persons derives directly from a salvific, spousal act made in time in and through the Bridegroom's gift of himself to the Bride. God's Fatherhood *pro nobis* and our identity as His children, then, are mediated by a marriage: by a man and a woman, husband and wife, by a human womb fecundated by divinity.

In Christ, God is a Bridegroom as well as a Father. It is by Christ's uniting to his Church that we are conceived and generated. The Fatherhood of God, therefore, is mediated by a husband (Christ) and a wife (Church). The Fatherhood of God is joined to an ecclesial Mother (Mary-Church). It is mediated by a properly nuptial or spousal relationship. The waters of baptism—the waters that make us children—are also *nuptial waters*, the womb of the ecclesial Bride and Mother.[4] The Spirit that is received here and in the sacrament of confirmation is the same Spirit already present and active in fecundating and sealing the nuptial relationship of Christ and Church, who becomes an abiding presence in the life of the baptized, completing in them the work of conversion so that they may become perfect, like their heavenly Father (cf. Matt 5:48). Not for nothing, then, does the *Catechism* say that "already Baptism, the entry into the People of God, is a nuptial mystery; it is, so to speak the nuptial bath which precedes the wedding feast, the Eucharist."[5]

---

4. "The Church is the mother of the sons of God; it is in baptism that she brings them forth. So the symbolic meaning of the rite is ready at hand: the baptismal bath is the maternal womb in which the children of God are begotten and brought forth" (Daniélou, *Bible and the Liturgy*, 48).

5. *Catechism*, 1617. For the nuptial symbolism of baptism, see Daniélou, *Bible and the Liturgy*, 191–92, 206, 217; Scheeben, *Mysteries of Christianity*, 374, 543–44; Ouellet, *Divine Likeness*, 212–13.

And as John Paul II puts it, "the one who receives Baptism becomes at the same time—by virtue of the redemptive love of Christ—a participant in his spousal love for the Church."[6]

Note again that this nuptial generation of the sacramental person means that our generation does not take place as a univocal parthenogenic birth directly from the Father or from the intratrinitarian relations themselves minus a definitive principle of mediation. Before and while we are trinitarian persons, we are christological and ecclesial persons: filial and nuptial persons, born from the union of Christ and Church, from the supreme relation of difference. Our existence comes from the Cross and the font, not from the sky, as it were: from the work of the Father in salvation history in the Son (Bridegroom) through the Spirit, in the fecundation of Mary (mother) and Church (bride). Our genealogy is therefore first *historical*—the work of the Father, Son, and Holy Spirit in time and space—before it belongs to anything we are capable of saying about the immanent Trinity. This means that the conditions for the sacramental person's incorporation into the Trinity are to be found, in any truly meaningful way, *in history*, not ontology (whether the ontology of human nature or the ontology of the divine nature), in relation, not substance. The sacramental person whose nature has by baptism been re-signified with the ultimate eschatological figurations which from the beginning constituted it is nevertheless reborn to live this new identity in history, according to the historical forms laid down by the Son in his relation to the Bride. Trinitarian identity is consummated in sacramental and ecclesial expression.

In this way, we can now speak of the individual person, whether male or female (for both bodies are baptized, both become children of God) as the filial fruits of the hypostatic drama of a nuptial love set in motion by the Father, constituted and realized in the divine initiative of Christ the Bridegroom who calls humanity to himself as his bride, and from this union gives birth to unique individuals, children—male and female—through the fruitful anointing of the Spirit. Each of us, as children of this nuptial union, then, thus bear its gendered "DNA" in our flesh. We are "related" to the Father, now, by adoption, in the most eminent way, the totality of which is illustrated by the original *total immersion* of baptism. And we thus have, however derivatively and distinctively, the same filial and nuptial marks and capacities as the divine archetype. The doctrine of the *imago Dei* thus lives most fully here, in the dynamic historical event of adoption and not as a static, default ontological status.

---

6. John Paul II, *Theology of the Body*, 482 (91.7).

At this point we can pause and take stock of a few key things that have been established so far in preparation for our goal to articulate the baptismal character of sexual difference and its import within a baptismal economy. First, we know that both man and woman always and everywhere experience the pull of original solitude. To each belongs the fundamental existential experience of lack and an insatiable appetite for the eternal that no temporal source can satisfy. Second, within the sacramental economy we witness both man and woman coming into the presence of an answer to this original lack, an answer that comes in the form of filial and nuptial categories. By this, we see man and woman pulled into the orbit of a divine drama of filial and nuptial love which is given to them as the answer to their solitude. But third, at no point does this revelation remain something extrinsic to them. Rather, this revelation—in its definitive gendered character—reveals anew the corresponding structure of signification in the bodily dimension of created masculinity and femininity, fatherhood and motherhood, a structure that has in the forms of the sacramental economy now received the full vision of what it signified from the beginning. Without saying that man and woman could ever possess the fullness of this vision in their pre-redeemed state (i.e., by "nature"), it is nevertheless true that they bear in their flesh and in their relation to one another as man and woman the typological and phenomenological foreshadowing of the ecclesial revelation of nuptial and filial forms, accessible phenomenologically in experience, both human and in Christ now sacramental.

In this sense, the revelation of christological and ecclesial nuptiality and filiality may therefore be indicating a deeper and lasting significance of what it means to be created male or female in this life, even within the context of both man and woman by baptism becoming sons in the Son and having their fundamental point of orientation shifted to the heavenly and eternal. That is, there is a reason why the grammar of sacramental faith involves a whole host of gender designations (father, mother, husband, wife, son, daughter, brother, sister) and not just "persons." And further, this suggests that the human meaningfulness of being male and being female may not cease to have value even in light of the properly ecclesial and eschatological fulfilment of the bodily structure of original solitude in baptismal adoption. Man might still need and be incomplete without woman, and vice versa, even if each as individuals have by baptism received the sacramental and eschatological grammar of the fullness of union which their bodies signify.

For it remains that case that becoming a person in Christ does not abrogate the fact that in their spiritual and bodily constitutions man and woman are still *made for marriage* as they were from the beginning, and that they still live in a world that has not yet been brought to its full eschatological destiny. In their psycho-somatic constitutions, man and woman are still primed for a particular nuptial relation to one another, despite the fact that they now enjoy the highest filial union with the Father in Christ by baptism. Precisely what, then, will happen to this primordial male-female relationship within a baptismal economy? Will it have only an extrinsic, relative, and conditional value, perhaps such that a heroic fidelity to it no matter the cost cannot be expected? Or will it be placed "inside" the archetype from which it came, and thus acquire a new sacramental value, dignity, mission, and the grace to be faithful?

The End of Sexual Difference in Light of the Eschaton?

To answer this question, we continue with an exploration of the way a baptismal perspective sheds new light on the full range of the experience of original solitude. We are now edging back towards deeper analysis of the second meaning of original solitude, "*the one deriving from the relationship between male and female*,"[7] as John Paul puts it. We have just hinted that the baptismal forms of the new economy represent the eminent historical and eschatological consummation of the primary inscription of original solitude, that is, our fundamental infrastructural need for and incomprehensibility without God which was discerned by man and woman on the basis of the body as per the Genesis beginning. The ultimate answer to the crisis of solitude was the full gift of nuptial and filial love in its properly and archetypally divine character, one that in the beginning was by the sexual difference "fleshed" out or given incipient content by man and woman's perception of the gendered other: "This one, at last, is bone of my bones and flesh of my flesh" (Gen 2:23). In our previous chapter, we saw how the second meaning of solitude and the unity achieved on the basis of the man-woman one-flesh relationship in some way constituted the visibility and contents of the first. That is, the man-woman relationship functioned as a mysterious sacramental icon or pre-christological vision of the person's primary relation to divinity which, in the Genesis accounts, is masked by the radical ineffability of God.

But now, within the new sacramental economy, the divinity has in baptism been revealed to us first-hand in unimaginable intimacy as a Father and as a Spouse. Encountered and received in the font, then, is the full reality which the original unity of man and woman signified proto-sacramentally. In this sense, by baptism we have now seen the signified. We have now seen

7. John Paul II, *Theology of the Body*, 147.

everything that the original man-woman relationship pointed to in its "primordial" constitution.

Now if this is the case, then it might be thought (contrary to what we have been implying so far) that this should in fact mark the *end* of the original created significance of being male and female, the *closure* of that original sign of the one-flesh union of man and woman, of the meaningfulness of the horizon of the second meaning of solitude, of all that the sign of sexual difference originally portended in the primordial beginning. For if nature has been "crossed out" or replaced by divinity, destroyed in the font, as it were, and if what it originally signified has now been *fulfilled* in the new archetypal expression of sexual difference in the ecclesial and eschatological figuring of gender in the new economy, then perhaps it stands to reason that the anthropological figures which incipiently signified the fullness of the mystery are simply superseded, made functionally irrelevant.

Put another way, perhaps we are all now, in the new dispensation of salvation history awaiting the fullness of eschatological consummation within what Louis-Marie Chauvet calls the "presence of the absence"[8] or the "empty place"[9] of a world whose forms of meaning have been destabilized or "crossed out" by grace such that it is no longer possible to speak of the created order as possessing an enduring post-resurrection metaphysical intelligibility and meaningfulness per se. Perhaps, then, we are called to live in a radically eschatological way, one that involves relativizing or eschewing the forms of a world that is passing away, that have been superseded by the event of Christ. Perhaps this relativizing of the created order includes a reduction of the *telotic* and sacramental meaningfulness of the one-flesh relation between man and woman. We pause and engage with this interpretation, as one way or another it today represents a profoundly common hermeneutical presupposition in the domain of theological anthropology.

If certain sects within early Christianity declared the end of created marriage in view of the belief in the imminence of Christ's second coming, today it is feminist and "queer" theologies[10] which stridently proclaim the end of the theological significance of sexual difference, not in the name of any imminent coming, but rather in the gnostic sense described by Eric

---

8. Chauvet, *Symbol and Sacrament*, 98.

9. Chauvet, *Symbol and Sacrament*, 70.

10. Queer theology is a contemporary interdenominational theological movement that attempts to think gender, and concomitantly, the Trinity, the Church, and theology in general, outside of the constraining features of "heteronormativity," or "binary" gender, where (for the latter) sexual difference (masculinity and femininity), heterosexual marriage, and procreative sex constitute the exclusive and normative framework of bodily intimacy. Cf. Loughlin, *Queer Theology*.

Voegelin in terms of the immanentizing of meaning and eschatology, or in popular parlance the "immanentization of the eschaton."[11] As one commentator puts it:

> There is only one identity stable enough to hope in. At death my church teaches me that all my secular identities are placed under eschatological erasure. They are not matters of ultimate concern. At my death all that has been written on my body will be once again overwritten by my baptism as it was a few weeks after my birth when I was immersed in the waters of death and rebirth and a new character was given to me which nothing can ever destroy. In the end (anticipated every time the Eucharist is celebrated) before the throne of grace everything will dissolve except that identity. Gender, race, sexual orientation, family, nationality, and all other culturally constructed identities will not survive the grave.[12]

Here, typically, created realities (significantly now cumulatively called only "cultural") begin to be left behind ("overwritten"), *here and now*, in light of their ultimate eschatological figuration, which is interpreted as a destabilizing rupture that overcomes and displaces the created reality that precedes it. The author above assumes that all anthropological identities are neutral or "secular" by default ("not matters of ultimate concern") and that baptism therefore represents *only* a disruptive break with these identities. It is here where Galatians 3:28 is commonly invoked as the definitive proof-text of this claim, as the ultimate scriptural warrant for deconstructing any enduring theological significance of sexual difference this side of the eschaton.

Now, clearly I too have suggested that there is a real death of nature and natural identities that occurs in the baptismal font. Galatians 3:28 really does refer to a new eschatological reality that changes the here and now of existence. However, I have also been suggesting that what is *not* put to death, but rather brought to the *fullest life* precisely by the baptismal death of nature, are those deeper signifying possibilities of the body that belong to its primordial inscription by the Mystery, possibilities which await a new baptismal release, and which are so released in the gendered forms of the sacramental economy. It is thus that we must begin to make a critical distinction between the body of "nature" with all its false and partial identities, and the body of the primordial beginning, whose "echoes" become fully accessible to the new person remade in Christ, in the baptismal person who is graced fully with the reality that those echoes seek after (and which will

---

11. Voegelin, *New Science of Politics*, 117–32.
12. Stuart, "Sacramental Flesh," 74. Cf. Ward, "There Is No Sexual Difference."

thus allow us to properly reclaim and *intensify* everything true and legitimate in the original horizon of creation). That is, while it is true that the post-lapsarian *historical* body—the body of nature, of culture, the fallen body—bears any number of false inscriptions and accretions accumulated within the hermeneutical perspective of alienation born from the curse of Genesis 3, it is nevertheless the case that the original *fundamental sacramental signification of the body*—all those primordial elements encoded in Genesis 1 and 2—is precisely what is brought to new life in and through the baptismal rebirth of the person by being immersed in the filial and nuptial forms of Christ's salvific economy. The baptismal person thus *reacquires* the mystery of the gendered beginning, only now in the *totality* of its fulfilled signification: in its fully christological, ecclesial, pneumatological, and eschatological signification according to the new forms of Christ and the Church as read through the sacraments.[13]

So, if this new person still bears this (recreated) primordial sacramentality of the beginning and if after their baptismal transformation they are sent back *into* the world rather than immediately *out* of it (i.e., to its and their ultimate eschatological consummation in the life of the world to come), then this means that the original anthropological inscription of the Mystery will not lose its *raison d'etre* in this life. Instead, the anthropological structure of sexual difference will become the Mystery's signifying engine and mediating point, its sanctified site in the world, its domestic liturgy, working in tandem with its newly appreciated archetype, the Christ-Church relationship and the ecclesial body. Via the baptized body, man and woman in sacramental marriage are sent back into the world to continue to be a sign of the Mystery as they were in the beginning; only now as a sign also of its *baptismal and eschatological fullness*—one re-written in their flesh by baptism,—and as the means of sanctification both for themselves and the world.

And so if baptism gives the ultimate answer to the first meaning of solitude (the theological question of our primary relation to God), it also gives a new and ultimate meaning to the second (the anthropological question of our relation to each other as man and woman), a meaning that I will argue holds an important key for discerning the deeper bases upon which the question of conjugal politics stands.

I will thus now move towards a baptismal rereading of the experience of the discovery of the other, first recounting the second creation account of Genesis (2:18–24) and the anthropological implications therein, beginning

---

13. John Paul II's discussion of "spiritualization" and "divinization" helps to draw this claim into greater relief. Cf. John Paul II, *Theology of the Body*, 379–412 (64–72).

with consideration of the primordial structure of difference as it appears in a broad anthropological context.

Sexual Difference According to the Primordial Beginning

First recall how in the Genesis narrative the original unity of man and woman is described in terms of Adam's declaration of recognition of the woman: "bone of my bones and flesh of my flesh" (Gen 2:23). Adam recognizes in the woman a common humanity within difference.[14] This John Paul II describes as "somatic homogeneity."[15] Before considering man the male or female, his point is that to exist in the visible world is to be fully human: it is to be marked with the sign of origin from God and to bear the capacity to express and reveal the Mystery of that origin. It will be within this bodily homogeneity that differentiation will then take shape as the two precise theological modes of expressing and revealing the Mystery.[16] At this point, however, the pope's point is simply that the body's capacity qua body to reveal origin and solitude is a "fundamental anthropological issue that is in some way prior to the issue raised by the fact that man is male and female."[17] Particularly pertinent within this emphasis is his affirmation that "*the woman is created in a certain sense based on the same humanity*,"[18] important in that it will underwrite the notion that woman is man's creational equal. Woman too, like man, is adopted by the Father.

From this foundation in a common humanity before God, John Paul II then moves to consider the point of *difference* within the unity of body-persons. In this, a theology of the body is specified or "fleshed" out by a "theology of sex, or rather, a theology of masculinity and femininity, which has its point of departure here, in Genesis."[19] Because of *difference*, the somatic homogeneity of man and woman is not such that man and woman simply stand side by side with each other dispassionately facing their creator

---

14. Balthasar observes: "Had God not formed Eve from Adam but (like him) from the dust of the earth, their unity would have been an external one, and Adam would not have recognized her as 'flesh of my flesh'" (Balthasar, *Person in Christ*, 285).

15. John Paul II, *Theology of the Body*, 161 (8.4).

16. He speaks here of how "their *unity* [i.e., as sharing a common humanity] *denotes above all the identity of human nature; duality, on the other hand, shows what, on the basis of this identity, constitutes the masculinity and femininity* of created man" (John Paul II, *Theology of the Body*, 161 [9.1]).

17. John Paul II, *Theology of the Body*, 148 (5.3).

18. John Paul II, *Theology of the Body*, 160 (8.4).

19. John Paul II, *Theology of the Body*, 165 (9.5).

without, as it were, looking at each other. Or, because of *difference*, their relation is not reducible to a "*communio* of the pub" or "*communio* of the academy," as it were.

Rather, somatic homogeneity and the first meaning of solitude are in a specific way "magnetized" horizontally, you might say, in and through the creative tension of difference which turns the man and woman into a face-to-face relationship, one that will also be magnetized vertically. This act of turning to face the other, far from a turn away from their primary relation to God, one that will lock them in the intracosmic sphere of idolatry,[20] is instead a turn deeper into the sacramental heart of the mediation of the ultimate christological and trinitarian difference: it will thus help to open the person to the full discovery of difference in their being from and for the Father as it will be expressed fully in the new sacramental experience of bodily love in the filial and nuptial forms of ecclesial existence in Christ. That is, the first meaning of solitude (relation to God) is enclosed within the folds of anthropological mediation according to the second meaning of original solitude (the relation of the man to the woman on the basis of the sexually differentiated body). The first meaning is played out here, visibly, sacramentally, corporeally, dramatically, in the flesh, in relationship, in time, in the domain of human freedom's conscious appropriation of the mystery via the modality of the person who acts.

Accordingly, were we to extrapolate phenomenologically the broader anthropological conclusions from this, the man and woman who in the modality of nuptial love open themselves to each another in sickness and in health, who lovingly accept children, who embrace the created and redeemed structure of family life, will thus position themselves to experience the deep wound of transcendence that seeks to evangelize them, that demands that they seek out the face of God ever more deeply and urgently, that calls them to relentlessly plumb the depths of the much deeper solitude that the joys and sufferings of their union inevitably suggest but cannot themselves erase. Intimate proximity to the other sex within the radical conditions of the drama of nuptial love, of the mystery of desire, begetting, birth, motherhood and fatherhood, all ripe with the tense experiences of joy, ecstasy, steadfast fidelity, betrayal, suffering, fallenness, sin, life and death all played out in marriage force man and woman in a particular way to existentially confront their own incompleteness as individuals. It makes them aware of and forces them to confront (even if it does not in and of itself guarantee an overcoming of) their own narcissism and selfishness which can be much more readily masked by the autonomy, comfort, and security

---

20. See my discussion in Sweeney, *Sacramental Presence after Heidegger*, 215–19.

of the individual, substantial self who may more easily erect barriers that insulate them from the dramatic call of the other.

In an acute way, then, this structure of difference forces you to make room for the other, it demands that you account for difference—that which is *not* your own subjectivity, *not* your own desires, *not* your own preferences, *not* your own gendered self. Fabrice Hadjadj accents how the difference of sex is thus the fundamental engine of transcendence. He explains that

> I truly become a man only when I am turned toward a woman, but I fulfill myself only by not being ever fulfilled. This is paradoxical. Something like this is called transcendence. Transcendence is not exteriority, it is something that is radically Other, but simultaneously "is here." It is an otherness, but not one that is non-present and it is not foreign. My deepest thesis is the claim that in the sexually endowed human body there comes about an opening onto transcendence.[21]

The anthropological structure that underwrites marriage is thus the call of difference as a perfection; an existential pedagogy of conversion born from sexual difference's original mediation of the mystery of the first meaning of solitude that leads to *the* transcendent culmination of that solitude given in the sacramental economy. It is an opportunity for and path to the conversion and holiness that comes from this ultimate difference. Marriage, so closely tied to issues of relation, difference, origin, generation, transcendence, contingency, lack, time, history, and the like in both its created and fallen reality thus primes and pressurizes the universal restlessness provoked by the first meaning of solitude. And the implication is that when marriage becomes a sacrament in Christ, the whole drama and salvation history and the mystery hidden in God from before all ages now also becomes concretized in the human form of marriage.

It is of course true that many do not take up this piercing wound of transcendence offered by the anthropological structure of marriage. If marriage is the icon, it can by the opposite potential of our freedom become the idol, specifically, through the distortion or eradication of the tension of difference, so essential as the sacramental mediating point of the mystery. If marriage can be refused and deconstructed, it can also become a surrogate by which we take refuge in the sign so as to *avoid* or postpone the more radical hope of ecclesial and eschatological filiality and nuptiality in the signified. Moreover, the greatest hope can, in the context of fallenness and sinfulness, become the greatest despair. But the point to be argued is that the anthropological structure of marriage *is and remains* the primordial testing

21. Hadjadj, "Sexuality as Transcendence." Cf. Hadjadj, *La profondeur des sexes*.

ground, the sacramental vision, the relational frame and place within which the drama of salvation will take place and where freedom will be tested and realized one way or the other.

And so the implication is that that sexual difference is not insignificant within the anthropological structure of created reality as well as the perspective of faith which fulfils it. Quite the contrary, it belongs and remains ingredient to the structure of unity, albeit a unity of tense transcendent aim. It is unity's condition and realization, and it remains such in the in-between time, the baptismal time of Jesus Christ. Difference *as such*, with all its tension and complexity, lies at the heart of salvation history, at the heart of the filial and nuptial revelation of divinity in Jesus Christ. We thus seek to eradicate, diminish, or re-symbolize it at our existential peril. For now, we can affirm that the unity of the face-to-face relationship of man and woman will remain within the essential structure of baptismal personhood.

Sexual Difference Within the Baptismal Relation

Now, we continue to move deeper into the existential question of what happens to this second meaning of original solitude, "*the one deriving from the relationship between male and female*,"[22] within the full context of the baptismal and eucharistic revelation of the Mystery in Christ as it is given to the baptized man and woman.

To start, in the enactment of a sacramental marriage in Christ, as in the beginning, we continue to see in its basic anthropological structure two persons, male and female, who stand face to face, gazing in wonder at each other, desiring to make a gift of self to each other, participants in the original created dimension of sexual difference. Note again, then, that baptism does not eradicate gender. Empirically speaking, baptismal adoption certainly does not de-eroticize the structure of attraction and desire that drives the second meaning of solitude. It does not cancel out the significance of the primordial forms of identity given in the beginning and the dynamisms that mediate them. Thus, it remains true to say that baptismal man and woman *are still man and woman*.

The difference within the structure of attraction and desire *inside* the baptismal relation, however, of which a man or woman may not be consciously aware is, to put it most simply, *history*: an event which by baptism has broken into the heart of the anthropological fiber of existence and experience. That is, these two who gaze at each other in wonder and desire now do so *as two baptismal persons*, as brother and sister in Christ,

---

22. John Paul II, *Theology of the Body*, 147 (5.2).

common offspring of the marriage of Christ and the Church, sharers in the Son's hypostatic personhood, inhabiting His relation to the Father as divine Son, and thus bearers and witnesses of an historical reality both anticipated and now made a full reality in their flesh. In other words, within the very structure of solitude *in a baptismal context*, in its continuing anthropological dynamism of *ekstasis* and reciprocity, the living forms of salvation history itself are themselves present and active. In the created, creaturely experience of the baptized, acting person, man or woman, we see also the living history of Jesus Christ, and in this, not just the universal experience of ontological creatureliness as it existed from the beginning and continued to be mediated in the experience of historical man. For now, in the flesh and subjectivity of the person, *this* man or *this* woman, baptismal adoption has broken any rigid or merely formal relation between nature and grace, ontology and history which, if still in place, would mean that there would be nothing different going on in the experience of a baptized or unbaptized person when it comes to the structure of solitude.

At the heart of this otherwise completely natural, completely normal experience, then, history—history *par excellence*—has been made present; and is being incarnated anew in and through the experience of man and woman. And precisely *what* is being made present, in and through the new baptismal relation in the flesh of man and woman, in an eminently personal way—and if spiritually attuned, *experiential* way as well—is the historical fulfilment, the personal archetypal reality of maleness and femaleness as revealed in Christ and the Church. What this means, accordingly, is that the baptized man and woman receive and experience (each in a unique way, as we will see) a new pattern of signification, one whose content is the living history of the Word made Flesh, the Word made "Bridegroom," so to speak. In their bodies, man and woman experience and embody not just the mystery of filial adoption (that they are born and generated from the nuptial mystery, that they belong to Christ, that they inhabit the Son's relation to the Father), but also the very originating forms and mechanisms of that theological mystery of spiritual fruitfulness in Christ and the Church. In other words, as children, they themselves also have the capacity to become *parents*, to share as *originators* in the very mystery of which they were the recipients, to "re-play," in sacramental form, the very story from which they themselves were born.

It is in this way that sexual difference and the marriage that it makes possible are "re-symbolized" according to the event of salvation, to the supreme and original archetype of marriage, Christ and the Church, brought wholly into the baptismal relation of total abiding in Christ. For adoptive, filial childhood comes already impressed with the "DNA" of its parents, with the capacity to marry, to love one's spouse, to unite so as to become one-flesh, to conceive, to give birth to new life, to love and raise one's children in a properly *spiritual* way, correlative to and iconic of Christ's spousal love and the Father's filial love. In *sacramental* marriage, there is a concrete and specific re-alignment of the now spiritual character of all union and generativity in Christ, and the original primordial order of this life in the world. Unlike consecrated celibates, who aim the new nuptial potential given to their bodies by baptism directly back to its spiritual source, as it were, in sacramental marriage (still lived in and from the world), a particularly *sacramental* way of aiming towards Christ and the Church is discovered, which is by the person's baptismal share in Christ's perfect hypostatic personhood a genuinely ontological as opposed to merely imitative reality. Here, in the one-flesh unity of the conjugal bond, the finite and the temporal are fused with the infinite and the eternal in the new economy of the baptized body, thus constituting in this world a new sacramental sign of the mystery hidden in God from all eternity and manifested fully in the history of Jesus Christ. Thus, almost inconceivably (and certainly, as a shock and a scandal—cf. Matt 19:10) each "frail, sacred union"[23] in Christ bears within itself the full weight of the mystery, whether the believer knows it or wants it.

Now, a man and woman who consent to enter this most peculiar new creation—who as a couple immerse their individual selves in a particular way in the humanity of their spouse and the divinity of Christ—do so, not as a command (i.e., getting married is not a requirement of Christian life) but as a choice. That is, getting married is not necessary for salvation. Indeed, as St. Paul recognizes, marriage comes with a whole host of tensions and anxieties which he is frank in warning the Corinthians of (cf. 1 Cor 7:28). The new spiritual value of marriage does not mean that it is now easy. And in a world that is passing away, that is destined for the fullness of perfection of heavenly glory, even marriage in its sacramental fullness, as a sign of the eschatological world to come, will pass away when that world comes to be. There is thus for the believer the option *not to get married*, to pursue a purely spiritual holiness and perfection in actualized anticipation of the purely spiritual union and fruitfulness of which marriage is a sign. This choice for consecrated celibacy and service Scripture sees as the "better" choice (cf. 1 Cor 7:38), one where the aspect of special charism and mission has always figured prominently, inasmuch as it is a sacrificial departure from the norm in the pursuit of eschatological fullness.[24]

---

23. Harper, *Shame to Sin*, 161.

24. John Paul II calls continence for the kingdom of heaven a *"charismatic choice."* John Paul II, *Theology of the Body*, 414 (73.4).

However, it is also true that the choice to *get* married in Christ is not for that matter something to blindly or deterministically fall into or denigrate, however subtly or "realistically." For indeed, when the sacramentality of marriage is seen as more than an extrinsic "add-on," it appears more properly and more radically as a state of life and vocation of holiness, one that in a certain sense is the sacramental source and embodiment of that mystical reality of union that the consecrated celibate is now able to embrace at its font. In this sense, just as marriage in the beginning was an inchoate fleshing out of who God is in himself, so too does sacramental marriage continue to flesh out the nature of this God, further illuminating the Godhead in and through the now fully historical symbolics of the body. Sacramental marriage thus furnishes the "form" of the consecrated celibate's vocation, just as the consecrated celibate reveals the eschatological completion and perfection of this form by witnessing to the reality of the world to come.[25]

The point being made here is that a sacramental marriage also has a proper dimension of charism or mission, inasmuch as it belongs deeply and profoundly to Christ's own saving mission. It is neither natural nor secular. Ouellet characterizes Balthasar's understanding of mission, describing it as the "temporal modality" or expression of the person's entry into the eternal "filiation-mission of the Word made flesh,"[26] through which the person's temporal sphere of acting becomes expressive of the eternal mission of the Son in his offering of everything to the Father. This is similar to Wojtyla's account of the "acting person," where it is in the act born of conscious freedom that the individual subject realizes him or herself. We might say that it is when a subject's acts flow from and embody a conscious freedom fully immersed in and iconic of the baptismal reality of childhood that their "personhood" is fully realized; that their existence and the acts therein, great or small, acquire the marks of sacrificial love and obedience offered as a gift to the Father in the Son, in and through the sanctifying mediation of the Spirit.

---

25. "On the background of Christ's words one can assert not only that marriage helps us to understand continence for the kingdom of heaven, but also that continence itself throws a particular light on marriage viewed in the mystery of creation and redemption" (John Paul II, *Theology of the Body*, 425 [76.6]). Fleshing this out, John Paul II continues: "spousal love that finds its expression in continence 'for the kingdom of heaven' must lead in its normal development to 'fatherhood' and 'motherhood' in the spiritual sense . . . in a way analogous to conjugal love, which *matures in physical fatherhood and motherhood* and is confirmed in them precisely as spousal love. On its part, physical generation also fully corresponds to its meaning only if it is completed by fatherhood and motherhood *in the spirit*, whose expression and fruit is the whole educational work of the parents in regard to the children born of their bodily conjugal union" (John Paul II, *Theology of the Body*, 432 [78.5]).

26. Ouellet, "Christian Ethics," 237.

As a consequence, the couple is called to live their marriage as a mission in this profoundly spiritual and existential sense, in a particularly "great" (cf. Eph 5:32) way, as a corporate extension and particularization of the universal mission given in baptism. Accepting marriage as a properly baptismal (christological, ecclesial, trinitarian) mission (and not in the sense of any species of mere "add-on") means that at its heart it is for the couple a vocation of specifically *embodied* prayer and worship, a shaping and conforming of the distinct activities of husband and wife, father and mother, into the image of their properly spiritual archetypes.[27] The activities proper to marriage can therefore be neither denigrated nor downgraded to just an extrinsic and conditional "shell game" which does not really express a meaning beyond the human and visible dimension. Rather, they belong fully to the same form of perfect conversion and holiness (Matt 5:48) to which every baptized person is called as an individual, to participation in Christ's mission to reconcile everything to the Father through himself (cf. Col 1:20; 2 Cor 5:18).

And so when a baptized man and woman give themselves to each other in marriage, their unique actions as husband and wife become a corporate expansion of mission; specifically, a mission in which the proclamation of the very inner workings of the nuptial mystery is of the essence. As already suggested, a man and woman in Christ, already "produced" as fruit of the Son's mission of salvation, and now bearing the "genetics" of this mission in their flesh, consent to take on the *further* task of "reproducing" in their own common life the very drama of espousal and marriage that birthed them as children of the filial and nuptial love of the Father in Christ, and doing so for the glory of the Father.

It should not be difficult now to connect the dots as to what this will mean for sexual difference in a baptismal frame. In short, it means unequivocally that gender is freighted even *more* significantly with the forms of divinity, just as from the beginning it has always been freighted with the mystery hidden in God from eternity. Gender is now weighted with the specific forms of salvation history that consummate and reveal that mystery, a microcosmic sign of the "gendered" identities and relationships that pervade the categories of sacramental faith, generating persons

---

27. This does not mean, however, a denigration or replacement of the human qua human, *viz.*, in distinction from divinity proper. Consonant with the logic of the ontological difference or better, the Chalcedonian logic of "no confusion, no change, no division, no separation" between Christ's human and divine natures, the union of humanity and divinity established in the baptized person by sharing in Christ's relation to the Father as Son does not for all that absorb or collapse the uniqueness and specificity of the spouse' unique relationship in both its ontological and historical character.

and persons-in-relation in Christ. In this way, within the corporate mission shared by the couple as a single gift and task, there are also the individual charisms born by virtue of the masculinity and femininity of each respective spouse. This corresponds to the essential forms of *difference* inherent in faith itself, forms which are unique and distinct ways in which the content of faith is revealed, i.e., God as Father, Mary-Church as mother, Church as bride, Christ as Son and Bridegroom. It is from these forms that the baptized person receives the "genetics" of his or her generative archetype, bearing them in baptized flesh, and employing them in and through the performance of the corporate mission of marriage.

Thus it is that masculinity and femininity will continue to place husband and wife in a specific configuration vis-à-vis sacramental marriage. In it, the "inseparable intertwining of sexual difference, love, and fruitfulness,"[28] which in salvation history is revealed fully according to its divine archetype, remains inextricably tied up with the unique capacity of a man to become a husband and father, and a woman to become a wife and mother. These capacities are in Christ revealed in their full glory, and read as the properly baptismal, properly spiritual dynamisms that they are, play out in and according to an arena of action well beyond both a "complementarian" and "egalitarian" hermeneutical configuration. By this, we hope to transcend both a "naturalistic" reduction that both hardens and reduces the significance of difference to terms set by a closed, intracosmic analysis, and an "eschatological" reduction that detaches the significance of difference as borne by the male or female body and self.[29]

All of this will be of the utmost significance when we turn in the final chapter to consider more concretely the "politics" of the relation of husband and wife as it pertains to the question of behavior and roles in marriage. Much more will be said there about the specific contents of our baptismal affirmation of sexual difference as theologically meaningful. For now, what matters is that baptismal adoption definitely does not mean the eradication or flattening of sexual difference per se. Rather, it instead re-dimensions or re-symbolizes difference inside the preeminent theological forms communicated in baptismal adoption, "saturating" its original primordial value with the absolute theological missions that flow from participation in the christological and trinitarian forms of life in Christ.

---

28. Scola, *Nuptial Mystery*, xx.

29. Regarding the eschatological reduction in relation to the question of the ontological and theological significance of sexual difference, it is worth looking at Roberts's incisive critique of three thinkers (Graham Ward, Eugene Rogers, David Matzko McCarthy), each of whom embody variations of this reduction. See Roberts, *Creation and Covenant*, 185–231.

With this foundation in place, we turn now to more deeply reconsider the specific point of difference that arrives with blunt insistence from the textual foundation of conjugal politics.

Reconsidering the Textual Foundation of Difference

My working assumption to this point has been that cultivating a baptismal conception of Christian existence from a point of departure in what the sacramental rites (here, particularly baptism, the eucharistic liturgy, and marriage) themselves signify and make present will generate and has generated a vision of man and woman that grounds their conjugal relationship in the deepest kind of a genuinely *sacramental* and *dramatic* (that is, neither strictly metaphysical nor strictly historical-critical) belonging and unity. By this, in stressing the deep sacramental unity that emerges within a baptismal conception of the person, male and female, I hope to have painted a convincing backdrop and frame from which to now pursue the more perplexing questions and implications raised by the principle of difference within the spousal relationship.

In the preceding section, our treatment of difference did not yet move into the more contentious areas of conjugal politics (*viz.* headship and submission). We have, on broader anthropological grounds, thus far merely confirmed the *theological* significance of the difference that may yet affirm or deny a corresponding politics. The reader will note to this point in my pursuit of a conjugal anthropology in baptismal key a glaring avoidance of confrontation with the more contentious implications of the *Haustafeln* text itself, the motherlode of difference, particularly as it bears on the question of masculine and feminine "roles." This has been deliberate, for as important as this text—and others like it, e.g., Col 3:18–4:1 and ancillary texts such as 1 Tim 2:8–15; Tit 2:1–10; 1 Pet 2:13–3:7—is in regard to a full confrontation with the question of difference, a deeper hermeneutical set of tools needed to be acquired if we were not to risk the two reductive approaches to this question that we characterized in chapter 1.

With this, I obviously presuppose that neither strict historical-critical exegesis nor the hermeneutics of a substantialist metaphysics can suffice for what I presume in advance to be a deeper meaning carried by the text. *Pace* Schillebeeckx (cf. chapter 1), then, I thus take it for granted in principle that the scope of a scriptural text always offers a deeper *theological* or *sacramental* meaning beyond the strict limits of both the immediate intentions and motivations of the human author, and the proximate contextual conditions that a teaching may have had as its primary motivation to address. Both of these horizons are only the visible tip of a much deeper, broader, and universal iceberg of sacramental meaning.

This means that well before we make claims about what any given text may or may not say it is always incumbent on the interpreter to embody a properly ecclesial first movement to a text: *lex orandi, lex credendi*, and here what I have tried to articulate in a more specifically defined baptismal-anthropological sense. The interpreter must presuppose that in principle there is in *any given text* an "excessive" meaning that goes beyond historical-critical or metaphysical possibilities. The ultimate grounds for this claim, I propose, are to be found in the baptismal person him or herself. For if we hold it to be true that the sacramental rites communicate the *actualized word and acts of God* (not just the "idea" of God) then we can see that the first and most significant interpretation of the text *has already been performed in our baptismal flesh*, something along the lines of what has been argued so far throughout this book. The baptismal person is always already a recipient and an inhabitant of the text of salvation history. This person is a living hypostatic text of *the* Text which has already spoken here. This person bears the beating heart of the central mystery of faith given for the life of the believer, that is to say *adoption*, the organic reality and fruit of our salvation in Christ.

And this then means first, that for this person the approach to any text—in our case, the *Haustafeln*—must necessarily bring with it these deeper *core* and *prior* theological convictions of who Christ is and what it means to be in Christ *baptismally, eucharistically*, and *nuptially*, the fundamental reality communicated in the *res* of the sacramental rites. In other words, this is to say the primary "text" of faith—Christ's historical person—precedes the text of the Scriptures, even as the text of the Scriptures becomes the faithful, living embodiment of the text of Christ's person. Because of the *sacramental* reality of faith—the faith given as an actualized, historical living reality,—encountered well before the *textual* discovery of this actualized faith in the Scriptures (with all the necessary complexities contained therein), the believer has already encountered Jesus Christ. They have already encountered the Christ who always precedes the text.

This first interpretive moment thus confirms the sacramental depth and possibility contained in the text, for the baptismal transformation of the person sets a standard and criterion from which to measure and assess a text in its basic theological import. It confirms that, in principle, there is a meaning in the text that by definition transcends any hermeneutical strategy that would, according to deficient hermeneutical commitments, reduce it to general norms, abstract truths, or provisional teaching that could hang outside of a real immersive and bodily transformation of the Christian. A *baptismal* approach to a text begins from the presupposition that the text in question will in principle always contain more possibilities than the textual conditions and motivations that belong to its genesis. This is not to say that this first baptismal approach will bring with it an immediate epistemological and interpretive clarity so as to make further textual exploration redundant, but it will provide what we might say is the core theological sensibility and motivation which must never simply be bracketed out. It would seem that nowhere is this kind of approach more applicable than in those texts which relate directly to matters of Christian identity.

On the above claims, it is important to notice how the majority of contemporary exegetes of the *Haustefeln* largely accept that the author of the text pretty much meant what he said in assigning various subordinate roles for certain parties, e.g., wives, children, slaves. For example, one says: "Attempts by commentators to take the patriarchal sting out of Eph 5:22–6:9 have generally proved unconvincing. . . . The primary purpose of Eph 5:22–6:9 is to provide theological justification and motivation for the subordination of wives, children, and slaves to the head of the household."[30] Another argues similarly that it "is not possible to take the sting out of the insistence that wives are to 'be subject' by contrasting their status with that of children and slaves, who are required to 'obey.' The verb *hypotassein* has the connotation of a subordinate, submissive role."[31]

Moreover, exegetically speaking, it does not seem possible to completely "smooth over" the above conclusion by simply appealing to any alleged egalitarian framing set by verse 21:

> mutual submission coexists with a hierarchy of roles within the household. Believers should not insist on getting their own way, so there is a general sense in which husbands are to have a submissive attitude to wives, putting their wives' interest before their own, and similarly parents to children and masters to salves. *But this does not eliminate the more specific roles in which wives are to submit to husbands, children to parents, and slaves to masters.*[32]

---

30. MacDonald, *Colossians and Ephesians*, 341.

31. Talbert, *Ephesians and Colossians*, 140–41. "Further, Titus 2:9 and 1 Pet 2:18 use *hypotassein* for slaves as well as for wives. Moreover, 1 Pet 3:1, 5–6 uses 'submit to' and 'obey' interchangeably. The shift from 'submit to' to 'obey' in Eph 5–6 is stylistic only. Wives are asked to do the same thing as children and slaves" (Talbert, *Ephesians and Colossians*, 141).

32. Lincoln, *Ephesians*, 366 (emphasis added). Whether or not it can be smoothed over theologically, *a la* John Paul II, is another matter which we are moving towards.

However, most commentators also stress that driving this text is a parenetic rather than strictly theological motivation, even if the latter dimension is clearly invoked in the text[33]: "paraenesis is his [the author's] primary concern, and in the end the christological and ecclesiological formulations serve that purpose."[34] Read with an emphasis on paraenesis, when a theological rationale is invoked it is done so in response to a certain situation or need within the community. The impression is given as a consequence that the perceived constructive and pragmatic motivation on the part of the author (domestic harmony) means that any theological precedent derived from and enlisted for that aim may therefore carry only an instrumental and provisional value that can and should be called into question from different points of view or different contexts. So it is that Galatians 3:28 tends to be adduced as the ultimate conditioning fact for us today,[35] one that comes with the strong ethical imperative to resist patriarchal and hegemonic interpretations of the Ephesians *Haustafeln*: "it is important to acknowledge that the text presents a vision of household relationships, rooted in an ancient setting, that is considered unjust today (and, in the case of slavery, completely immoral)."[36]

From the point of view of a purely textual horizon in the historical-critical sense, all of this would force an uncomfortable choice: either we cling to what appears to have been the author's own convictions in his own time and place about the importance of headship and submission, but apply them to our own time and place on apparently thin or dubious theological

---

33. "The beginning, middle, and end of this passage [Eph 5:21–33] contain exhortations in the form of direct imperatives or similar (stronger or weaker) verbal forms. All these exhortations, except the last pair, are supported by a single motivation: Christ" (Barth, *Ephesians*, 652).

34. Lincoln, *Ephesians*, 389.

35. Placing Ephesians and Galatians next to each other "involves a refusal to apply the household codes inappropriately to the modern Christian family" (Talbert, *Ephesians and Colossians*, 153).

36. MacDonald, *Colossians and Ephesians*, 341. As an aside, I would say that an exegete's integrity would be far better served were they to resist the temptation to offer such extrapolations beyond the intentionally narrow limits they set for their enquiry; limits which seem far too narrow to warrant drawing universal conclusions from the text, but which most seem unable to resist doing, at least in the context of sexual politics. The approach of Marcus Barth seems wiser: "The question whether the change of time and culture permits or requires present-day Christians to reject the injunctions of 1 Cor 7 and Eph 5 cannot be treated in this commentary; only literal and historical problems can be taken up in the following" (Barth, *Ephesians*, 652). Were an exegete to entertain a more broadly theological consciousness that would incorporate other sources of the faith into their research, then there would be no difficulty with the performance of such extrapolations.

grounds, or we go the way of most exegetes today and conclude that the *Haustafeln* provides "spirit" without "form," and thus write off more or less entirely any capacity of the text to speak of a theologically significant difference between man and woman. In the first, to accept the premise about the theological bases of the teaching being merely parenetically and contextually motivated, means that any attempt to universalize the text's teaching will run the risk of merely inflecting an essentially time-bound human conception of difference (with all of its attendant risks) with a certain theological qualification under conditions that by no means guarantee that said theological inflection will be strong enough to prevent the kinds of ontological subordination of woman that we saw in chapter 1. Here, you would safeguard difference, but you might do so for an intracosmic rather than a properly theological difference.

If one chooses the second option, the risk is that the act of relativising the *Haustafeln*'s imperatives tends to produce and itself be the product of an already very thin, merely moral or psychological account of difference, whether we are talking of a theological or anthropological account of difference. Thin anthropologies are logically (and thus almost invariably) paired with thin ecclesiologies, and vice versa. In the end, both seem to rule out the possibility of a genuinely *theological* anthropology operative in the text.

My own contention is that there is a legitimate way out of this impasse, but only if we approach the text *baptismally*, in light of the meaning that the baptized person already bears in his flesh; a meaning which will set certain fundamental parameters for deeper interpretative possibilities in the text. As I have shown, baptismal persons bear above all a *christological* meaning in their flesh, not merely a moral, pedagogical, or imitative Christology, but a living ontological and hypostatic Christology: an actualized Christology within and by which they have become a theological person. In this sense, my suggestion is that the deepest interpretation of difference is contingent on the benchmark of this prior christological flesh—prior, not in the sense that it is formally distinct from or excludes the contents of its textual foundation, but rather in the sense of an organic actualization and vision of those contents via the realized text of the sacraments—converging with its fundamental textual foundation in Ephesians. When the two realities converge, I believe that it becomes possible—indeed, *demanded*—to affirm a difference that includes a real headship and submission as a genuine and universal feature of the text, *but only in a properly theological manner*.

In making this claim, I am fully aware that I am crossing certain "sacred" limits of critical exegesis in automatically espousing the theological dimension as the first and deepest horizon of the text. But crossing these limits is precisely the point.[37] Some of these limits need to be crossed, just as some of the limits of a substantialist notion of the person need to be crossed, as I argued in chapter 3. Let me now try to explicate further the logic of and rationale for this crossing.

Exegetically speaking, I am quite comfortable in entertaining the theoretical possibility that the author of Ephesians (let us just call him St. Paul again) may not himself have had *full* appreciation of the significance of linking anthropology to Christology in the context of the conjugal *Haustafel*—although in principle I think it always wise to give far more credit to a human author's own intelligence and perception: they, in their own intimate proximity to the Christ-event and as recipients of the Spirit's work in and through them, seem eminently more trustworthy than all of our sophisticated "scientific" methods of exegetical retrieval.[38] For the sake of argument, let us imagine that in his own mind St. Paul was only motivated by a functional desire to ensure that the spousal and familial relationships were well-ordered and harmonious in the Christian community at Ephesus. Let us also suppose that he simply took it for granted that woman was the natural inferior of man, and that it was this conviction, along with his pragmatic and procedural desires for order, that influenced his decision to enlist an elaborate theological justification for the order of the sexes. In other words, let us assume that up to a point it may well be true that St. Paul's proximate motivations were not entirely theological.

---

37. Ratzinger's 1988 Erasmus lecture remains just as relevant for us today. Consider: "The exegete must realize that he does not stand in some neutral area, above or outside history and the church. Such a presumed immediacy regarding the purely historical can only lead to dead ends. The first presupposition of all exegesis is that it accepts the Bible as a book. In so doing, it has already chosen a place for itself which does not simply follow from the study of literature. It has identified *this particular literature* as the product of a coherent history, and this history as the proper space for coming to understanding. If it wishes to be theology, it must take a further step. It must recognize that the faith of the church is that form of "sympathia" without which the Bible remains a *closed* book. It must come to acknowledge this faith as a hermeneutic, the space for understanding, which does not do dogmatic violence to the Bible, but precisely allows the solitary possibility for the Bible to be itself" (Ratzinger, "Biblical Interpretation," 22–23).

38. For "even when the sacred writer makes use of modes of expression that prevailed in his time, he uses them according to a new perspective. His thought can never be reduced to that of the profane authors from whom he often drew inspiration. Even when it is materially similar or identical to its Jewish or pagan models, his text takes on a *new sense* in the *new context* of Scripture" (Potterie, "Biblical Exegesis," 36). Further, "the argument that the household lists were merely historically conditioned would need to have a question mark appended to it. Early Christianity did not blindly adopt behavioral models from its social environment, but in each particular case considered very precisely which aspects of general ethics were to be taken over unchanged, given new form, or discarded altogether" (Hauke, *Women in the Priesthood?*, 352).

Now if, for the strict contemporary exegete, it can be demonstrated that this is indeed the proximate motivation driving St. Paul, then it must be the case, first, that headship and submission are only of relative value (if any value at all), and then, probably, that the very notion of a "high" theological-sacramental anthropology (certainly of the kind that I have proposed) in general must be discarded. But even if it could be indubitably demonstrated that this were the case, ambiguity remains. In the first place, this conclusion presupposes by default that divine authorship of a text cannot imbue what might otherwise be thought to be an imperfect or even dubious "literal" aspect to a textual utterance with a deeper message. Otherwise stated, exegetical strategies that reify human motivations and conditional circumstances tend to lock out the possibility that it might be the case that "God writes straight with crooked lines." *Pace* Feuerbach, it might be the case that God speaks just as much through the veiled and humanly imperfect as through the explicit and divinely transparent. If it is true that the interpreter "should carefully investigate what meaning the sacred writers really intended," it is also true that they must attend to "what God wanted to manifest by means of their words"[39] And if we were to follow this logic, then, it may be the case that *from God's point of view*, the teaching that the husband is head of his wife could bear what we might call a "saturated" meaning[40]: a meaning that explodes the strict contextual conditions and imperfect authorial intentions of its utterance, that in fact bears a paradoxical and transgressive theological meaning which transcends both those interpretive reductions we have been considering in this book.

So it is that when the baptismal person approaches Eph 5:21–33 they must have as their first disposition openness to the fact that even the presence of what may appear to our contemporary sensibilities an unnerving or indeed indefensible teaching may in fact bear a deeper signification. To be faithful, a saturated meaning must be presumed as possible. Moreover, as we will point out further, this presumption seems all the more appropriate when we consider the obvious fact that the politics of conjugal difference is housed in such a christological context, as well as that its fundamental claims are further corroborated by a network of ancillary texts. If one takes seriously the belief that God may write straight with crooked lines and that Scripture teaches "solidly, faithfully and without error that truth which God wanted put into sacred writings for the sake of salvation,"[41] then it would be

---

39. Second Vatican Council, *Dei verbum*, 11.

40. In describing what he calls a "saturated phenomenon," Jean-Luc Marion speaks of "the impossibility of attaining knowledge of an object, comprehension in the strict sense," not "from a deficiency in the giving intuition, but from its surplus, which neither concept, signification, nor intention can foresee, organize, or contain" (Marion, "In the Name," 39–40).

41. Second Vatican Council, *Dei verbum*, 11.

imprudent, not to mention hubristic, to reduce such a direct and therefore seemingly *God-sanctioned and approved* inclusion in the text to mere authorial oversight, agenda, or social circumstances. In this case, confronting Ephesians 5:21–33 as both meaning what it says *and* bearing a universal meaning beyond the context of its utterance, is essential.

The risk at this point is if the act of accepting a text in its givenness *is not simultaneously a baptismal act*. That is, the temptation will always be to interpret the acceptance of givenness and saturation according to a hermeneutics of simplicity and transparency, approaching the text "in its literal purity, just as it stands and just as the average reader understands it to be."[42] For it is also true that the "average reader," no less than the critical interpreter, will bring certain hermeneutical criteria to the text, here, perhaps the demand for clarity or order, and in this, not necessarily openness and the motivation of fidelity come what may.[43] However, in contrast to both a false sophistication and a false simplicity—both of which try to control the text in their own ways,—a *baptismal* acceptance of givenness should be both childlike/Marian in disposition *and* rigorous and sophisticated in mode of interpretation. The two should not be thought of as contradictory. Instead, the simplicity of genuine faith should by definition be docile to a deeper expansion, a deeper immersion into the profound and complex glory of the Mystery. When this happens, conditions for a truly saturated interpretation of the text become possible.

I will now turn to explain what the convergence between the actualized Christology borne by the baptized person and the textual affirmation of headship and submission might represent in terms of the question of difference. We know that the actualized Christology borne by the baptismal person represents a certain living embodiment or actualized interpretation of the text, and therefore in a certain sense its hermeneutical standard. In this, within the horizon of baptismal personhood, the adoptive and christological horizons have become the definitive standard of what it means to be human; what it means to be man and woman. And here, their unity as a couple within this standard has emerged as a specific sacramental perfection of our adoptive relationship to the Father through life in Christ.

---

42. Ratzinger, "Biblical Interpretation," 3.

43. This points to the general *human* impossibility of pure objectivity without presupposition in the act of any kind of interpretation. "Pure objectivity is an absurd abstraction. It is not the uninvolved who comes to knowledge; rather, interest itself is a requirement for the possibility of coming to know" (Ratzinger, "Biblical Interpretation," 7); "Reason can only move towards being genuinely universal and impersonal insofar as it is neither neutral nor disinterested" (Macintyre, *Three Rival Versions* 59–60); "One never confronts the subject matter in a 'neutral' fashion: *not being neutral* is synonymous with *having lived*" (Schindler, "History, Objectivity, and Moral Conversion," 577).

This affirmation allows us to say that if headship and submission belong properly to the text as *God-sanctioned and approved realities* according to the rationale just articulated above, and if we must simultaneously hold that any "political" connotations therein cannot be the product of and directed to the "old man" of nature (even notwithstanding any *possible* motivation or intention in this sense on the part of the human author), and if we take the conditions of the baptismal person as a definitive living embodiment of the text, then it must be the case that the frame through which the text's meaning will become manifest is *fully and completely christological*. As Marcus Barth expresses it, "every 'ought' contained in verses 21–33 is supported by a Christological and ecclesiological 'is.' Paul appears intent on saying nothing to the two partners in marriage unless he can show a Christological and ecclesiological reason."[44]

With this, we have established that the meaning of headship and submission (whatever that yet may be more precisely in its anthropological iteration) will therefore be originally and properly christological. The meeting of the baptismal person who appropriates the text within and according to his or her baptismal existence, provokes a fusion of the christological horizon embedded in each. The actualized Christology borne by the baptized person authorizes as definitive and normative the christological horizon of the text, which in turn obligates us to take the christologically defended teaching of headship and submission as normative in principle. Authorized to read the text as properly and originally christological, we can thus say that when Eph 5:21–33 presents conjugal politics as grounded in and supported by a christological politics, *it means what it says*: when the text points to a real "subordination" (*hypotassein*) of the Church to Christ, there must be an equally real "subordination" of the wife to the husband. This must simply be affirmed from the point of view of the textual criteria we have generated thus far.

On this basis, still prior to concrete analysis of the gnitty gritty of the teaching (*viz*. does or does not headship equal male "authority" in a practical, operational sense? If so, to what extent?) we can affirm that the text functions at a deeper level as a concrete attestation of the centrality and importance of difference in the sacramental structure of faith. I think that the order of difference in the 5:21–33 pericope, then, must be thought of first as a kind of blunt or stark reminder of the central importance of difference in general in the structure of faith, one that is pervasive and systematic. Here, difference serves the very existence of the economy of

---

44. Barth, *Ephesians*, 652. A christological reading of the text permits us to confirm that even if the same verb (*hypotassein*) is used in each *Haustafel* to articulate the relationships of subordination between wives, children, and slaves respectively, one must suppose that in the primary *Haustefel* (21–33) *hypotassein* is uniquely qualified by its distinctively sacramental and christological structure.

salvation. The Incarnate Word is essential for the purification of the Bride (Eph 5:25–27). The receptive response and assent of the Church in her docility to Christ, archetypally embodied in the "yes" of Mary, is the fertile assent required as the counterpart to the initiative of the Incarnate Word, for the redemption and sanctification of the world. Without this creaturely "yes" grace could not take root. And any subsequent corruption of this mystery, in both its divine and human pole, obfuscates our ability offer our unconditional yes to this grace.

More specifically, it is an affirmation of the central importance of difference as ingredient in the unity of the couple inasmuch as the couple is birthed from and participate in this structure. St. Paul thus commits his readers to think theologically about difference. He exhorts his readers to think *sacramentally* about difference, to take seriously the missions of difference within the frame of a baptismal existence in Christ. In this, the conjugal politics of difference here should be thought of as a function within and for the greater unity of spousal love. It should be thought of as a dynamic of initiation and response, of calling and answering, that corresponds to two unique instantiations of and vocations to the same love. And it should, on the basis of St. Paul's own words, be taken seriously.

The important thing to affirm before embarking on an interpretation in our final chapter about just what this may mean for the way headship and submission play out in a marriage, is that the "saturated" hermeneutics that we are proposing here disqualifies the two "secular" reductions of difference that we have been encountering throughout this book. We are permitted neither to harden difference into merely natural and hierarchical roles where Christ figures only as a justifying and legitimating "add-on," nor to collapse difference into a hegemony of egalitarian identity that consummates christological extrinsicism with the de-ontologizing and de-sacramentalizing of the entire sacramental structure of faith. Both reductions reduce and supplant the genuinely sacramental shape and depth of Christian faith. Both make filial adoption and nuptial communion mere ornaments within an alternative meta-narrative.

Against these reductions, I hope to have shown how there can only be the *sacramental* iteration of difference within the horizonal saturation and excess of the perspective of the baptismal person. What remains to be done is to articulate an account of conjugal politics within the living baptismal fabric of the relation of man and woman in marriage, as they take up and rehearse and replay the mystery of their sacramental unity each and every day in and through the sacramentality of their domestic church. It is to this task that we turn in the final chapter.

5

Conjugal Politics in the Baptismal Relation

I hope by now to have demonstrated that because of baptism we must take seriously the christological and ecclesiological rationale for conjugal politics and the theological significance of the sexual difference that underwrites it. And my preliminary conclusion therein is as follows: we must accept a real headship and submission within this politics, but we will be permitted to do so *only* on adequately christo-baptismal grounds, e.g., according to the actualized Christology of the baptized person conceived as the fundamental frame and hermeneutics of the text. This is to say that St. Paul's affirmation of a difference and an order of relation between husband and wife must be accepted as a clear aspect of a theology of real difference, but *only* from the point of view of a genuinely theological—that is, baptismal—saturation. The only way we can thereby assess and interpret the character of this affirmation is by doing so from "inside" the multivalent perspective of the saturated baptismal person who has in their subjectivity and sexually differentiated flesh already been given the living core of the christological and ecclesial reality of which the Ephesians text speaks, affirms, and offers its own specification of.

My intention with the foregoing chapter has been only to argue that we must allow the broader anthropological and theological perspective of the baptized person, particularly in both its filial and nuptial iterations, to more deeply inform the textual foundation of conjugal politics. This has led us to a relatively "traditional" affirmation, but with the possibility of a richer, more "saturated" *interpretation* for it. On the one hand, our argument has progressed to the point that we have been led back to a more or less simple or "plain" affirmation that yes, St. Paul teaches headship and submission in perfect fidelity to the Mystery of which he speaks. On this score, beginning from a new hermeneutics—a baptismal theology of relation and baptismal anthropology—has led us back to retrieve the original and unanimous orthodox intuition that has driven the Tradition at least up until *Casti connubii*: St. Paul means what he says, and as such, the order of man and woman in Christ must therefore be an important and meaningful *theological* element of the conjugal relationship.

At this point, of course, opposition from various egalitarian, feminist, and historical-critical perspectives will likely be deafening. But by now I am happy simply to shrug this off. If the absurdity of the event of Christ is true, faithfulness to the word of God must take priority over every other consideration and prevailing social and cultural imperative. If what I cling to is Christ, then I must preach it.

On the other hand, however, if the affirmation of conjugal politics remains "traditional" in the sense described above, the same may not exactly be said of its interpretation. For the orthodox and historic teaching that we affirm is at the same time brought more fully within the baptismal space of election and adoption. Far from being arbitrary or motivated purely by the ubiquitous "modern man needs this or that" imperative, my claim is that this argument rests on the more timeless imperative that belongs to the Gospel itself: conversion to Christ crucified (cf. 1 Cor 2:2). A "saturated" interpretation proceeds from the premise that what every man and woman *really* need is always to be found at a deeper and higher point beyond every reduction and corruption of power, and that our responsibility as interpreters of God's word must take this seriously. This deeper point I have argued to be the christological and ecclesial horizon of the baptismal person, which, if followed radically (*viz.* baptismally) enough, I contend will open up a new horizon of interpretation, one that in leading more deeply into to the mystery via a higher sacramental synthesis, will free conjugal politics from the hermeneutics of both complementarianism and egalitarianism.

The "saturated" interpretation that I will seek to perform in this chapter will therefore be one in which the basic structure and data of faith is respected. Having staked my claim on the christological integrity of the various "texts" of faith, I suppose no post-critical hermeneutic of suspicion or deconstruction when I approach classic themes and sources of faith. All I suppose is that our interpretation of said themes and sources can be much deeper and richer, that we can be drawn much closer to the mystery in a much more sacramental and existential manner. I suppose interpreting difference and unity from within the baptismal subjectivity of the person who is already inside the Johannine and Pauline "reversal," already a child of God in the deepest theological and eschatological sense. I suppose, without transgressing the limits of the greater unlikeness between Creator and creatures that, having received filial adoption through the Son in his spousal union with the Church, by the anointing of the Spirit, that the believer has become a trinitarian person, that in the Son they inhabit Christ's very hypostatic mode of relation to the Father. I suppose that all of this, while a gift truly given to the person and one that immerses them completely in the sacramental world of Christ, nevertheless requires the free response and assent of the one who receives it, a response and assent possible only as the life-long task of conversion and conformity to Christ crucified. I suppose that baptismal existence is only truly received and completed when the baptismal person takes it up consciously, joins it to the sacrifice of the Son, and with the Son, in the Spirit, takes up the mission of returning one's entire self as a living offering back to the Father. Baptismal existence must thus take the shape of vocation, discipleship, conversion, and mission, of a return-gift of everything to the Father in the Spirit of Christ. I suppose that in sacramental marriage—the marriage of the primordial beginning remade and re-signified with the fullness of Christ's gift of self to the Church to which the baptized person is granted new access—read through the lens of baptism and the Eucharist, is discovered the fundamental anthropological grammar of existence as a gift received to be offered back to the Father in gratitude and praise. I suppose that, because of baptismal adoption, the return-gift to the Father in Christ of the spouses in sacramental marriage already takes place "inside" the Christo-ecclesial-trinitarian relation, and that it is this characteristic that makes and defines it as a uniquely sacramental state of life and mission. I suppose that at the heart of this mission of self-gift is the presence of the Spirit, who seals the relationship of the couple, interceding for them with "groanings too deep for words" (Rom 8:26).

So it is that when a baptized man and baptized woman embark on marriage they embrace a way of life that demands much of them, even as it brings the graces that will make faithfulness a real possibility. In this, what will matter most for a deep and faithful living of their conjugal relationship—in particular, for the proper integration of the dimension of conjugal politics—will be a shared acceptance of and commitment to the radicality and depth of the journey they are taking up. To this end, my interpretation will begin with the experience of the couple who approach the altar, and from this point it will then continue to expand and integrate the diverse sources of faith that inform what a common life in Christ looks like in the sacrament. It is within this context that an interpretation of conjugal politics will be fleshed out.

A Spirit-Filled State

The first critical step for the possibility of a truly theological discovery and appropriation of conjugal politics is that both spouses must existentially perceive and "buy in" to the state of life they are embarking on. That is, they must arrive at a baseline awareness and belief that what they are entering into is a state of life that is much more than anything related to nature or to freedom. Regarding conjugal politics, they must recognize that in this sacramental state of life there is no place for "normal" binary and competitive notions of first and second, better and best, commanding and following, leading and obeying, and the like; for they have been remade in the newness of baptismal faith. It is not a relationship of merely human unity where the meaning of difference is only natural, nominal, relative, instrumental, functional, and constructed, or where the Christ-Church relationship is only to be "imitated." It is a relationship where both uninflected hierarchicalism and flat egalitarianism are inadequate. It is, in a word, a relationship where God's call on them as male and female and as a couple is total and absolute.

The couple who grasp this will come to recognize the extent to which their new sphere of existence is dramatic. That is, they will comprehend how their sacramental state of life has broken and is breaking the logic of all false binaries and monisms within the regime of sin that work to alienate God from mankind and man from woman. They recognize that by baptism and marriage, through Christ's eucharistic gift of himself to the Church, the filial and nuptial meanings of their bodies have been liberated from a closed naturalistic interpretation and from an all-determining bondage to the categories of violence, power, and to "pastoral" concessions to sin that constrict and falsify the greatness to which they have been called. The first gift of faith is the gift of a relation that "crosses out" nature and shatters the legions of excuses and self-justifications that pervade a life lived within a merely imitative understanding of faith and which therefore preclude a full appropriation of a baptismal life in Christ.

Above we spoke of sacramental marriage as a state of life possessed of a unique and specific manner of expressing the sincere gift of self[1] and pursuing the holiness to which all the baptized are called. Here, the return of everything to the Father is realized from within the interpersonal relation of man and woman who are together, through sacramental insertion into Christ's mode of relation to the Father (sons in the Son), in the mediation of the concrete *communio* of the Church, Bride of Christ, already placed "inside" the trinitarian relations themselves (albeit, still "existentially" me-

---

1. Cf. Second Vatican Council, *Gaudium et spes*, 22.

diated by baptismal, christological, and ecclesial forms) by a supreme gift of the Father. It is from here, together as a sacramental couple, that they offer themselves to the Father.

Essential in a successful labor of reception and internalization of the Mystery demanded of the couple is the role of the Holy Spirit, the one who lies at the heart of every gift given, every gift received, and every gift offered back in praise and thanksgiving. The Son sent by the Father is accompanied by the Spirit: "When the Father sends his Word, he always sends his Breath."[2] Anointed by the Spirit, the Son is proclaimed "beloved" by his Father (cf. Matt 3:16–17). Together with the Spirit, the Son takes up his mission of offering himself as a living sacrifice for all mankind, so that every person might be reconciled with God. Upon completion of his saving mission, the Son returns to the right hand of the Father, and together with the Father sends the Spirit to complete the redemptive work began on earth.

As a consequence, our adoption—both as gift and mission—does not exist in a vacuum: the work that Christ accomplished, the relation to the Father established, continues by the sealing in the Holy Spirit, in the reception of the "Spirit of adoption" (Rom 8:15). It is because of his Spirit that we can cry "Abba! Father!"[3] "For you did not receive the spirit of slavery to fall back into fear, but you have received the Spirit of adoption as sons, by whom we cry, "Abba! Father!" (Rom 8:15). It is this dynamic presence of the Spirit—the one who anoints the adopted son or daughter, who seals their relation to Christ, who capacitates their ability to live and act in Christ—that allows the baptized person to live faith "existentially." It places them in a *living* relation with Christ, perfecting their participation in his sacrifice of praise (cf. Heb 13:15) so that, joined to his perfect and living sonship, they too might come to be worthy of the Father's words: "This is my beloved Son, in whom I am well pleased" (Matt 3:17).

In this way, the Spirit lies at the heart of the appropriation and realization of a genuinely non-imitative christo-baptismal existence. The Spirit is at the heart of the perspective of the acting, *baptized* person. Without the Spirit, a living existence in and with Christ would not be possible. The event of Christ and the promise of adoption would never truly enter the horizon of the individual as a *living* and *dynamic* presence. Because of the gift of the Spirit, by contrast, the entire work of adoption is really and truly efficacious. Sacramental grace can truly "work" because in it is the Spirit's personal living

---

2. *Catechism*, 689.

3. The *Catechism* says that "the mission of the Spirit of adoption is to unite them [God's children] to Christ and make them live in him" (*Catechism*, 690).

proximity to the person, touching their heart, calling them to conversion, making Christ's personal presence a concrete reality.

This is so for all of the baptized in their walk of faith. The grace they receive from the sacraments in which they participate is actualized in and through a person, a person who enables them to offer their "bodies as a living sacrifice, holy and pleasing to God" (Rom 12:1). The Spirit exhorts and compels the adopted Christian to truly embrace and live the gift of their relation to the Father in the Son, to take up their mission and offer it back to him in fullness and perfection in "true and proper worship" (Rom 12:1). The Spirit does so, from the "inside," so to speak: from within the possibilities of the "new man" (Eph 4:24). He does so, in other words, in and through the new forms of life in Christ, in and through the efficacy of sacramental grace. The Spirit's animating breath within his "joint mission" with Christ to bring each person to their full baptismal potential that he shares with Christ, is what will allow a full and conscious conforming of self to Christ and the full offering of one's self to the Father, one "perfect and complete, lacking in nothing" (Jas 1:4).

All of this is no less true for the married couple, the baptized man and woman who together in Christ constitute an original sacramental unity, and who thus participate in the Son's return of everything back to the Father as a couple. But what is *unique* about this married couple's participation in the Son's gift is the extent to which the Spirit must work overtime, as it were, in order to lead the couple to the conversion necessary to realize the unity required for them to offer themselves *as a couple* to the Father. No one needs to be told that by anyone's standards this is no easy feat. At the best of times, learning to negotiate an intimate life in common with a person of the opposite sex is difficult. At the worst of times, in a culture that reifies individual choice and autonomy and is opposed to a life-long sacrificial fidelity that might cut into said choice and autonomy, genuine unity may appear well-nigh impossible. And we should also note the baptismal intensification of this challenge, given that the couple in Christ is called to much more than a functioning natural unity. *Sacramental* marriage by its nature calls man and woman to much more. It calls them to a full and conscious mission to offer themselves as a couple to the Father.

Given the many obstacles, it should not be surprising to discover a high failure rate. Today, the first challenge is simply to make married couples' *aware* of the mystery in which they are participating, even before the challenge of then getting them to consciously buy into it and discover its living forms in their fullness. Moreover, if our argument in chapter 3 is worth anything, there is a close connection between an imitative approach to the person and the broader contemporary cultural embrace of the nihilistic completion of the person in the configurations of modernity/postmodernity. We should not be surprised if one of the consummations of this paradigm is a pastoral response to difficult situations in marriage that does not ask for greatness, but rather accommodates to weakness or to the social status quo. If grace merely only "hovers" over the person, without truly descending, then various forms of nihilistic reductions will always present as possibilities and perhaps as perverse imperatives. If one is not prepared to challenge people with baptismal personhood, then a pastoral program of accommodation is usually what one will necessarily be left with.

The whole point of our baptismal approach to the person, however, is that man and woman *must* be challenged by the Gospel, and by those entrusted to its care; they must be challenged to buy in completely, not as a function of power or authority but because of the intrinsic truth of the norm itself. Though few may be chosen (i.e., actually become saints), the many are nevertheless always called to the long road of conversion (cf. Matt 22:14). John Paul II's words in *Veritatis Splendor* remain more relevant than ever. Speaking in the context of moral theology, he warns (presciently, almost prophetically) against a pastoral approach based on accommodation:

> some authors have proposed a kind of double status of moral truth. Beyond the doctrinal and abstract level, one would have to acknowledge the priority of a certain more concrete existential consideration. The latter, by taking account of circumstances and the situation, could legitimately be the basis of certain exceptions to the general rule and thus permit one to do in practice and in good conscience what is qualified as intrinsically evil by the moral law. A separation, or even an opposition, is thus established in some cases between the teaching of the precept, which is valid in general, and the norm of the individual conscience, which would in fact make the final decision about what is good and what is evil. On this basis, an attempt is made to legitimize so-called 'pastoral' solutions contrary to the teaching of the Magisterium, and to justify a 'creative' hermeneutic according to which the moral conscience is in no way obliged, in every case, by a particular negative precept.[4]

The whole point of a *baptismal* conception of existence as I have articulated it is that the doctrinal and the existential are woven into the deeper perspective of the sacramental "now," within the dimension of the baptized person who acts within the encounter with Jesus Christ, one efficaciously mediated in and through the sacramental forms of the Church.

---

4. John Paul II, *Veritatis Splendor*, 56.

There cannot be a separation between the two for the person who has received the grace of adoption and the gift of the Spirit. As I have tried to emphasize throughout, baptism involves not just the conditional or relative sanctification of consciousness, mind, or abstract "processes," but also the sanctification of *the body*: the corporeal "space" whereby the baptized person lives and acts; hence John Paul's notion of a "theology" of the body. Baptismal space is the space of adoption, of God's time penetrating the entire spatiotemporal world of the person, making their world a dramatic sacramental space where thought, word, *and deed* now participate, express, and signify *God's* time and space.

The point of this is to say that the "negative precept" or the uncomfortable truth (in this instance, conjugal politics) demands that we go deeper into union with the Beloved if we are to have any hope of being faithful. This is the only legitimate option for the baptismal person. If the text seems to suggest that headship and submission are ingredient for spousal unity and a faithful realization of their mission to return their relationship to the Father, the couple must fully submit to Christ if they are to have any hope of submitting to the text. And the only hope that they have for fully submitting to Christ is found in the gift of the *Holy Spirit*, the one who heals their wounds, drawing them nearer to one another by sealing them every more deeply in their relation to Christ in his perfect kenotic relation to the Bride, interceding for them with "wordless groans" (Rom 8:26). In other words, only with the Spirit can a couple hope for a deep enough conversion to the sacramental real to perceive the theological saturation of difference and accept the mission given to them as man or woman as a consequence of this difference.

Discovering Conjugal Politics in the Action of the Spirit

So let us imagine that the couple, in and through docility to the Spirit who has brought the Mystery to them, have now cognitively or imaginatively "bought in" to the state of life which they are embarking on as the first fruits of that docility. They now stand open, ready to receive their missions, ready to hear the word of God from a vantage point inside the drama. What now? From the point of view of a christo-baptismal state of life accepted and placed "inside" the relation of the Father and the Son and animated by the living breath of the Spirit, how might the specific spousal missions of husband and wife appear as a lived reality at the level of concrete action within this context?

The first thing we can say is that if we wish to encounter a truly living and saturated appreciation of conjugal politics, we must place its concrete interpretation within the perspective of the person whose acts will take place "inside" the baptismal relation. Otherwise put, if the Christ-Church paradigm is thought of as effectively penetrating the man-woman relationship baptismally (i.e., if it has become more than a merely imitative reality thereby prone to any number of reductions and distortions), then it must be both perceived and *enacted* (that is, at the level of action) by the couple from a deeper, existential, living point. It is only from within the perspective of the baptized person who acts, the one who is animated by the living presence of Christ in their midst in and through the grace of the sacrament, mediated in and through the work of the Holy Spirit, that the gap between the Christ-Church relation as ideal and the real conjugal relationship can be bridged in a living synthesis, a genuine fusion of horizons in the space of the sacramental middle. It is only from their new identity as son and daughter of a Father really present to them (in the Son and the Spirit, in the ecclesial mediation of the body of Christ) that the logic of conjugal politics will be unveiled in a truly dynamic and saturated way.

This is to underscore my conviction that conjugal politics will always be more "in the relation" than "in the substance," whether the substance pole is either the "natural" framing of the man-woman relation or the bare structure of the sacramental form of the relationship of man and woman in Christ. It will not be enough to understand conjugal politics from within a merely static or theoretical conception of marriage's sacramental form, i.e., according to a "christomonism." Life in Christ must be more than a new series of laws, virtues, or ends, however original and profound. It must be more than a blueprint that one might find in a manual and achieve by a correct sequence of procedures or steps. It must be more even than grace understood merely as a power, a medicine, a thing, or a substance sufficient in abstraction from a relational, real-time exchange of persons. To say that conjugal politics must take place "in the relation" is not to say that "substance" will not have anything to do with it, but rather to highlight how any new mark of the baptismal person, any remade or new ontological characteristic given in the relation, will only be as good as that mark and characteristic's insertion into the horizon of the acting person: of the one who experiences and discerns the call of Christ from within the midst of the Spirit's "real time" gift of Christ to them in each historical moment, within the Spirit's animation of the multiple points within the relation that inform the sphere of action.

What is needed for an interpretation of conjugal politics, therefore, is the articulation of an adequate theory of *baptismal* action; an adequate account of the way that the concrete acts of the baptismal subject receive a more than exemplary or imitative framing by virtue of the existential actualism of life in Christ as mediated by the Spirit—how they actually mediate and accomplish the new baptismal identity that the person carries in their flesh and lives as a mission. We can begin by noting that for the baptized the sphere of action or "ethics" has infinitely expanded.[5] The one who acts is a theological person: all action is called to take place within an efficacious discernment and communication of the subject who inhabits the dramatic space of a real relation to and with the Father, who receives his call and inspiration in the present through the Son, in the Spirit via the dramatic "stage" of salvation in the mediation of Christ's ecclesial body, the Spouse of the Word and all of the theological relationships therein amongst Her children (including marriage). All action, every act, is thus dramatically charged with the living current of God's trinitarian presence to the one who acts. Action is not static or closed. The theological person acts *within the architecture of the baptismal relation*; not as a natural person whose acts' sole referents are the relations of a closed system of human virtue (even the best kind of virtue ethics[6]) or divine law extrinsically understood (*viz.* as a law extrinsic to the person understood formalistically as principles or precepts[7]). For the Christian, at no point can action appear according to an abstract norm or perspective not placed entirely within the *real personal and historically present relation* established and discerned in the sacramental experience of Christ present and active. Actions here are performed as children subject to God the Father, inside the gift of election and adoption, inside the sacramental relationships in the Church, inside the relation of the Son to the Father, in docility and openness to the Spirit who brings these gifts to the person in the concrete, in the moment of discerning, in the moment of acting.

This means that conjugal *politics*—or "ethics," i.e., the domain of action—must always be interiorly constituted by a relation that explodes our effort to govern and order our "roles" by a freedom that functions autonomously, whether it presupposes as its object and sphere of reference a closed

---

5. Important directions in this regard can be found in: Ouellet, "Christian Ethics"; Melina, *Sharing in Christ's Virtues*; *Epiphany of Love*; Pinckaers, *Sources of Christian Ethics*.

6. Cf. MacIntyre, *After Virtue*.

7. Melina describes "legalism" and "extrinsicism" as understood by the post-tridentine manual tradition in the following way: "On the philosophical level, law was seen as not as the expression of a truth about the Good, but as a principle of obligation deriving from the will of a lawgiver. On the theological level, the moral dimension was conceived as autonomous and extrinsic with respect to faith and grace" (Melina, *Sharing in Christ's Virtues*, 4).

teleologism (i.e., complementarianism) or a practical nominalism (i.e., egalitarianism). The couple cannot live the christological and ecclesial character of their relation to one another (e.g., the norm of the Christ-Church relationship) as merely a closed carbon copy of its archetype. This means, first, very practically, that headship and submission cannot be interpreted simply by cataloguing the characteristics of Christ's headship and the Church's submission and then neutrally and statically superimposing them over-top of the spousal relation of husband and wife, without considering the dynamic mode of communication between the two realms via the action of Christ and the Spirit in the life of the couple, the action which may in fact deeply qualify and/or relativise key features of that relation when it is transcribed into the life of *this* concrete couple. Because the action of the baptismal person is always the action of *a son in real relation to the Father* (and not simply an autonomous rational agent who chooses goods on the basis of internal powers according to some immanent notion of human flourishing), an internal principle of relation to a person becomes its fundamental reference point. Aspects of this perspective are captured well by Livio Melina:

> The encounter with Jesus Christ does not obstruct desire or stop action (see 2 Thess 3:10). However, the disciple's action unfolds in a new context—the constitutive tension toward fulfillment is oriented toward a future that is well defined as a goal and that, in some way, is already anticipated in the present. The future is determined in the promise and rescues action from insignificance, while its mysterious anticipation in the present gives action its driving force.[8]

A further *baptismal* specification of this perspective on action would place the acts of the person in an even more intensely *existential* sacramental context. The act performed by a baptized son or daughter of the Father is at its deepest point framed by the person's *immediate and present participation* in the new dramatic filial space of intimate communication with the Father given by the Son and the Spirit in their joint mission of reconciling the person to God. Sacramental/baptismal action is the action of the one called, named, and chosen to participate fully in the trinitarian relations *here*, *now*, in this moment of time, in this act of discernment (and not, therefore, only according to the horizon of general orientations or motivations). Thus it is that human action is placed "inside" divine action. To act in the fullest sense is to let one's actions be shaped by the "real time" involvement of divinity in your midst; not only as a "structure" or informing backdrop/moral code which must then be integrated and applied by your own prudential

---

8. Melina, *Epiphany of Love*, 19.

judgment, but rather dynamic dialogue with the living breath of the Spirit's communication of Christ and the Father.

And so we now have both the dramatic staging, structure, or backdrop against which conjugal politics will be played out (i.e., the sacramental perspective of the deeper conjugal unity of the baptized man and woman in Christ), and the living personal grammar through which this structure can be practically "interpreted" into the lived reality of the spousal relation with all the necessarily qualifications, attentive to both the similarities but also the *maior dissimilitudo*. In this light, let us now attempt a tentative and to this point still provisional sketch of how conjugal politics might appear in this context.

"For the Husband is Head of His Wife, just as Christ is the Head of the Church . . ."

We have determined, in a specific sacramental way, that it is the relation to the Father in the Son that grounds and informs the action of the baptismal person. This is more than a formal and structural relation inasmuch as it is a *living*, real-time relation in the existential present given to the man or woman in the Son and the Spirit. As such, the baptismal person who acts must, if said acts are to be true and faithful at the deepest level, do so in real-time "conversation" or communication with the Father, in the perspective of his or her own ongoing conversion. In regard to the husband and the wife, this is to say that they must live and express their spousal relation *to each other* from inside this dynamic filial mode.

This would be to say that *the husband can discover and exercise his headship only insofar as he is a son and a brother, while the wife can discover and exercise her submission only insofar as she is a daughter and a sister*. To be and to act as a spouse, husband or a wife, is to at all times submit oneself and one's acts to the standard of a theologically *more basic identity* as son or daughter, an identity called to become ever more actualized, ever more conformed to and "existentialized" in the Father in the perspective of the "now" of the sanctified present in Christ and the Spirit. It is this dynamic horizon that will shape both the theory (the "what") and praxis (the "how") of headship and submission.

It must be noted again that what is most novel regarding this perspective is not so much that within it we will discover original exegetical data regarding some of the key variables associated with the structure of difference in ecclesial and christological faith. It will still be the case that the same archetypal logic and rhythm of the Christ-Church relationship continues to pervade the various levels of life in Christ. We have already shown in principle how the man-woman relationship will not be exempt from this logic; a feminist hermeneutic has been rejected. What *is* novel, by contrast, will be the model of "communication" between the theological archetype and the anthropological image. As already suggested numerous times, it is in the sacramental middle that the discovery of a new relation will be made, and with it, a more saturated notion of man and woman's presence to each other and Christ. So in what follows the reader should assume novelties, not in dogmatic content, but in a baptismally intensified interpretation of this content.

We begin with a provisional first sketch of what male headship might look like given the above perspective. First, we can accent the deepest animating *source* of what we already know to be the husband's goal of unity with his wife and the return of their communion back to the Father. Headship, we can posit, in its properly christological realization, is at its root a specific theological responsibility given to the husband. This is so, not so much or first for him to "lead" his wife or to have "authority" over her as a feature intrinsic to his own natural and autonomous masculine identity, one proscribed for the purpose of a merely intracosmic harmony or order within the relationship, but rather as the prerogative for him to take what we might begin by describing as the *active part* and the *main responsibility* for baptismally perfecting the relationship of the couple—immersing it ever more deeply in the font, as it were—so that it might be offered in fullness and perfection to the Father in the Son, and so that every member of the domestic church entrusted to him in this mission might see God face to face and know him as Father.

Now, because this is a mission given to him from *inside* the baptismal relation—because it is not from its animating ministerial or vocational point a feature governed by nature or by a merely extrinsic conception of mission—this means that it is not first and foremost a feature that belongs to a property of his essence which could then be effectively carried out by him according to principles intrinsic to this property. This feature, in its natural iteration, has been "crossed out" by baptism. Any prerogative that remains has been reshaped and given to him from the Father as a properly baptismal mission, thus radically changing the basic terms of the "operation" of his masculine specificity.

It is important to continue to affirm, however, that this does not mean that his masculinity does not carry certain symbolic signs and anticipations of its *baptismal* iteration which will remain within that iteration. There is a real natural/creational (ontological) reason why the mission of headship is given to the man and not the woman. As *male*, the husband is in his "nature" from the beginning ontologically equipped and disposed for this mission (inasmuch as his masculinity is from creation itself already patterned on the model of Christ and the Church, even if in Christ he now learns that he must place his mission entirely in the hands of the Father). It is not possible for man and woman to ever live "beyond nature" in an empirical sense. Its primordial inscription in the horizon of Being will continue to pull and shape their existences. It is necessary to recognize and affirm that as a consequence of its primordial character, nature, under the sign of the body, *does* carry the signs and anticipations of its baptismal fulfilment, and that these will continue to exert a powerful effect on the hearts, minds, and behavioral patterns of all men and women, baptismal persons or not.

In this sense, to say that the baptismal iteration of nature is absolute is not to deny that there is something meaningful expressed in the empirical instincts of human nature (not least in the complexity of its primeval and evolutionary history). For instance, there is something real being expressed in the male instinct to provide and protect or to slay and dominate. The "energy" expressed here cannot be reduced to contingent social conditioning, but has roots in both a genuine theology of sexual difference in the beginning, and in its fallen expression in the perspective of the Genesis curse (Gen 3:16). Idealism and ideology are inevitable if this is no longer recognized. I do not wish to give the impression that this broader anthropological context, in all its infinite complexity and nuance, could ever be merely extrinsic to the baptismal rationale I am seeking to articulate here.

As a consequence, one supposes that before a husband can find the strength and redemption required for what is the peculiarly *kenotic* form that his headship over his wife will take, he must have in a distinct way confronted and wrestled with the empirical reality of masculinity in its anthropological specificity, and in a non-dualistic way—that is to say, in a way that does not deal with masculinity by feminizing it, but rather by shaping its power in a truly redemptive form of strength. In other words, let us say that the capacity to express masculine strength as an act of submission to the Father, one that will open his "initiative" to the response of his wife (which we will explore further in a moment), but without a concomitant "feminizing" of his strength (e.g., where his masculinity is reduced to femininity or androgyny so as to be redundant) requires that he must have first inhabited, wrestled with, and subdued (but without breaking) the primeval temporal reality of his anthropological masculinity.

A man must, one might say, have grasped the handle of an axe. He must have slain the proverbial dragon. He must have tested his strength, courage, and honour in moments of trial. He must have entered and begun to conquer the darkness and chaos of his own psycho-somatic self. He must have achieved self-mastery of his sexuality. He must have begun to extirpate the enervation and dissipation of lust, narcissism, intemperance, sloth, and resentment.

What I mean by all of this is that at the level of the man's confrontation with *himself*, as male, the particular "energy" associated with masculinity demands a certain pattern of redemption commensurate to it. It requires meeting strength with strength and, even if the source of this strength lies in Christ's redemptive act, the way it manifests for a man in his confrontation with himself has something to do with struggle, conflict, valour, strength and the like; spiritual *warfare*, in a real sense. All believers are of course called to warfare of this kind, but my point is that for a man it will have something of the precise character of a raw and forceful wrestling with existence itself, in a manner that corresponds to the specific defining primeval and evolutionary characteristics of masculinity.

In this sense, achieving excellence as a man requires something like that seen in the following excerpt from J.R.R. Tolkien's *Lord of the Rings*. In it, King Théoden of Rohan has just been awakened from psychological bondage to the manipulations of the wizard Saruman and his henchman Grima Wormtongue. Upon his release, the wizard Gandalf counsels the still weak and indecisive Théoden to take up his sword.

> Slowly Théoden stretched forth his hand. As his fingers took the hilt, it seemed to the watchers that firmness and strength returned to his thin arms. Suddenly he lifted the blade and swung it shimmering and whistling in the air. Then he gave a great cry. His voice range clear as he chanted in the tongue of Rohan a call to arms.
>
> *Arise now, arise, Riders of Théoden! Dire deeds awake, dark is it eastward. Let horse be bridled, horn be sounded! Forth Eorlingas!*[9]

Perhaps we could say that it is the resolute, courageous, and disciplined capacity to grasp and wield a sword, to fight the demons of the self and to take responsibility to fight the demons that threaten those entrusted to his care, that is ingredient to a man's capacity to then experience and transmit power, authority, and responsibility as *cruciform love*. The one without the other is insufficient: for a man, strength risks becoming domination, while cruciform love risks becoming passivity and redundancy. My point here is to say that a man cannot escape and forgo confrontation with the specific demands that the primeval and evolutionary features of his anthropological masculinity impose on him. As both ontological and historical realities, they cannot be escaped, save by wrestling with them from within. He must non-dualistically

---

9. Tolkien, *Lord of the Rings*, 540.

control, master, and harness this strength, for it is precisely this strength that will enable him to realize the strength required for *kenosis*.

Without therefore in any way espousing a theological idealism wherein all of the above considerations are irrelevant, my goal in what follows is nevertheless to focus on the way in which masculine strength will find a new shaping and potential in the spousal mission of faith. Here, the instincts proper to masculinity find a new outlet and mode of expression, a new level of "humanization," we might say. In this context, the man as husband must now learn to place his instincts wholly and exclusively at the disposal of the other. They must be *subordinate to* and *organized by* the new mode of spousal love that has become available to the person by the baptismal relation. For the husband, then, it is thus a question, not so much of *eliminating* the strength proper to his primordial masculinity, but rather of how to access and shape it in a way which avoids both its outworking in patterns domination and violence, or concomitantly, in the egalitarian tendency to reduce its missional and vocational significance. Again, it is a question of seeking a *saturated* meaning that gives full weight to natural instincts but precisely by reinscribing them in the baptismal relation so that they can attain what they are already inchoately signifying and groping towards.

If the husband's specific mission of headship is given to him from within the horizon of baptismal personhood, then this means that when it comes to the question of *how* he is to take the active part and main responsibility for his conjugal union and domestic church he must first recognize that before headship can be exercised on his part, *it must be received*, and as a gift and a mission. More specifically, it must be placed within *a constant existential labor of reception*. For him to have any hope of faithfully realizing the new *baptismal* recapitulation of his masculinity, or indeed, of even seeing and comprehending its novelty at all at this level, he must first recognize headship as an existential call of the Father on *himself as a husband* to order his own existence and his acts wholly and completely in light of his dramatic relation to the Father in Christ. From this point of view, headship can first be thought of as belonging to the grammar of God the Father's specific claim on the husband, a mode incarnated archetypally in the absolute authority that Christ has over the husband by virtue of the latter's properly creaturely and baptismal sharing in the mode of the Marian-ecclesial Bride.

In this sense, headship is in its first iteration *more for the husband than it is for the wife*, a specific modality of the more basic stance of creaturely submission and receptivity proper to the person in his or her identity as an adopted son of the Father in Christ and as sanctified Bride of Christ. Before it is a term of relation or order between the husband and the wife, it is a term of relation or order *between the husband and the Father* as a specification of the absolute subordination that every believer owes to Christ. The injunction to take the active part and main responsibility for the spousal relationship and domestic church thematizes the husband's identity vis-à-vis the Father, *before* it does that of the husband vis-à-vis the wife.

From the point of view of headship vis-à-vis the Father, we could say that headship is given to the man as a baptismally shaped vocational answer to his unique masculine identity, to the legitimate but inchoate drives that characterize him as a man. It is a baptismal mission generated from inside the baptismal relation, one that responds to and shapes the specific male instinct to provide and protect, that gathers up all of the unique "energy" associated with being a man and inserts it into the redemptive perspective of Christ the Bridegroom and God the Father. Headship in its first movement is thus a radical vocational summons that calls the existential ground and identity of the man into question so that it may begin to be reshaped to the particular task of being a faithful husband and father according to its new theological coordinates. It should thus serve to rupture a man's sense of self and what he may take to be "normal" masculine and husbandly behavior. In this sense, we could say that at the heart of any priority he may have over his wife must be a much deeper subordination of himself to the Father.

Here we can point to an interesting discussion in the first part of the Theology of the Body where John Paul II discusses original innocence. He notes how here it is "the woman, who in the mystery of creation 'is given' by the Creator to the man" and who is "'welcomed' or accepted by him as a gift."[10] This suggests that the first primordial "stance" of masculinity vis-à-vis femininity must, if it is to fully realized according to the eternal mystery hidden in God, be existentially placed in an even more *primordial* receptive stance vis-à-vis the Father, a response to *the one who has given the gift*. The man here stands in a sequence of gift-reception, having first received his own being as a gift of his Creator. As a second movement within the first, woman is created, i.e., literally from the side of the man. In this, woman belongs to the first movement of gift, but is also from the first placed in a specific kind of relation to the man as one entrusted specifically to him, according to the original logic of the man's own creation. She is, as John Paul II puts it, "entrusted to his eyes, to his consciousness, to his sensibility, to his 'heart.'"[11]

The point to bring out here is that the giving of the woman as gift to the man implies the necessity of a unique stance and labor of receptivity *on the part of the man* both in relation to the gift and the gift-giver. The performance

---

10. John Paul II, *Theology of the Body*, 196 (17.5).
11. John Paul II, *Theology of the Body*, 197 (17.6).

of his mission depends on living his own existence as gift. Even if in the horizon of the face-to-face relationship of husband and wife we might say that it is the *woman* who is the one more associated with receptivity in relation to her husband (a fact which, in a closed, intracosmic perspective easily fosters the sense of the feminine as subordinate due to some ontological defect), from the point of view of the man who receives the woman as a gift from the Creator we discover that receptivity could in a deeper, more ontologically primitive sense be called the defining mark *of the husband* vis-à-vis the Creator inasmuch as to him is apparently given the specific responsibility of receiving and safeguarding the gift (one which, incidentally, Adam fails completely and utterly when he stands by idly—perhaps playing on his Xbox—while Eve is tempted by the Serpent [cf. Gen 3:1–7]). Correlative to greater responsibility comes the need for a *greater* "subordination" to one's task and the source of this task. For the husband to receive the gift according to the measure with which it is given, he must submit himself fully to the first pattern of the sequence of gift-reception, i.e., to the one who has given the gift, the Father. To be a husband within the baptismal relation, then, is to constantly labor for a more faithful reception of *one's own baptismal existence* from the Father so that one can ever more faithfully receive and welcome the wife given as a gift by the Father.

Headship thus ups the stakes and heightens the drama of the man's baptismal journey of faith. By giving the man the active part and the main responsibility of overseeing the unity of the spousal relationship and taking the major part in mediating its offering back to the Father, the Father also gives to him a uniquely *urgent* imperative of conversion and holiness. It is only by embracing the dramatic vocational shape given to his masculinity that he can enter fully into the mystery of spousal union and love of his wife according to the measure of Christ and the Father's love for her. Headship, we can thereby submit again, is first more for the husband than for the wife. It is the means by which his baptismal existence is further shaped by the imperative to accept the gift of his wife only according to the measure of the Father's gift.

With all of this in view, we can now speak of headship as a paradoxical mission of subordination, reconciling, welcoming, and acceptance in terms of what it demands for the basic stance of the husband who can only then take up its "active" dimension from a point inside this prior stance. The first movement of headship vis-à-vis his wife must therefore have the character of his deeper recognition of her as gift. The man's first "posture" in relation to the woman must be at the deepest level a receptive, grateful, and adoring one. She is the gift of the creator. She is one willed for her own sake. His mission is one, first of obedience to the One who gives the gift, and then born from this, to facilitate her fullest realization as a daughter of the Father. This means that any act of the man in relation to the woman must first be an act breathed through and through with this more primitive logic of reception and contemplation. And it is only in accepting and welcoming her according to the measure of the gift that the man will be able to become his full spousal self. There is no "activity" or "priority" on the part of the man in relation to the woman not always already circumscribed by the fact that the man's fundamental activity is to welcome and accept woman as woman, as one who is the gift of a prior love. To welcome and accept his wife is to recognize and affirm her distinct identity as a daughter of God, a sister in Christ, to welcome and accept what makes her unique as a woman. This would be to say that headship imposes on the husband the imperative to learn, without compromising or reducing his own masculinity, to "adapt" himself to her spiritual, physical, emotional, and psychological uniqueness. In turn, the husband's mission of welcoming and accepting is shaped further by his wife, who both in the form of her femininity and in her conscious personalized response to her husband's welcoming and acceptance enriches, deepens, and *completes* her husband's distinctive mission, thereby becoming *joined to his mission* of offering their relationship back to the Father in praise and thanksgiving. The full range of the specific mission of the wife will be explored shortly.

We should at this point stress that it would be incorrect to regard this masculine dimension of subordination or receptivity as reducible merely to a generic feature of a mutual submission shared univocally by husband and wife. It would be inadequate to interpret any sense in which the husband's prior receptivity belongs to an interchangeable dimension of the horizon of mutual love in which each are to be subordinate to one another in reverence for Christ (Eph 5:21), i.e., to that subordination that John Paul II described as "not one-sided, but mutual."[12] For what we have seen above would seem to belong *uniquely and exclusively* to the mission received by the husband from the Creator. In this, if he must be "subordinate" to his wife in light of this responsibility of welcoming and accepting her as gift, he must be so as a *consequence* of the specificity of his distinct role as head, and therefore within the territory marked out by Ephesians 5:25. This cannot in any way be thought of as collapsing the specificity of male headship into a generic horizon of mutual subordination. His specific mission belongs to him and to him alone, a consequence of the baptismal iteration of his primordial masculinity, even if the full realization of this mission will involve an expansion of woman into it.

---

12. John Paul II, *Mulieris dignitatum*, 24.

If we want to speak of the significance of Ephesians 5:21 and the way that it might qualify and inform the specific missions of husband and wife, it seems better to do so by locating this kind of subordination, important in its own right, as ingredient to the common horizon of being brother and sister in Christ, in being children of the same heavenly Father. This horizon will of course bleed into the specificity of their individual spousal missions, placing each in a much deeper filial and eschatological horizon. It will be true that the husband's expression of headship over his wife must be placed within the deeper filial and brotherly and sisterly relation they share in their common filiation from and adoption into the Father. In this perspective, any priority of husband over wife will be informed, not only by the husband's existential relation to the Father and to his wife as gift of the Father, but also to the horizon of their common belonging to each other as adopted children of God. This is another important layer which we will consider below; but the point first to make clear is that this will remain *formally* distinct from the source and mode of each unique mission of the spouses. Mutual subordination will not replace or reduce the specificity of mission of either husband or wife.

This perspective is nevertheless important, however, inasmuch as it does represent the next crucial plank in our argument thus far. The perspective of husband and wife as brother and sister, son and daughter of the same Father further shapes the husband's main part and greater responsibility of the couple's shared vocation of perfecting the spousal bond so that it might be offered as a pleasing sacrifice of praise to the Father. The notion of his wife as sister deepens the husband's awareness of the personal identity of the gift of woman he has received from the Father. Here we can thematize the peculiar expression in the Song of Songs where the Bridegroom addresses his Bride as "My sister, my bride" (Song 4:9). John Paul II speaks of a "fraternal theme"[13] in the Song, linking it to a horizon of deeper "friendship" born of the fact that man and woman share a common humanity within their difference: "The expression 'sister' speaks of union in humanity and at the same time of feminine diversity, of the originality of this humanity."[14] Further, he goes on to comment how the love of the spouses—a love which in the Song seeks to transgress the borders of death (Song 8:6–7)—drives the couple to discover a deeper common foundation for their love:

> Love . . . pushes both to seek the common past as though from infancy they had been united by memories of the common hearth. In this way, they reciprocally feel as close as brother and

---

13. John Paul II, *Theology of the Body*, 568 (110.5).
14. John Paul II, *Theology of the Body*, 562 (109.4).

sister who owe their existence to the same mother. *A specific sense of common belonging follows from this.*[15]

Placed in a baptismal setting, the baptized son and daughter become acutely aware that they *are* united by memories of the common hearth, that they *are* brother and sister within the deepest folds of their relation to God as Father. From the point of view of the husband, this is another attestation that woman is a gift, not only as a wife, but also as a sister, as one who though different occupies the same filial horizon and plane of adoption. The husband must live his spousal relation to her from within this deeper adoptive plane of connection which, by marriage in Christ, has been corporatized in the one-flesh union of *this* man and *this* woman, but without abrogating their deeper relation as brother and sister. The gift that he has received from the Father is from this point of view never specifically his as one could possess an object; she is a being, a person, outside of the fact that she a gift for the man. To recognize her as *sister*, is to perceive her as God the Father's *daughter*, as He perceives her: as willed and love for her own sake. She remains in this sense a "garden closed," a "fountain sealed" (Song 4:12) even while she gives herself completely to him in love.

It is thus to remember the sovereign limits on the husband's own missional activity vis-à-vis his wife. At no point can he treat her *only* as his wife; her status as sister and daughter are two more existential points of contact with the sacramental structure of their spousal unity as a couple and with the mission given to the husband. They are thus additional reminders to him to remember the greater drama which he participates in. This, we might suggest, can serve to deepen their relation to one another, expanding it well beyond the perspective of erotic love or domestic expediency, shaping their love in the direction of filial fellowship and genuine interpersonal friendship.

At this point we have fleshed out our claim that the husband's mission in general to take the "active part" and "main responsibility" for perfecting the spousal union and offering it back to the Father begins by expressing itself as a fundamental welcoming and acceptance of his wife as gift, as sister in Christ, a child of the Father with him. His relation to her is thus framed by a disponibility which has as its negative object the breakdown of his individuality, abstraction, and domination, and as its positive object the shaping of his primitive orientation to provide and protect into a theological mission. Headship presupposes and expresses both the husband's call to receive himself from the Father as a labor of conversion and transformation, and his call to express this fundamental act of reception as ingredient in his labor of reception of his wife. It is in this double labor of receptivity, expressed in

---

15. John Paul II, *Theology of the Body*, 566 (110.1) (emphasis added).

relation to his wife above all as attentive kenotic self-gift, that headship finds its form and *raison d'être*.

But we must now acknowledge the fact that we have yet to confront the thorny question that everyone seeks an answer for: does male headship presuppose a kind of "authority" over the wife in what we might term an "operational" sense? In other words, does what we have interpreted as the husband's more general primary responsibility to perfect spousal unity and offer it to the Father, but primarily from the point of view of his own filial sonship and adoptive belonging to his wife, retain also the more traditional interpretation of the husband possessing a certain "sovereignty" over his wife in the day to day living of the couple, as correlative to Christ's absolute authority over the Church?

Thus far, we have only really used the Christ-Church framing of the husband-wife relationship as the source of the barest intuition that the husband must have some kind of priority at the level of theological mission. We have fleshed out exactly what the heart of this priority might look like by placing it first within the multiple points of a baptismal perspective above, suggesting that here it appears first as a deeper submission of the husband to the Father in Christ and a receptive disponibility to his wife, each the product of his baptismal sonship. Now we need to return to the question of *authority* in priority vis-à-vis the wife if we are to confront the most difficult connotation of the notion of husband as head.

To begin, it should by now go without saying that any genuine authority borne by the husband will necessarily be derived, relative, mediated, and thus to a certain extent contingent on the degree to which he himself is existentially subordinate to the Father's claim on him—both in principle and at the level of discernment in the Spirit in the domain of concrete action. This is because the theological mission of masculinity in marriage belongs more to the relation (with all of its multiple existential claims) and less to the substance of the man's identity *in abstracto*, even in the case of a baptismal identity, which as really given to the baptized person thus bears a real ontological solidity. At its deepest level, however, the substance of identity *is the relation itself*. Identity is only fully itself within the relation. This is especially the case within *sacramental* relationships, where the domain of action and the integrity of action is *intrinsically* tied up with the existential relation of the actor to its sacramental source. Thus, the actions of a baptized husband that belong to the intrinsic core of sacramental relationships—in this case, the action of being head—must proceed from and be animated by the deepest point of their relation to Christ and to adoptive, filial existence in the Father in the existential perspective of action. To act, theologically, is to act as a son or daughter, with the Father, in Christ, and through the Spirit. It can be suggested that nowhere will it be more essential that the husband act as a son in this sense as in the actions that bear and manifest his authority as head.

From this point of view, any authority borne by the husband best appears as a kind of participation in Christ's dramatic mission of saving and purifying the Church, rather than a discrete function within a "command structure" whereby the husband would issue orders relating to the sphere of the practical functioning of the relationship understood in relative isolation from its dramatic footing. Following Trainor's language, it is in this sense that the authority borne by the husband is thus best understood as an "authority through" rather than an "authority over." In other words, in his role as head, the husband is the chief representative or mediator of the message of an absolute authority *that is not his*, the absolute authority of the Father/Christ, just as we might say that it will be the woman who is the chief representative or mediator of the response/internalization/bearing fruit of this message. In each case, both are *intrinsically* constrained and shaped by the message of a "third" (Father, Son, Holy Spirit) beyond them that calls and constrains them, that breaks open any tendency to limit their relational interplay to closed conditions of their own freedom.

In terms of the husband's mission of mediating the authority of Christ, he is tasked with faithfully communicating and transmitting the Word as its recipient, servant, and messenger, not its originator. His wife's submission to him, therefore, inasmuch as he faithfully realizes this task, will be at its deepest level a submission to Christ: "Wives should be subordinate to their husbands *as to the Lord*" (Eph 5:22, emphasis added). In submitting herself to her husband, the wife submits herself to Christ's authority *through* the authority which her husband bears in His name. Rather than fetishize the fact of the *limit* that this seems to impose on woman (i.e., the way her subordination to Christ is mediated by her husband), it is important to instead first accent the limit that this places on the *husband's* "authority," which, as little more than the icon of Christ's perfect authority over him as well as his wife, cannot therefore be independent and *total* like Christ's authority over the Church or the Father's authority over his creation, just as by the same logic the wife's submission to her husband cannot be *total* as is the Church's submission to Christ, inasmuch as her husband is not Christ. It is precisely this total authority of Christ and the Father to which the husband has been given the mission of protecting and transmitting, *not* owning or authoring. The husband is the *minister* of an authority that is not his, he is not its author and owner.

There are further elements which can be adduced that reveal the truly relational context of the husband's authority. Inasmuch as husband is joined to his wife in a real one-flesh relationship he too participates in the reception of the very authority that he is tasked with transmitting. In general, the husband, like his wife, is as a theological person the bride in relation to the Bridegroom, as one in need of the washing of water and the word, of becoming holy without blemish (cf. Eph 5:26–27). At this level, from the point of view of both his sonship vis-à-vis the Father and his "femininity" vis-à-vis Christ the Bridegroom, it is as normal for him to submit absolutely to the headship of Christ as it is for his wife.

But by the same logic it can be argued that he also shares in his wife's own submission to the authority that he himself bears in transmitting and radiating the Fatherhood of God. For love—the breakdown of the individual ego, the expansion of the self by the other, the mutual inhering of respective identities—provokes a kind of "sharing" of missions, inasmuch as each party is fully given to the other in and through the unity of Christ and the Church. While this does not mean that said identities are interchangeable, it does mean that to love means to deeply enter into and share the experience of the other. In the case of Christ and the Church, Christ deeply enters into the experience of his Bride, to the point of a *literal* identification with sinful humanity in its alienation from the Father. The Son *dies* for his Bride, experiencing the same suffering, abandonment, separation, and suffering, relinquishing his hold on his divinity, humiliating divinity by submitting to the fate of the creature. In this, the Son submits to himself as it were, to the work of salvation that he bears for the Church. He "becomes" the Bride, in a certain sense, by sharing in her condition of alienation, and in and through this deep identification with her existential condition, redeems and purifies her, reclaiming her for the Father.

In a similar manner, in participating in this, the Son's mission of salvific identification with the Bride, the husband enters deeply into identification with his wife's vocation of responsive welcoming to the Bridegroom, that which is distinctly characteristic of her own mission (which will be looked at shortly). In this, without losing the identity and mission that belong to him as a husband, love allows him to participate in and identify with the mission of faithful reception that belongs to his wife. John Paul II speaks of how

> Love not only unites the two subjects, but allows them to interpenetrate each other, belonging spiritually to one another, to the point that the author of the letter can affirm, "The one who loves his wife loves himself (Eph 5:28). The 'I' becomes in some way the 'you,' and the 'you' the 'I' (in the moral sense, of course).[16]

---

16. John Paul II, *Theology of the Body*, 485 (92.7).

Love, without effacing the specificity of identity or mission (hence the "moral" sense of unity within bi-subjectivity[17]), nevertheless blends and seals identity and mission with their relational counterpart, binding each in the service of a common aim that makes their individual function mutually inhere and co-penetrate with one another. Trainor's notion of "three sovereignties for each other" is pertinent here. The "sovereignty" that each might have in theory by virtue of their unique respective missions is only properly actualized when it takes into account the way that unity in Christ (the "third") makes each spouse a participant in the other's mission. This spousal joining provokes a certain paradoxical reversal of roles: the husband discovers that in leading and having authority over his wife he must be led and shaped by her response, just as the wife discovers that in being submissive to her husband, she is in fact informing and participating in his initiative.

The conclusion of all of this is to say that the authority of the husband cannot be unilateral at an operational level inasmuch as it is above all else a sacramental function within a common project of love that both husband and wife play their part and have a stake in. And so the husband cannot cling to his mission as exclusively and unilaterally his own, for love elevates the wife to a genuine participation in his authority just as it will incorporate the husband into her mission of response. The point is to say that the exercise of authority is mutual and dialogical, even if the dynamic of initiative and response is in the end "led" by the husband and wife respectively. The husband cannot on his own decide the right course of action without "submitting" himself to the prophetic measure of his wife's response, a response that in its own way belongs to the baptismal mission give to her as woman.

Make no mistake: the husband has the prophetic task of communicating Christ's headship as a living reality in the spousal relationship. But we would miss the mediated and derivative character of this task if we were to strip it of its participatory character and of the way in which the husband finds himself uniquely implicated in the response of his wife. In short, then, the husband bears genuine authority as head, but only within the dialogue of love that constitutes the triple sovereignty of man and woman in Christ.

---

17. Scola points out that "the dual unity of sexual difference does not mean an irenic and symmetrical reciprocity as Aristophanes supposed in Plato's *Symposium*. Man and woman are not two halves destined to merge so as to regenerate a lost unity. This is evident even at the phenomenological level of the state of life. Man lives relations not only of a spousal sort, but also of paternity, maternity, fraternity, etc." (Scola, *Nuptial Mystery*, 8).

"Wives Should Be Subject to Their Husbands as to the Lord"

The above, admittedly, may not yet completely satisfy. For one thing, there is still a certain level of ambiguity, abstraction, and idealism about what exactly it might mean for the husband to manifest his mission of headship at the level of concrete action. Moreover, what happens when we place the foregoing in a fallen context? What happens when the dialogue of love that grounds the exchange of conjugal missions breaks down, when one or both spouses fail (inevitably) in their baptismal mission to give glory to the Father? Much more needs to be said about all of this. But we can do so only once we have plumbed the depths of the relational counterpart to the headship of the husband, *viz.* the mission of responsive submission that is apparently given to the wife.

If, as we have seen, the husband's fundamental mission is suggested by a specific alignment with Christ, the wife's is discovered by her specific alignment with the Church. But here, the same species of qualification that nuanced and qualified the husband's status as head (i.e., a greater unlikeness to Christ than a likeness) also applies to the woman's linkage with submission. Any way that she participates in and resembles the mode of the Church vis-à-vis Christ passes through and is qualified by the deeper frame of her baptismal adoption, of her common filiation with her husband in the Son. But before we follow this through to its full flowering, let us begin—as we did with the mission of the husband—with a provisional first sketch of what the woman's textual identification with the Church in Ephesians might portend.

First, if it is true that the husband's primary mission is to take the active part and primary responsibility in perfecting spousal union and facilitating its return in wholeness to the Father, then it stands to reason—and is textually obvious—that the wife's mission will take its specific shape as a complementary response to the mission of her husband, one that completes and perfects his mediation of the will of the Father. This is to say that the wife's primary mission, if it is not to be collapsed or reduced in its specificity must be to *receive, answer, safeguard, or "make flesh" the word of her husband.* The mission of the husband makes no sense without this feminine answer.

This no doubt immediately places us in very "traditional" territory. For example, the motif of woman as answer, as fruitful "nature," as potency to the male's activity, as immanence to the man's transcendence, etc. have all been employed in various—often instrumental—ways by the tradition. Balthasar refers to the "omnipresent danger of equating the male, the heavenly, with the 'spirit,' and the female, earthly, with 'matter,' or at least with 'nature' in the modern sense, that is, the danger of depreciating the latter."[18] The risk here has always been to functionalize the receptive response of woman, reducing femininity to a mere moment that completes a masculinity otherwise quite sufficient in itself, thus leaving her with little identity in her own right.

The temptation, especially here in relation to woman, is thus to "emancipate" ourselves from this paradigm all together, locating woman's selfhood at a point beyond the risk of sexual difference. As we saw in our treatment of the symbolic substructure of masculinity, however, the solution is not to attempt to evade it, but rather to interpret it from a higher, more saturated point. All of the perceived feminine linkages with nature, immanence, receptivity, response, answer, and the like must—like all of the perceived masculine linkages with priority, transcendence, initiative, and the like—be placed within the baptismal relation.

Recall how the baptismal shaping of masculinity manifested primarily as the placing of limits on certain masculine characteristics related to the primordial "provide and protect" instinct. If the accent here is on how the baptismal relation to the Father *restrains* the energy of masculinity by placing it in the perspective of adoption and mission, we can suggest that the baptismal relation will *liberate* by way of excess what is distinctively feminine by expressly framing it within the horizon of the identity given to each person by Christ. Precisely what it liberates femininity from is the tendency to read reception, acceptance, answer, response, and nurturing from within the closed intracosmic and binary dialectic of transcendence-immanence wherein woman is persistently seen as passive matter or potency. Baptism saves created femininity from both modes of its denigration—linkage with an imperfect mode of creaturely existence and the contemporary rejection of the feminine in light of this perceived linkage—by revealing and allowing participation in the mode of receptivity offered in baptismal-Marian-ecclesial existence. Baptismal existence above all else reveals that to exist is to exist from and for the other, to gratefully receive one's existence and to be tasked with perfecting that existence so as to offer it back to its source in praise and gratitude. In a word, baptismal existence is the existence perfectly typified in the Marian fiat, in the indwelling of the Word in the feminine creature and of the new capacity of that creature's fruitful, creative word in response, wherein the Word becomes incarnate as spirit and life.

It was this broader theologically "feminine" identity and disposition of the creature vis-à-vis the Creator that drew the man into the deeper revelation of the receptive character of his own act of "priority" vis-à-vis his

---

18. Balthasar, *Man in God*, 367.

wife. Here, the baptismal shaping of masculinity appears above all else as the crucifixion of that in the man that seems "first nature" to him so that he might be led into a mode of existence that "by nature" seems foreign to him. The baptismal shaping of femininity, by contrast, seems to appear as a kind of dramatization of characteristics that are seemingly already more "first nature" to her. Woman's baptismal self is to a certain extent an expansion of those elements that were already crystallized in her as woman (at that inchoate primordial-archetypal-natural-symbolic level), those elements that find their ultimate expression in Mary-Church, in which is embodied the perfect fruitful creaturely response to the Bridegroom, and therefore the new baptismal pattern of femininity. It is above all else in woman, in bride and mother, that is found the sacramental visibility of the fruitfulness of the word, where the Word takes flesh.

This pattern of course has its archetype in the person of Mary (the anthropological archetype of the baptismal person, man or woman), in her free assent to the Holy Spirit—"Let it be done to me according to thy word" (Luke 1:38)—a responsive, welcoming assent through which the Word is in her made visible, made manifest in her flesh, in the womb which bore the Saviour, by whose prevenient graces she was saved (cf. 1 Tim 2:15), and through which the sin of Adam was reversed. The Word depends on Mary. The Word requires Mary's free assent, her life-giving womb, her nurturing breasts, her loving smile. The Bridegroom requires a woman who is wife and a mother, one with whom to raise a family—to raise the adopted children of the Father.

Even in the relation of divinity to humanity, of the perfect divine Bridegroom to the imperfect human bride, it is important to recognize the extraordinary ennobling elevation and dignity granted to the feminine archetype of the creaturely response to grace. Grace appears as a person, a man and a husband, but as one who submits divinity to a woman, who allows her response to become the ecclesial condition of his entry into the world and the door and mediation of the efficacy of his salvific mission. In emptying himself totally, in adopting the stance of responsive and self-abnegating readiness and availability, God in Christ fills the feminine creature with every grace and blessing. Note well: according to the Pauline and Johannine "reversal," the one being filled with grace and blessing first *is a woman*. It is woman who becomes the Mother of God and mother of all the living. It is woman who becomes bride of Christ. It is through woman that grace is—literally—born. It is woman who is allowed access to a relationship of utmost intimacy and who personally and uniquely experiences the love of the Father and the love of the Son in the most intimate depths of her person. It is woman, in a word, upon whom rests the fate of the world.

In all of this, then, it is woman's "fertility" that is ingredient to the actualization of the Word. It is therefore no coincidence or mere patriarchal or masculinist manipulation that fertility and procreation have figured—however reductively, at times—so prominently in the definition of the essence of the feminine. But what we can see from the above is that the unique feminine element of fertility is in its *theological* essence a *spiritual* dynamic that belongs to the heart of the baptismal drama of mission. That is, we will not understand the empirical phenomenon of "natural fertility" adequately outside of properly *spiritual* fertility. Its archetype is found first in Mary, the perfect woman who offers the perfect baptismal response to the mission given her by the Father via the angel Gabriel. Mary's response is the response of a child, of a daughter, *before* it is the bridal response of the bride to the Bridegroom. In this, it is *by being a daughter that she becomes a mother*: the Mother of God himself and of all believers in Him in the Spirit of Christ. Her obedient baptismal response to the Father is what gives her the truest fertility, a fecundity that reverses the curse of Genesis 3.

In her, then, we see exemplified the logic of *all* fruitfulness, the form of all creaturely responses to the word of God through which the crucified and risen Lord can become a Spirit-filled reality in the life of the baptized. Now, we have seen that in this perspective, the man—just as much as the woman—is "feminine" vis-à-vis divinity. But we also see in an acute and distinctive way how the paradigm of fruitfulness belongs in a unique and exclusive way to each woman *as woman*, by virtue of her baptismal participation in the same mystery fructified by archetypal yes of Mary. That is, from the point of view of Eve-Mary-Church the woman is the more perfect creature in a manner that is in a certain way inaccessible to the man.[19] Again, she is "by nature" (that is, according to the primordial symbolic structure of creation) a being whom already in her body bears the capacity to be "mother of all the living" (Gen 3:20), to be the fruitful principle of the salvation of the world, to save the world by childbearing (cf. 1 Tim 2:15).

In this, her being, as seemingly more essentially and perfectly creaturely, is not a "problem" in the same way that masculine being presents as such. This is why it is worth perhaps more greatly accenting the sense in which the man can only truly discover his identity and his mission in the feminine response of woman, in a bridal and maternal mediation. Until this point, his being as creaturely remains a problem, an anomaly, a crisis, where aspirations to transcendence easily terminate in egoism, idolatry, anger, or despair. In marriage—particularly *sacramental* marriage—the man (if he can "submit" to it)

---

19. Accordingly, "we would have to reverse the scholastic definition of woman as a *mas occasionatum* and define the male, rather, as the *femina occasionata*, a woman *manquée*" (Balthasar, "Word on *Humanae Vitae*," 442).

will discover a profound pedagogical answer to this crisis, one that fleshes out and complements the answer already given to him in his own adoption, giving him the ability to successfully complete his mission of subordinating himself to the Father. This we will see more of shortly.

But first, within the archetypical yes of Mary, the same vocational mission is given to every woman in her "microcosmic" sacramental living of the mystery as a baptismal person. *Every* woman who responds to her baptismal vocation as daughter, who freely assents to the creative word of the Father given in Christ through the Spirit with a welcoming response, becomes immediately *spiritually* fruitful, a mother, a unique and concrete sign of the Father's "seed" of grace alive and active in the world. John Paul II's notion of the "feminine genius" or the "genius of woman" is located here.[20] It is to woman that the mystery is first entrusted, it is women who were present to Christ, who ministered to him during his Passion, who were the first witnesses of the resurrection. By baptism, in becoming a daughter, *every* woman is granted a unique, irreplaceable and non-transferable sharing in Mary's motherhood.

For the *married* woman, who with her husband recapitulates the drama of creation and salvation (the same drama where it is Mary's fruitfulness that allows the Word to take flesh), this response and assent to the Father as daughter that capacitates the fruitfulness of motherhood takes on another dimension through the microcosmic sacramentality of marriage. Here, woman's baptismal capacity to proclaim and mediate the Word is specified and mapped out within the specific category of mission that belongs to sacramental marriage. And here, the spiritual capacity to receive, generate, and give birth to the Word given in her baptismal personhood *is made literal flesh* in a unique and particular way. In the conception of a child, there is a new fusion of the spiritual and the physical. The full and properly spiritual character of fruitfulness and motherhood that belongs to woman's baptismal existence is here given back to the pattern of signification given in the beginning but lost during the regime of sin. We can then immediately see how "fruitfulness" in marriage, namely, the woman's fruitful response to the word of her husband, belongs properly to Marian and ecclesial fruitfulness, which for the creature can be summed up according to the baptismal form of creaturely existence. A

---

20. In his "Letter to Women," John Paul II speaks of how "there is present in the 'womanhood' of a woman who believes, and especially in a woman who is 'consecrated,' a kind of inherent 'prophecy' [cf. John Paul II, *Mulieris dignitatum*, 29], a powerfully evocative symbolism, a highly significant 'iconic character,' which finds its full realization in Mary and which also aptly expresses the very essence of the Church as a community consecrated with the integrity of a 'virgin' heart to become the 'bride' of Christ and 'mother' of believers" (John Paul II, "Letter to Women," 11).

deeper baptismal interpretation of 1 Tim 2:15 in its anthropological import—"But she [woman] will be saved through motherhood, provided women persevere in faith and love and holiness, with self-control"—becomes possible here, if procreation is seen first and foremost as the expression of woman's baptismal identity, iconic of the spiritual fertility and motherhood that she bears as placed inside the baptismal relation.

From this angle, the first thing that needs to be stressed is that given its properly spiritual character, the first and fundamental fruitfulness of the wife vis-à-vis her husband is one that precedes (but of course in no way excludes or competes with, but is completed and made visible by) a conception of fruitfulness either in the sense that woman completes the man as a lover/"partner" or that she is capable of providing him with offspring. It goes far deeper than this. In its definitive baptismal iteration, the woman gives to the man the personal and spiritual response ingredient to the sacramental communion of *baptismal* persons, the response that gives "birth" to love. She gives him a response that activates the "third," the Spirit who seals and fructifies their relationship in Christ. In this, her response is, as it were, the gatekeeper of the Spirit. With her response, the Spirit can now seal the couple together in Christ. To her has thus been given the mission to shape and fructify the word of her husband, to pass his word—his kenotic opening and abandonment of himself to her—through the filter, as it were, of her consummate baptismal capacity for fruitful interiority, indeed *greater* in her—in the highest sense—as a consequence of her sacramental sharing in the mystery of Mary's perfect response to grace and therefore supreme interiority: "Let it be done to me according to your word" (Luke 1:38); "Mary treasured up all these things and pondered them in her heart" (Luke 2:19).

But just as the husband could not think of his priority as a kind of birthright due to him simply by virtue of his masculinity qua masculinity, nor should the wife think of her answer as a function only of her femininity qua femininity. That is, it is imperative that her vocation of response be just as shaped by docility to the Father in and through the Spirit's deepening of her relationship with Christ. It is only by virtue of a baptismally perfected response to a baptismally perfected word that a fully formed communion of *baptismal* persons can be made flesh in a manner worthy of the mystery in which it participates, and therefore worthy for a return to the Father. In this instance, the imperative for woman is that she fully accept the baptismal consummation of her womanhood, that she commits to accepting the full mystery of being baptismal woman, that she learns how to give and respond and answer in accordance with the indwelling of the Spirit in her. It is only then that her response can become worthy of the response of the archetypal woman, Mary; that it can be *spiritually* fruitful.

Here we can note that if the specific risk and temptation for the husband is that he refuses his wife entry into his mission, holding fast to it as his own exclusive and unilateral function, the specific temptation for the wife is to claim his role for herself, to deny him the scope to perform his own mission. To the distorted image of headship in the man who dominates his wife is the distorted image of submission in the woman who manipulates her husband. The wife can seek to usurp and abrogate the mission of her husband to herself, just as the word of the husband can trample over and replace the mission of response of his wife. The challenge for woman is to learn to see her husband's mission in its proper baptismal iteration. That is, the wife must learn to see the value and importance of a husband who is seeking to carry out his task of mediating the Father's authority, who sees his headship in terms of his own subordination to Christ and participation in His mission of returning everything to the Father. She must thus learn to see her husband as son, as one intent on doing the will of the Father, of carrying out the mission given to him by Christ. She must learn to see him as brother, as one for whom the mission of headship takes place within the shared ontological plane of brother and sister in Christ. Part of being "subordinate," then, is simply allowing her husband to be faithful to his own mission. But more than this, it is in fact giving him the positive, fruitful, and affirming spiritual "yes" that will in fact shape and reveal to her husband the deeper character of his mission.

What further detail can we add to the notion that the shape of the wife's response to her husband is first and properly spiritual? The key element here is that in a distinct and irreplaceable way, she is guardian and mediator of the communion of persons in that to her is given the responsibility of bringing the relationship to life. What she first "gives birth" to, then, is the love given to the couple by the Father in Christ and the Church. Her "fertility" receives the word and manifests it, a spiritual dynamism that is then corporeally completed by the gift of the conception of the child. In this, the word of her husband that on its own is incapable of fully comprehending itself finally finds itself fully in woman. Balthasar thus calls this fruitfulness of woman an "answering fruitfulness, designed to receive man's fruitfulness (which, in itself, is helpless) and bring it to its 'fullness.' In this way, she is the 'glory' of the man (1 Cor 11:7)."[21] As a consequence, he goes on to call her "the fruit-bearing principle of the creaturely realm."[22] The wife receives the baptismal word of her husband—the word that in its baptismal essence is a welcoming and opening of himself to her—and, in receiving it according to the measure

---

21. Balthasar, *Person in Christ*, 285.
22. Balthasar, *Person in Christ*, 286.

of her Marian-ecclesial answering feminine fruitfulness (*viz.* guarding, treasuring, and "incubating" it) allows it to take root in her and come to life as their shared communion with one another in the Lord.

From the husband's point of view, he can now see that to which his word always aimed, that is, the communion of persons, a word in relation, a word bound to and completed in the other. Prior to the response of his wife, the husband can only accept his mission on faith, as it were, perhaps experiencing his mission to welcome and open himself to his wife as a burden and imposition with only uncertain foreseeable fruit. Without his wife's answering fruitfulness, the husband's word remains to some extent invisible, unactualized, purely theoretical and abstract—almost a kind of clumsy, uncertain, and "blind" movement to the other that cannot be sure of its own meaning and terminus. Thus, every initiating stance of openness and welcoming in accord with his mission *depends absolutely* upon the unique capacity of woman to receive, bear, internalize, and literally give flesh to his word. The woman must, in a particular way, teach man his own masculinity, just as in receiving his masculinity she will in turn discover her own femininity in a new way. With her uniquely and definitively feminine form of welcoming and receiving, the word of the husband suddenly lights up. It becomes visible, both to his wife and to himself. His own mission is drawn into sharper relief in and through the response that makes the radiance of love manifest; that gives his movement flesh and form. The crucifixion demanded of him is no longer theoretical, but has an object, a face who responds to his word with a welcoming yes, and who allows his word to bear fruit. In the woman, in his wife, in her loving yes, the word becomes flesh.

Thus, the *communio* of persons, the sacramental unity of the couple comes into presence. The husband's word is received, sealed, and reciprocated. The response of woman is thus not just as a passive or purely instrumental vessel within which the masculine word might grow on its own terms and powers, unhindered or uninfluenced by her presence. Here we can point to how Mary is essential to the life and nurturing of the Christ-child, to how in and through her role as mother she is joined to the very mission that she was herself prepared for and a part of even before she had any conscious awareness of it. Through Mary, the Word binds itself nuptially to creation, bringing to birth a bridal and filial creature and incorporating that creature into the divine life. In this, Mary's yes is not simply left behind as a merely provisional stage or instrumental husk. Rather, she is granted the supreme and unimaginable dignity of becoming *Mother of God* and mother of all the living. She is called to participation in the Fatherhood of God in an unprecedented manner.

And it is this same model of participation and incorporation that is given sacramentally to the woman in relation to the word borne by her husband. In receiving this word, she completes his word and together his word and her response become a *new corporate word*, a new creation in which word and answer become reciprocal modes of the same reality (something concretized with the conception and birth of the child, who becomes a kind of "signifying" presence of the unity of the couple, of the fact they are more than simply two individuals). Here, just as we saw love make the husband a participant in his wife's response by drawing him kenotically outside of himself, requiring him to submit his word to her response, subjecting himself to the discernment of the Spirit, so too is the wife, as ingredient to the new word constituted by the couple, caught up into his mission of initiative and responsibility. In this, she does not remain trapped in the hermeneutics of her own response. Her response is called into a co-relation with his initiative such that, without losing the specificity of their own missions, each find themselves caught up in participation in the other's mission, sharing each in common, and thereby living their communion as a genuinely mutual partnership of love. The act of opening themselves to each other, whether in an "initiating" or "receiving" manner is saturated in communion, in an interpenetration and sharing of mission so that neither now clings to their mission as either something to be jealously guarded and which excludes the other (*viz.* the temptation in relation to masculinity), or something to be jettisoned as dehumanizing (*viz.* the temptation in relation to femininity).

Thus, in regard to what feminine subordination looks like in relation to the question of any distinct authority borne by the husband as head, we can suggest the following. To begin, recall our conclusion as regards the husband's authority. We suggested that his authority cannot be viewed as unilateral and one-sided, on the basis that at the heart of his mission is a welcoming of woman into his authority and sovereignty, an opening to her to share in the offering of their relationship to the Father. Now, having seen more fully the reciprocity of word and answer via the supremely important answering fruitfulness of woman, we can suggest that there can be no word of the husband that is purely and exclusively unilateral, i.e., that does not from the first bring his wife into a sharing of the discernment of his mission. Likewise, there is no answering word of the wife that is purely and exclusively unilateral, i.e., that does not also bring her husband into a sharing of the discernment of *her* mission. In each case, each mission begins in "consultation" with the other. Each must submit their mission to the conditions and scrutiny of the other in and through the mediation of each trinitarian Person if it is to be brought fully into the service of love. The word is always shaping the response, and the response the word. Every word already contains the answer, every answer the word. Each take place within the baptismal, eucharistic, and nuptial unity of the new life and love that comes from being a new creation in Christ, a son and daughter of the Father, brought to the fullness of communion in the Spirit.

Headship and Submission in the Ontological Difference

The final question that must be confronted is one that derives from the more practical, pastoral perspective. As flagged at the beginning of the previous section, a difficult question—the limit question, one might say—emerges when we consider all of the above within the exigencies of the human side of the ontological difference or real distinction between Being and beings, between God and man, even baptismal man; in the light of creatureliness, time, temporality, finitude, freedom, and the regime of sin that continue to shape and influence the sacramental expression of the Great Mystery. This is to say, first, that there are no guarantees that baptism constitutes an absolute immunity from sin. Second, it is to acknowledge that there will therefore emerge distinctly non-baptismal modes of behavior even amongst the baptized. It is precisely when the category of mission breaks down that headship and submission become points of conflict, threat, violence, and manipulation—the very antithesis of what we have presented them as being in their theological core. And finally, third, it is to say that, even absent of sin, the way in which a *concrete* couple realize and embody the reality expressed in and through the mode of headship and submission will not in each instance be identical. Nor does it presuppose the loss of uniqueness of the individualities and relationship of the spouses who express it.

The question has to do with how headship and submission function in light of such considerations. To pursue treatment of our first two points above, it is a question of whether the word of a husband in a situation of conflict and disagreement continues to carry the kind of theological authority that we have claimed it does within what should properly be a situation of mutuality and unity in the reciprocal exchange of word and response. The first thing to stress here is that a word borne by a husband, a word whose legitimacy flows from its existential fidelity to the word of the Father in Christ, and a word dependent in some way on the response of the woman, should probably not be thought of as a "trump card" in situations of disagreement. That is, my sense is that it would be problematic to think of the exercise of the husband's headship as the means to resolve spousal disagreement by means of a sovereign unilateral imposition of the husband's will over the wife's, even if this is only as a last resort. The temptation in the past has been to see the word of a husband as facilitating the unity of the couple by this sovereign means in precisely these kinds of limit situations. If unity and order cannot be achieved by other measures, so the position held, then the word of the husband must be the last word.

But *sacramental* unity cannot be the product of coercion or imposition. The word of one baptismal person cannot coerce a response of another. It cannot override the hermeneutics of the answer. To do so does violence to the supreme dignity and freedom of the feminine answer, an answer that occupies the same ontological plane and carries the same ontological value as the masculine word in the baptismal call and answer under the absoluteness of Christ's headship. Thus, in situations of conflict and disagreement, headship and submission issue the demand for a far deeper labor of reciprocal engagement and dialogue before any genuine resolution to a problem can be posited. This will not be to say that the politics of reconciliation and conflict resolution will take place outside of the specificity of each mission in a kind of egalitarian sameness. Rather, it is to say that headship and submission would here function precisely as the mechanism that would work to *restore* spousal mutuality so that the conflict or disagreement could *then* be resolved from a deeper baptismal complementarity.

What might this look like? First, I suggest that the primary function of the masculine word of the husband in this situation is to provoke a contemplative turn inward, rather than an activist one outwards in the direction of conflict resolution. That is, rather than seeing his word as the means to forcefully bend reality to his will, i.e., by "putting his foot down," the husband ought first to make thematic the status of his own faithfulness to the headship of Christ. The husband must confront the way in which he himself may have failed in his task of loving his wife, of accepting her as gift, of respecting and acknowledging her response, of being shaped by her giving of flesh to his mission. Headship thus here demands that he humble himself, both in relation to Christ and spouse; that he question the extent to which he may have slipped into non-baptismal modes of behavior.

Second, I suggest that headship imposes the demand for the husband never to seek resolution to a conflict from an autonomous and extrinsic point outside of the baptismal communion of persons. Let me be clear again: headship, understood baptismally, undermines any notion that the husband could invoke his status as head in a way that does not require the answer of his wife for its valid functioning. For without submission, it cannot truly be itself. It requires its relational counterpart, its answering fruitfulness, *by definition*. And this means then that the outward expression of the authority borne by the husband in situations of conflict and disagreement pertains first and foremost to *a mission of reconciliation*, to the restoration of the dialogue of call and answer within love. The husband must employ his mission here in the form of peacemaking, one radically distinct from what might be the fallen male tendency to "fix things" by the pure force of his word, i.e., "I'm sorry" through gritted teeth and without truly entering into the experience of his wife, uttered so as to move on without a genuine dialogue.

As a function of his headship, then, it is thus incumbent on him—given to him as a particular theological responsibility—to make the first move, to turn to his wife in humility, openness, gentleness, and tenderness. Crucially, to him belongs a particular imperative of *speech*, we might say. That is, he must resist and become the breaker of the silence of separation, isolation, and grudge-holding. Headship demands that he humiliate his ego and his insecurities by speaking first, by making himself vulnerable first, by *apologizing first*,[23] not to project a false and narcissistic humility so as to control and manipulate the situation, but to seek a truly mutual resolution. Perhaps this latter is in fact the supreme *practical meaning of headship*, and not without coincidence, the one that men likely find most difficult.

Consider the classic trope of male resistance and reluctance embodied in the so-called "Man's Prayer" from a Canadian comic sketch television show in the mid-1990's: "I'm a man, but I can change, if I have to, I guess." But it is precisely in headship that is found the Gospel imperative to humiliate the tendency to think of oneself as an entity distinct from the hermeneutics of the other, from the deeper communion to which your being belongs and is nothing without.

At its heart, then, the initiating word of the husband is aimed towards healing spousal communion. It must seek to heal the context of the call and answer of husband and wife. It must reject the temptation, both to abdicate responsibility from healing communion, and to seek resolution to conflict and disagreement outside of the full reciprocity and mutuality of the baptismal relation. Headship would thus look like the husband refusing to negotiate or impose his initiative on a plane other than love. It would look like him refusing the temptation to resolve the problem at the level of abstraction from a properly baptismal belonging to Christ and to spouse. But, equally of importance, it would also forbid him from standing passively on the sidelines, shuffling his feet and looking the other way, as perhaps was Adam's failure while the Serpent tempted Eve.

From the point of view of the feminine answer of the wife, submission would at its heart involve a similar kind of conversion and reconciliation

---

23. I am indebted to a colleague, Owen Vyner, for expressing headship in these terms in conversation.

seen in the function of male headship, but according to its specifically feminine, answering frame. Here, a contemplative return to the explicitly Marian shape of her mission is the first imperative. She must hold herself to account at the bar of the Father's claim on her as expressed through the archetypal Marian response of the Church. Submission is thus for her a variation of the same mission of reflection and contemplation given to her husband, a missional heightening of the universal call of holiness given to every adopted child of God. She too must confront the way in which she may have failed in loving her husband, in receiving and treasuring his gift of himself, in giving him space to offer himself to her. Submission thus demands that she consider the extent to which she may have fallen into non-baptismal modes of behavior.

For her, the positive expression of her submission would look like a similar refusal to resolve conflict and difference outside of the horizon of the baptismal relation. It would make reconciliation and peacemaking a prerogative for her as well. But here this prerogative would be expressed in a certain way as the relational shaping of her husband's mission of initiative. That is, it might involve a kind of pregnant silence, presence, and abiding nearness to her husband, subtle signals of an enduring, patient, and steadfast love, an expectation of and confidence in his free and loving turn to her, a willingness not to give up on him. In this, she would resist the temptation to abrogate his mission, to manipulate or force an apology out of him. She would instead creatively nurture his word in the bosom of her answering fruitfulness and, without violating its freedom, in this assist in drawing it more fully back into the baptismal center.

But let us be careful: this is *not* to say, in a literal sense, that she should never say sorry first or that the prerogative of her feminine mission must truncate or restrict interpersonal patterns of reconciliation and forgiveness however they might precipitate. It is not to equate this receptive mode with literal silence or impotent passivity, suggesting that she is little more than a doormat who must wait until her husband gets his act together—one imagines that every husband needs a sharp word or rebuke from his wife from time to time in order to stimulate his responsibility. Rather it is to say that she must resist the temptation to speak *for* her husband, to be his "mother" in the sense of managing, smothering, or forcing his word. The specific strength of her answer is that it has the capacity to enrich, complement, and arouse his word without manipulating or replacing it. Because of her, the word of her husband has the capacity to become something that it could not otherwise be on its own. In this sense, the responsibility on the part of the husband to act and take responsibility is, in fact, when the wife takes her mission seriously, always itself the fruit of her creative shaping, which in some sense is always shaping his word, running before it.

Her answering submission must therefore always be cognizant of not evading or reducing her own unique reconciling and peacemaking potential. Again, the goal is for each to return to a full, conscious, and active participation in the mission of spousal communion, to place their conflict and disagreement within the deepest baptismal point of their relationship. Headship and submission thus serve this goal. In moments of conflict and disagreement, they above all else call the couple back to the primacy of mission as service to love. In moments of crisis, they are the modes of mutual reconciliation through which the Spirit acts to offer healing, forgiveness, and a return to full *communio*.

The point is that all conflict and disagreement must be relocated evermore consciously into the dimension of baptismal existence; the solution cannot be found in temptations that belong to the hazards of fallen politics and nature. This would be to say that headship and submission, as *theological missions*, can only be explicated and function properly inside baptism. To attempt to resolve conflict or exercise authority outside of this, i.e., outside of the asymmetrical reciprocity of love and mission, would be to do so in the half-life or abstract zone of fallen nature and history, i.e., it would involve the couple abstracting from their baptismal identities and refusing to deal with the conflict as son and daughter, brother and sister, husband and wife—as *theological persons*.

All of the above is to say that headship and submission therefore serve to draw the couple into a deeper and genuinely *trinitarian* discernment of their relationship, according to the modes and gifts of love given to them by the Father, Son, and Holy Spirit. Headship and submission in Christ leads temporality and finitude—in all the glory of its freedom and specificity—into the folds of the deepest unity-in-difference in eternity and infinity.

But as our final point relative to the uniqueness and particularity of the mission of discerning headship and submission in the concrete, we can stress that, consonant with the logic of the ontological difference or real distinction[24] (especially when it is baptismally and hypostatically understood), even as headship and submission immerse the couple deeper into the trinitarian folds of Father, Son, and Holy Spirit, they never do so at the expense of the genuine freedom and uniqueness of the creature. First, *participating* in, rather than merely *imitating* the mystery—a point I have stressed throughout this book—does not simultaneously mean that one must dualistically renounce a distinctively human way of embodying the mystery. In other

---

24. Cf. Balthasar, *Realm of Metaphysics*, 613–27.

words, it does not mean pantheistically losing oneself in God, giving up all claim to possessing an act of existence irreducibly unique and one's own. For adoption, sharing in Christ's hypostatic personhood, does not eradicate "real" distinction, but in fact protects it beyond measure; the creature remains an adopted son—a son in the Son, and therefore not *the* Son,—one who is created (not eternally begotten), always in this sense irreducibly distinct from the trinitarian mystery of Father, Son, and Holy Spirit, even as called fully into its communion. In this way, the creature never loses genuine creatureliness, a genuine distinction from God and others, though granted the most perfect communion with God and others.

Consonant with this distinction is the abiding ontological value of the person in all of his or her particular historical character and specificity. That is, what is saved, redeemed, and sanctified—made capable of "adding," as it were, to the divinity itself—is not the "individual substance of a rational nature," i.e., the abstract or generic self, but rather *this* self, in all its specificity, color, and historical uniqueness. I speak of those considerations that scholasticism somewhat pejoratively labelled the "accidents" of the human person, but which personalism correctly judges to be an essential dimension of personal existence.[25] From this point of view, the self's incorporation into Christ's body, into his relation to the Father as Son does not constitute a loss of "personality." Rather, you are incorporated into Christ's relation to the Father and to his body as *you*; and with your spouse, as *we*. The color of your existence is not washed out.

Clearly, there are things about ourselves and our relationships that we would rather not have for eternity—dysfunctions, weaknesses, addictions, any number of embarrassing and destructive behaviors. But I suspect there is a real place, not only for the truly personally unique, but also for joyful oddness, idiosyncrasies, and "colloquial" aspects of personality, all of which are in some sense essential for what makes you, *you*, and what makes we, *us*. It is within the dynamic historical and relational matrix of existence that the subject and relationships come to be. *My* personality and *our* personality is in this sense as much the product of relationality (including much of its uncanniness and peculiarity) as substantiality. It arises from the mediation of temporal existence in time and space, in the contingent interplay of freedom (both my own and others'), events, and material forces; of enigmatic as well as more transparent or obvious factors and realities. All of this combines to produce *me*. Baptism does not so much eliminate all this as place it inside the baptismal relation, restumping and reanimating that which is "me" and "us" within the context of union with Christ, the image of the eternal Father.

25. Cf. Patterson, *Chalcedonian Personalism*.

Thus, as regards the spousal relationship, it is precisely in the fact that my marriage with my wife is irreducibly particular and unique—that it has to be *me* and it has to be *her* so that it can be *us*—that is found a constitutive dimension of what is absolutely "essential" and "real" about it. We love each other precisely because of the unique interweaving of time, place, personality, and shared experience that have shaped and continue to shape our co-existence. I love her because she is *not* someone else, as she does me, and it is that which makes our relationship unique and exclusive.

If the argument thus far is sound, then all of this will also have some effect in terms of how the mutual exchange of headship and submission is practically shaped. That is, given the entirely legitimate and appropriate factors of personality and the particular "styles" of each couple, headship and submission will not look like a "one-size fits all" prototype that is identically and mechanically performed by each couple. Rather, it may from this perspective look far more customized. The word-response dynamic may in any given relationship be weighted or calibrated differently. Given each other's strengths and weaknesses, spouses may in different ways supply what is lacking in each other. In this sense, that the concrete realization of headship and submission may not appear strictly "conventional" is in no way a default or necessary indication that its essential theological character is not being lived and expressed in faithfulness. Each concrete expression of headship and submission will be unique, and this "diversity" may be entirely legitimate, a fruit of the genuine and particular *communio* of the couple.

This is also why in the end headship and submission cannot simply be reduced to a division of labor within the realm of domestic life. They will certainly inform and shape this life, but they cannot impose themselves absolutely on it, for it may well be the case that *this* wife or *that* husband may or may not have the capacity or may fail in the practical aspects of their respective missions, a fact which may relativise, up to a point, more "traditional" gender roles and distinctions as regards the practical support of or running of a household. Moreover, changing social structures and expectations will not be an irrelevant factor either, in terms of the concrete "how" of conjugal politics as it relates to practical expression in personal and social life.

This is not to deny that headship and submission will and should shape a shared life together in certain ways familiar to more traditional arrangements. For example, it remains true that woman in her genuine baptismal mission will exhibit more concrete links to domestic nurturing than will the man. It flows from the Marian character of woman's baptismal mission to take up the mission of receiving and nurturing the word, a vocation intrinsically tied up with a "real presence" to the raising of children and the maintenance of a home, something that belongs in a particularly acute and specialized way to woman. The mother's smile is emblematic of this essential dimension of baptismal motherhood,[26] and much is lost when this smile no longer irradiates the domestic sphere in all its living reality. The point is rather that the genuine differences which create certain normal divisions and differentiations within the domestic world belong, first, to the category of dynamic theological mission, not static natural role, and second, as such can never be thought of as radically distinct spheres that exclude the other from participation. This is a further application of the way that the distinct missions of masculinity and femininity expand into each other, calling them to a real participation in a mission that is otherwise than their own, and thereby relativising the *absolute* distinction between the roles or vocations born from the category of mission. It is here we can speak of the importance of the sharing and supplementation of missions, especially in situations where one spouse is not able to fulfil his or her mission. Each spouse can learn to expand and stretch their capacity for and expression of love, intimacy, and service. Again, the specificity of mission means that it is not simply interchangeable; but this will never preclude a genuine sharing of mission in love.

Finally, we might even go so far as to say that in some way all of the unique and irreducible human ways of bearing and expressing the mystery given to us by adoption is therefore in some way a manifestation of a mystery of novelty, creativity, and freedom in the Archetype itself. That is, the "color" of each relationship, if ontologically valid, therefore perhaps uniquely expresses aspects of a divine mystery of love that is truly infinitely and eternally concrete, particular, and creative; not simply a reality where "pure act" is conceived as a kind of stasis in which "surprise" or "eventfulness" no longer play any part. Perhaps the particularity of temporal existence and relationship may allow us to countenance something more of an eternal richness of divine existence and relationship than a metaphysically substantialist approach has allowed. At the same time, a more robust *baptismal* account of the person helps to prevent this insight from becoming the occasion for an anthropological reduction of God to the level of the human pole of the real distinction. In the end, a *hypostatic* logic located in the sacramental ground

---

26. "The child's 'I' awakens in the experience of a 'Thou': in its mother's smile through which it learns that it is contained, affirmed and loved in a relationship which is incomprehensively encompassing, already actual, sheltering and nourishing. The body which it snuggles into, a soft, warm and nourishing kiss, is a kiss of love in which it can take shelter because it has been sheltered there a priori" (Balthasar, *Realm of Metaphysics*, 616).

of baptism seems to me the only truly effective way to safeguard the unity and difference of humanity and divinity.

In conclusion, this chapter has sought to show how it might be possible to more theologically (and hopefully, more faithfully) construe headship and submission as signifiers of a much deeper sacramental participation as child of the Father in the Son. I have argued that the grace of a new "hypostatic" relation to divinity in baptism and in sacramental marriage received by the believer constitutes a new ground of relation for the respective gendered missions of husband and wife. In this context, headship and submission are terms of relation that relate to the full theological dramatization of human identity in Christ. The husband and wife faithful to Christ, filled with the Holy Spirit, and obedient to the will of the Father, thus discover a mode of relation that exceeds the hermeneutical limitations of the politics of both complementarianism and egalitarianism. In the politics of the baptismal relation, they discover the hope and possibility of new freedom in a truly trinitarian love and communion.

Conclusion

My hope is that, however tentative, exploratory, and therefore provisional it may yet be, I have nevertheless within the frame of an anthropological vision shaped by baptism delineated a vision of headship and submission credible enough to provoke further conversation. I have presented conjugal politics as making the most sense when interpreted in and as a dynamic of communication and relation ordered to love, one that takes place inside the baptismal relation of man and woman to the Father in the Son. I have read headship and submission above all else as terms of relation, as missions given to husband and wife that express a baptismal existence and personhood that must be fully conformed to Christ, all so that each in their own way may give of themselves to the other more fully, not so that they might lose their selves in the other, but so that they may infinitely gain both the other and their own self according to the great mystery of God's own trinitarian love.

I have throughout stressed that the only sure way of interpreting and harnessing the energy linked to the primordial designations of masculine and feminine—those designations that have persistently linked the feminine with "earth" and the masculine with "heaven,"—is to remap them within the dramatic world of baptism, the word and reality that sums up and unifies the christological, ecclesial, eucharistic, pneumatological, and Marian radiations of the trinitarian mystery as they take concrete shape for the creature in the nuptial trilogy of baptism, the eucharistic liturgy, and marriage. As a consequence, I have consciously stepped away from the bottom-up or imitative task of trying to link a natural hermeneutics of sexual difference with the Gospel. My goal has been to stress the baptismally specified category of theological mission as the only possible perspective that can save nature from distortion, particularly in social and cultural situation typified by various hermeneutical celebrations of the death of God.

But, as also clarified, this should not be thought of as suggesting that the baptismal missions given to man and woman simply hang nominalistically in the void, bearing no connection to their pre-baptismal being and nature. Rather, the designations given here are the shaping of masculinity and femininity into their ultimate, perfected, dramatic form. Baptismal personhood belongs to the ontology of spirit, so to speak, the ontology of the deification of the age to come that begins here and now in the new sacramental forms of life in Christ.

Thus, if I have tended to downplay an ontologization of difference and role from below (nature), and if I have also stressed as a consequence headship and submission as terms of relation inexplicable apart the mutual co-inhering of baptismal masculinity and femininity, we must nevertheless continue to strongly affirm that baptismal existence gives to the man and woman an identity and mission in fundamental ways inaccessible to the opposite way of being human. In this, given the way in which it has today been downgraded, one should explicitly affirm that a unique and irreplaceable existence and grace has been given to the husband to mediate the word of authority of the Father in Christ, to bear this word in his person and to transmit it to his wife and family for the unity of the domestic church, and for the return of the spousal and filial *communio* to the Father as a living sacrifice of praise and worship. Even if I have stressed the somewhat relative character of this existence and mission, inasmuch as the initiative of the husband is simultaneously bound to both the Father's headship over him in Christ and to his wife's participation in his own mission, it nevertheless remains the case that his baptismal masculinity, as masculine and as a new creation, bears within itself the capacity for true greatness, true love, service, respect, courage, glory, honour, dignity, and strength. There should be no reason to deny that the best of the natural iterations of masculinity continue to belong to and inform baptismal masculinity. Nothing that we have said should be interpreted as meaning that a husband somehow ceases to be a man, can no longer legitimately enjoy masculine things, is no longer called to a distinctly human kind of masculine strength, excellence, and discipline, and is no longer attractive to his wife on precisely this basis. I have sought only to show how the specific task of headship, as a theological mission, shapes and trains a man to a new realization of what his masculinity is capable of. It reveals the greater mission to which he is called, how he can become worthy of Christ's dramatic mission for the Church, able to love, to guard, to protect, and yes, to "lead" the woman who has been entrusted to him.

I fully recognize that much more could and should be said in terms of more adequately explicating the shape of the masculine mission. But I have largely limited myself to accenting that what matters most for both husband and wife and what will frame any further sense of the uniqueness and specificity of their respective missions is that they never lose sight of the new baptismal organization of masculinity and femininity. Whatever the precise shape of masculine and feminine missions of husband and wife, they can only be explicated from a point deep inside the love that made them son and daughter, brother and sister, husband and wife in Christ.

At the heart of my account of conjugal politics has been an anthropology rethought according to more radical notions of person and baptism. To this task I devoted two chapters. I have argued that what is imperative—especially within a secular context that ritually celebrates possibilities that emerge from the death of God—is that we develop a deeper sense of human persons as they are born from and occupy what I have been calling the "sacramental middle." By this I have meant the sources of identity for the person that cannot be reduced either to nature or divinity, but belong rather to the perspective of the interweaving or "marriage" of these realities in the hypostatic personhood of Christ. The dramatic and baptismal identity that has emerged here is one premised on the notion of person as child, as son or daughter, and only then as male and female in any truly theologically meaningful way. This person now lives "inside" the trinitarian relationship, but only through the fundamental mediation of *ecclesia* and its sacramental life. A person for whom time and freedom remain "live," the baptized son or daughter realize themselves the extent to which they live their existence as mission, as a labor of worship and conversion centered on giving themselves more and more completely as a Spirit-filled offering to and in praise of their heavenly Father. The nuptial relationship represents a "corporatization" of this mission, an insertion of a couple into the spousal relationship of Christ and his Church and a worldly calling to radiate Christ's love for the Father and for humanity to the entire world. This becomes part of the realization of the spouses' vocation of worship and conversion as together they perfect their communion with one another in the Lord, anticipating that future time of the fullness of trinitarian communion in the life to come.

All of this has meant that I have approached the possible trinitarian foundations of headship and submission from within the sacramental infrastructure of baptism. More than anything else, the Trinity has emerged at the heart of the mission of conjugal politics, not as a static or imitative reality, but as the living personal presence of Father, Son, and Holy Spirit as each in the unity of their communion assist the couple in the task of holiness and conversion. In this, I do not suggest that I have employed this sacramental infrastructure only as a kind of prudential, manufactured protective mechanism to prevent possible pollution of the divine archetype by the human image. Rather, I have suggested that any participation in or appropriation of trinitarian existence must be properly located within the deepest "existential" point of our belonging to the Father in the historical actions of Christ and the Spirit. This is what it means to be *imago trinitatis*. It means to belong to the Godhead in the *communio* of the Church, in the corporate relating to the Father in Christ and the Spirit from within the theological relationships that flow from being sons in the Son. It is by being son and daughter, brother and sister, husband and wife, father and mother that we attain the deepest likeness to the trinitarian God. It is the notion of a *baptismal anthropology* that is fundamentally crucial in this regard.

I hope that by speaking of the Trinity through the sacraments—particularly according to the nuptial trilogy of baptism, the eucharistic liturgy, and marriage, read in the terms of the Pauline and Johannine reversal—I have both protected the distinction owed to the divinity, as well as revealed the specific trinitarian impress within the filial and nuptial structure of anthropology which man and woman take up sacramentally in Christ. By this attention to the sacramental "middle," I hope to have contributed to and complemented Trainor's chapter.

In the end, the task for husband and wife must be to "immerse" themselves ever more deeply into the mission of conjugal love understood above all as baptismal worship, as a kind of "liturgy." It is for them to offer their filial and spousal childhood as a sacrifice of praise to the Father. Near the end of the Theology of the Body, John Paul II begins to speak of the marriage relationship in the language of liturgy and prayer. In discussing the relationship of Sarah and Tobias in the Old Testament book of Tobit, he draws attention to how the experience of God working in their lives transforms their love into a prayer. God's intervention in their dire situation causes them to open their face-to-face relationship to intrinsically include and be encompassed by the divine Third. The pope refers to how the prospect of death, the ultimate "limit" of love, "brings *the loving dialogue of the spouses in some way to silence*."[1] That is, the couple recognizes that only in opening their relationship to the infinite and eternal can they be saved. This recognition peaks in the couple's common turning to the Lord in prayer, where they offer up their relationship to him:

> In this dramatic moment of the history of both, Tobias and Sarah, when on the wedding night it was their due, as new spouses, to speak reciprocally with the 'language of their body,' they transform this language into a single voice. That unison is prayer. This voice, this act of speaking in unison, allows both of them to pass beyond the 'limit situation,' beyond the threat of

1. John Paul II, *Theology of the Body*, 600 (115.3).

evil and death, inasmuch as they open themselves totally, in the unity of the two, to the living God.[2]

The limit placed upon their relationship by death (a death that all relationships must face and confront, albeit perhaps not always in as immediate and dramatic a situation as Sarah and Tobias) here provokes them to turn to the Lord as a couple, to fix their gaze on his priority and initiative. They find themselves met by God's merciful intervention, and as a consequence dedicate themselves in gratitude and praise wholly to him. In this, Sarah and Tobias discover his living presence in their lives, learning that their relationship belongs not to themselves but to him. And so their wedding night (and their whole marriage) becomes a hymn of praise, a prayer, a liturgical offering to the God who has delivered them, the occasion of their total gift of themselves to God as a couple and thus the sanctification and hallowing of their spousal relationship.

It is only here that conjugal politics can insulate itself from the risk of domination and humiliation. Only when the primordial signification of masculinity and femininity is re-dimensioned in Christ, placed inside the baptismal relation, sealed and fecundated in the Spirit, and animated by a mission ordered towards worship of the living God, can the relation of man and woman attain the highest trinitarian heights from which it has been born and to which it is destined. May every marriage become such a hymn of praise and love.

---

2. John Paul II, *Theology of the Body*, 602–4 (115.6).

Bibliography

Allen, Prudence. *The Concept of Woman: The Aristotelian Revolution, 750 BC–AD 1250.* Grand Rapids: Eerdmans, 1985.
Ambrose. "Hexaemeron." In *The Human Couple in the Fathers*, edited by Giulio Sfameni Gasparro, et al., 223–26. Boston: Pauline, 1999.
———. "On Paradise." In *The Human Couple in the Fathers*, edited by Giulio Sfameni Gasparro, et al., 218–23. Boston: Pauline, 1999.
Ashley, Benedict. *Justice in the Church: Gender and Participation.* Washington, DC: Catholic University of America Press, 1996.
Athanasius. "Four Discourses Against the Arians." In *The Nicene Creed and Post Nicene Fathers of the Christian Church*, vol. 4, edited by Philip Schaff and Henry Wace, 303–447. Grand Rapids: Eerdmans, 1971.
Augustine. "The Excellence of Marriage." In *The Works of Saint Augustine*, vol. 9, edited by John E. Rotelle, 33–60. Translated by Ray Kearney. New York: New York City, 1999.
———. *Expositions on the Book of Psalms.* Edited by Philip Schaff. Grand Rapids: Eerdmans, 1956.
———. "Lectures or Tractates on the Gospel According to St. John." In *The Nicene and Post-Nicene Fathers of the Christian Church*, vol. 7, edited by Philip Schaff, 7–452. Grand Rapids: Eerdmans, 1956.
———. "On the Literal Meaning of Genesis." In *The Human Couple in the Fathers*, edited by Giulio Sfameni Gasparro, et al., 265–66. Boston: Pauline, 1999.
———. "On Marriage and Concupiscence, Bk. 1." In *The Human Couple in the Fathers*, edited by Giulio Sfameni Gasparro, et al., 266–68. Boston: Pauline, 1999.
———. "Sermon 9." In *The Human Couple in the Fathers*, edited by Giulio Sfameni Gasparro, et al., 268–71. Boston: Pauline, 1999.
———. "Sermon 132." In *The Human Couple in the Fathers*, edited by Giulio Sfameni Gasparro, et al., 271–72. Boston: Pauline, 1999.
Balthasar, Hans Urs von. *Creator Spirit.* Vol. 3 of *Explorations in Theology.* Translated by James L. Houlden. San Francisco: Ignatius, 1993.
———. *Epilogue.* Translated by Edward T. Oakes. Einsiedeln: Johannes Verlag, 1987.
———. "The Fathers, the Scholastics, and Ourselves." *Communio* 24 (1997) 34–96.
———. *Love Alone Is Credible.* Translated by D. C. Schindler. San Francisco: Ignatius, 2004.

———. *Man in God*. Vol. 2 of *Theo-Drama: Dramatis Personae*. Translated by Graham Harrison. San Francisco: Ignatius, 1976.

———. "On the Concept of Person." *Communio* 13 (1986) 18–26.

———. *The Person in Christ*. Vol. 3 of *Theo-Drama: Dramatis Personae*. Translated by Graham Harrison. San Francisco: Ignatius, 1991.

———. *Prayer*. Translated by A.V. Littledale. London: Geoffrey Chapman, 1961.

———. *The Realm of Metaphysics in the Modern Age*. Vol. 5 of *The Glory of the Lord: A Theological Aesthetics*. Translated by Oliver Davies, et al. San Francisco: Ignatius, 1991.

———. *Seeing the Form*. Vol. 1 of *The Glory of the Lord: A Theological Aesthetic*. Translated by Graham Harrison. San Francisco: Ignatius, 1982.

———. *A Theology of History*. San Francisco: Ignatius, 1994.

———. *The Theology of Karl Barth*. Translated by Edward T. Oakes. San Francisco: Ignatius, 1992.

———. *Truth of God*. Vol. 2 of *Theo-Logic*. Translated by Adrian J. Walker. San Francisco: Ignatius, 2004.

———. "The Unknown God." In *Elucidations*, 35–45. Translated by John Riches. San Francisco: Ignatius, 1998.

———. "A Word on Humanae Vitae." *Communio* 20 (1993) 437–50.

Barth, Karl. *Church Dogmatics*. Translated by G. T. Thomson, et al. 31 vols. Edinburgh: T. & T. Clark, 1936–77.

Barth, Marcus. *Ephesians: Translation and Commentary on Chapters 4-6*. The Anchor Bible. New York: Doubleday, 1974.

Basil. "On the Spirit." In *The Nicene Creed and Post Nicene Fathers of the Christian Church*, vol. 8, edited by Philip Schaff and Henry Wace, 1–50. Grand Rapids, Eerdmans, 1971.

Benedict XVI. *Deus Caritas Est*. Holy See, December 25, 2005. http://w2.vatican.va/content/benedict-xvi/en/encyclicals/documents/hf_ben-xvi_enc_20051225_deus-caritas-est.html.

Bilezikian, Gilbert. *Beyond Sex Roles: What the Bible Says about a Woman's Place in Church and Family*. Grand Rapids: Baker Academic, 2006.

Boethius. "Treatise Against Eutyches and Nestorius." In *Theological Tractates/The Consolation of Philosophy*, 73–127. Loeb Classical Library. Cambridge, MA: Harvard University Press, 1918.

Bonaventure. *The Breviloquium*. Vol. 2 of *The Works of Bonaventure: Cardinal, Seraphic Doctor, and Saint*. Translated by Jose De Vinck. Paterson: St. Anthony Guild, 1963.

Browning, Don S. *Marriage and Modernization: How Globalization Threatens Marriage and What to do About It*. Grand Rapids: Eerdmans, 2003.

Burke, Cormac. "A Postscript to the 'Remedium Concupiscentiae.'" *The Thomist* 70 (2006) 481–536.

Butler, Sara. *The Catholic Priesthood and Women: A Guide to the Teaching of the Church*. Chicago: Hillenbrand, 2006.

Cantalamessa, Raniero. *Loving the Church: Scriptural Meditations for the Papal Household*. Translated by Gilberto Cavazos-González and Amanda Quantz. Ohio: Servant, 2003.

Catechism of the Catholic Church. Ottawa: Canadian Conference of Catholic Bishops, 1994.

Cere, Daniel Mark. "Marriage, Subordination, and the Development of Christian Doctrine." In *Does Christianity Teach Male Headship? The Equal-Regard Marriage and its Critics*, edited by David Blankenhorn, et al., 92–110. Grand Rapids: Eerdmans, 2004.

Chauvet, Louis-Marie. *Symbol and Sacrament: A Sacramental Reinterpretation of Christian Existence*. Translated by Patrick Madigan and Madeleine Beaumont. Collegeville: Liturgical, 1995.

Christians for Biblical Equality. "About." *CBE International*, 2019. https://www.cbeinternational.org/content/about-cbe.

Clarke, W. Norris. *Person and Being*. Milwaukee: Marquette University Press, 1993.

Clement of Alexandria. "Paidagogos." In *The Human Couple in the Fathers*, edited by Giulio Sfameni Gasparro, et al., 174–75. Boston: Pauline, 1999.

———. "Stromata." In *The Human Couple in the Fathers*, edited by Giulio Sfameni Gasparro, et al., 171–72. Boston: Pauline, 1999.

Compendium of the Social Doctrine of the Catholic Church. Washington, DC: USCBB, 2005.

Cooper, Adam G. "Marriage and the 'Garments of Skin' in Irenaeus and the Greek Fathers." *Communio* 33 (2006) 215–37.

Council on Biblical Manhood and Womanhood. "About." *CBMW*, 2019. https://cbmw.org/about/mission-vision.

Cyril of Jerusalem. "Mystagogical Catechesis 2." In *Documents of the Baptismal Liturgy*, edited by E. C. Whitaker and Maxwell E. Johnson, 31–32. Collegeville: Liturgical, 2003.

Daniélou, Jean. *The Bible and the Liturgy*. Notre Dame: University of Notre Dame Press, 1961.

Doyle, Robert. "Are We Heretics? A Review of *The Trinity and Subordinationism* by Kevin Giles." *The Briefing* 307 (2004) 11–19.

Erickson, Millard. *God in Three Persons: A Contemporary Interpretation of the Trinity*. Grand Rapids: Baker, 1995.

Fitzmyer, Joseph A. *Paul and His Theology: A Brief Sketch*. Englewood Cliffs: Prentice Hall, 1989.

Frame, John. *The Doctrine of God: A Theology of Lordship*. Phillipsburg: P & R, 2002.

Francis. *Amoris Laetitia*. Holy See, March 19, 2016. https://w2.vatican.va/content/dam/francesco/pdf/apost_exhortations/documents/papa-francesco_esortazione-ap_20160319_amoris-laetitia_en.pdf.

Gadamer, Hans Georg. *Truth and Method*. New York: Crossroad, 1992.

Geisler, Norman. *Systematic Theology*. Vol 2. Minneapolis: Bethany, 2003.

Giles, Kevin. *Jesus and the Father: Modern Evangelicals Reinvent the Doctrine of the Trinity*. Grand Rapids: Zondervan, 2006.

———. *The Trinity and Subordinationism*. Downers Grove, IL: InterVarsity, 2002.

Girard, René. *Battling to the End: Conversations with Benoît Chantre*. Translated by Mary Baker. East Lansing: Michigan State University Press, 2010.

———. *I See Satan Fall Like Lightning*. Translated by James G. Williams. Maryknoll, NY: Orbis, 2001.

Grenz, Stanley. *Women in the Church: A Biblical Theology of Women in Ministry*. Downers Grove, IL: InterVarsity, 1995.

Grudem, Wayne. *Evangelical Feminism and Biblical Truth*. Sisters: Multnomah, 2004.

———. *Systematic Theology: An Introduction to Biblical Doctrine*. Grand Rapids: Zondervan, 1995.

Grudem, Wayne, and Piper, John. *Recovering Biblical Manhood and Womanhood: A Response to Evangelical Feminism*. Wheaton: Crossway, 1991.

Hadjadj, Fabrice. *La profondeur des sexes: Pour une mystique de la chair.* Paris: Éditions du Seuil, 2008.

———. "Sexuality as Transcendence: An Interview with Fabrice Hadjadj." Translated by Artur Sebastian Rosman. *Ethika Politika,* April 14, 2015. https://ethikapolitika.org/2015/04/14/sexuality-as-transcendence-an-interview-with-fabrice-hadjadj.

Hanby, Michael. "A More Perfect Absolutism." *First Things,* October 1, 2016. https://www.firstthings.com/article/2016/10/a-more-perfect-absolutism.

Harper, Kyle. *From Shame to Sin: The Christian Transformation of Sexual Morality in Late Antiquity.* Massachusetts: Harvard University Press, 2013.

Hart, David Bentley. "God or Nothingness." In *I Am the Lord Your God: Christian Reflections on the Ten Commandments,* edited by Carl E. Braatan and Christopher R. Seitz, 55–76. Grand Rapids: Eerdmans, 2005.

Hauke, Manfred. *Women in the Priesthood? A Systematic Analysis in the Light of the Order of Creation and Redemption.* San Francisco: Ignatius, 1986.

Healy, Nicholas J. *The Eschatology of Hans Urs von Balthasar: Being as Communion.* Oxford: Oxford University Press, 2007.

Henrici, Peter. "The Philosophy of Hans Urs von Balthasar." In *Hans Urs von Balthasar: His Life and Work,* edited by David L. Schindler, 149–67. San Francisco: Ignatius, 1991.

Heidegger, Martin. *Identity and Difference.* Translated by Joan Stambaugh. Chicago: University of Chicago Press, 2002.

———. "What is Metaphysics." In *Martin Heidegger, Basic Writings,* edited by David Farrell Krell, 93–110. London: HarperPerrenial, 2008.

Illich Ivan, and Cayley, David. *The Rivers North of the Future: The Will and Testament of Ivan Illich, as told to David Cayley.* Toronto: House of Anansi, 2005.

Jerome. "Commentary on the Epistle to the Ephesians." In The *Human Couple in the Fathers,* edited by Giulio Sfameni Gasparro, et al., 243–50. Boston: Pauline, 1999.

John Chrysostom. "In Praise of Maximus." In *The Human Couple in the Fathers,* edited by Giulio Sfameni Gasparro, et al., 323–26, 339–43. Boston: Pauline, 1999.

———. "On the Epistle to the Ephesians." In *The Human Couple in the Fathers,* edited by Giulio Sfameni Gasparro, et al., 318–20, 343–46. Boston: Pauline, 1999.

———. "On the First Epistle to the Corinthians." In *The Human Couple in the Fathers,* edited by Giulio Sfameni Gasparro, et al., 331–36. Boston: Pauline, 1999.

———. "On Genesis." In *The Human Couple in the Fathers,* edited by Giulio Sfameni Gasparro, et al., 316–18, 329–31. Boston: Pauline, 1999.

———. "Stavronikita Series 2." In *Documents of the Baptismal Liturgy,* edited by E. C. Whitaker and Maxwell E. Johnson, 43–47. Collegeville: Liturgical, 2003.

John Paul II. *Familiaris consortio. Holy See,* November 22, 1981. http://w2.vatican.va/content/john-paul-ii/en/apost_exhortations/documents/hf_jp-ii_exh_19811122_familiaris-consortio.html.

———. "Letter to Families." *Holy See,* February, 2, 1994. https://w2.vatican.va/content/john-paul-ii/en/letters/1994/documents/hf_jp-ii_let_02021994_families.html.

———. "Letter to Women." *Holy See,* June 29, 1995. https://w2.vatican.va/content/john-paul-ii/en/letters/1995/documents/hf_jp-ii_let_29061995_women.html.

———. *Mulieris dignitatum. Holy See,* August 15, 1988. http://w2.vatican.va/content/john-paul-ii/en/apost_letters/1988/documents/hf_jp-ii_apl_19880815_mulieris-dignitatem.html 1988.

———. *Ordinatio Sacerdotalis. Holy See,* May 22, 1994. http://w2.vatican.va/content/john-paul-ii/en/apost_letters/1994/documents/hf_jp-ii_apl_19940522_ordinatio-sacerdotalis.html.

———. *A Theology of the Body: Man and Woman He Created Them*. Translated by Michael Waldstein. Boston: Pauline, 2006.

———. *Veritatis splendor*. Holy See, August 6, 1993. http://w2.vatican.va/content/john-paul-ii/en/encyclicals/documents/hf_jp-ii_enc_06081993_veritatis-splendor.html.

Käsemann, Ernst. *Perspectives on Paul*. Philadelphia: Fortress, 1982.

Knight, George. *New Testament Teaching on the Role Relationship of Men and Women*. Grand Rapids: Baker, 1977.

Krell, David Farrell. "General Introduction: The Question of Being." In *Martin Heidegger, Basic Writings*, edited by David Farrell Krell, 3–35. London: HarperPerrenial, 2008.

Lacoste, Jean-Yves. *Experience and the Absolute: Disputed Questions on the Humanity of Man*. Translated by Mark Raferty-Skehan. New York: Fordham University Press, 2004.

Leithart, Peter J. "Trinity and Headship." *Leithart* (blog), September 7, 2011. http://www.patheos.com/blogs/leithart/2011/09/trinity-and-headship.

Leo XIII. *Arcanum Divinae*. Holy See, February 10, 1880. http://w2.vatican.va/content/leo-xiii/en/encyclicals/documents/hf_l-xiii_enc_10021880_arcanum.html.

Letham, Robert. *The Holy Trinity in Scripture, History, Theology, and Worship*. Phillipsburg: P & R, 2004.

Lincoln, Andrew T. *Ephesians*. Word Biblical Commentary 42. Nashville: Thomas Nelson, 1990.

Lossky, Vladimir. *In the Image and Likeness of God*. London: Mobrays, 1975.

MacDonald, Margaret Y. *Colossians and Ephesians*. Sacrina Pagina Series 17. Collegeville: Liturgical, 2000.

Macintyre, Alasdair. *After Virtue: A Study in Moral Theory*. Notre Dame: Notre Dame University Press, 2007.

———. *Three Rival Versions of Moral Enquiry: Encyclopaedia, Genealogy, and Tradition*. Notre Dame: University of Notre Dame Press, 1990.

Marion, Jean-Luc. *The Erotic Phenomenon*. Translated by Stephan E. Lewis. Chicago: Chicago University Press, 2007.

———. *Givenness and Revelation*. Translated by Stephan E. Lewis. Oxford: Oxford University Press, 2016.

———. "In the Name: How to Avoid Speaking of 'Negative Theology.'" In *God, the Gift, and Postmodernism*, edited by John D. Caputo and Michael J. Scanlon, 20–41. Indiana: Indiana University Press, 1990.

Mattheeuws, Alain. *Les 'dons' du mariage: Recherche de théologie morale et sacramentale*. Brussels: Culture et Verite, 1996.

Mead, Margaret. *Male and Female: A Study of the Sexes in a Changing World*. Harmondsworth: Penguin, 1974.

Melina, Livio. *The Epiphany of Love: Toward a Theological Understanding of Christian Action*. Grand Rapids: Eerdmans, 2010.

———. *Sharing in Christ's Virtues: For a Renewal of Moral Theology in Light of Veritatis Splendor*. Translated by William E. May. Washington, DC: Catholic University of America Press, 2001.

Methodius of Olympus. "The Banquet of the Ten Virgins or Concerning Chastity VI." In *The Ante-Nicene Fathers*, edited by Alexander Roberts and James Donaldson, 309–55. Grand Rapids: Eerdmans, 1997.

———. "Two Fragments, Uncertain." In *The Ante-Nicene Fathers*, edited by Alexander Roberts and James Donaldson, 402. Grand Rapids: Eerdmans, Michigan 1997.

Miller, Monica M. *Sexuality and Authority in the Catholic Church*. Scranton: University of Scranton Press, 1995.

Moltmann, Jürgen. *The Trinity and the Kingdom*. New York: Harper and Row, 1981.

O'Donovan, Oliver. *The Desire of the Nations: Rediscovering the Roots of Political Theology*. Cambridge: Cambridge University Press, 2003.

The Order of Celebrating Matrimony English Translation according to the Second Typical Edition. Collegeville: Liturgical, 2016.

Origen. "Commentary on Gospel of Matthew." In *The Human Couple in the Fathers*, edited by Giulio Sfameni Gasparro, et al., 192. Boston: Pauline, 1999.

———. "Homily on Joshua." In *The Human Couple in the Fathers*, edited by Giulio Sfameni Gasparro, et al., 191. Boston: Pauline, 1999.

Ortland, Raymond. "Male-Female Equality and Male Headship: Genesis 1–3." In *Recovering Biblical Manhood and Womanhood: A Response to Evangelical Feminism*, edited by John Piper and Wayne Grudem, 95–112. Wheaton: Crossway, 1991.

Ouellet, Marc. "Co-operators of the Truth of the Human Person." In *God and Eros: The Ethos of the Nuptial Mystery*, edited by Colin Patterson and Conor Sweeney, 212–25. Eugene, OR: Cascade, 2015.

———. *Divine Likeness: Towards a Trinitarian Anthropology of the Family*. Translated by Philip Milligan and Linda M. Cicone. Grand Rapids: Eerdmans, 2006.

———. "The Foundations of Christian Ethics According to Hans Urs von Balthasar." *Communio* 17 (1990) 375–401.

———. *Mystery and Sacrament of Love: A Theology of Marriage and the Family for the New Evangelization*. Translated by Michelle K. Borras and Adrian J. Walker. Grand Rapids: Eerdmans, 2015.

Patterson, Colin. *Chalcedonian Personalism: Rethinking the Human*. Oxford: Peter Lang, 2016.

Paul VI. *Humanae Vitae*. Holy See, July 25, 1968. http://w2.vatican.va/content/paul-vi/en/encyclicals/documents/hf_p-vi_enc_25071968_humanae-vitae.html.

Paulinius of Nola. "Carmen." In *The Human Couple in the Fathers*, edited by Giulio Sfameni Gasparro, et al., 290–94. Boston: Pauline, 1999.

Peterson, Jordan B. "The Psychological Significance of the Biblical Stories." Youtube videos (playlist), 2017–2018. https://www.youtube.com/playlist?list=PL22J3VaeABQD_IZs7y60I3lUrrFTzkpat.

Pettersen, Alvyn. *Athanasius*. New York: Morehouse, 1996.

Pinckaers, Servais. "Ethics and the Image of God." In *The Pinckaers Reader: Renewing Thomistic Moral Theology*, edited by John Berkman and Craig Steven Titus, 130–43. Washington, DC: Catholic University of America Press, 2005.

———. *The Sources of Christian Ethics*. Translated by Mary Thomas Noble. Washington, DC: Catholic University of America Press, 1995.

Piper, John. *This Momentary Marriage: A Parable of Permanence*. Wheaton: Crossway, 2009.

Pius XI. *Casti connubii*. Holy See, December 31, 1930. https://w2.vatican.va/content/pius-xi/en/encyclicals/documents/hf_p-xi_enc_19301231_casti-connubii.html.

Potterie, Ignace de le. "Biblical Exegesis: A Science of Faith." In *Opening Up the Scriptures: Joseph Ratzinger and the Foundations of Biblical Interpretation*, edited by José Granados, et al., 30–64. Grand Rapids: Eerdmans, 2008.

Pseudo-Jerome. "Letter to Celantia." In *The Human Couple in the Fathers*, edited by Giulio Sfameni Gasparro, et al., 299–304. Boston: Pauline, 1999.

Ratzinger, Joseph. "Biblical Interpretation in Crisis: On the Question of the Foundations and Approaches of Exegesis Today." In *Biblical Interpretation in Crisis: The Ratzinger Conference on Bible and Church*, edited by Richard John Neuhaus, 1–23. Grand Rapids: Eerdmans, 1989.

———. "Concerning the Notion of Person in Theology." Translated by Michael Waldstein. *Communio* 17 (1990) 437–54.

———. *Introduction to Christianity*. Translated by J. R. Foster. San Francisco: Ignatius, 2004.

———. "Letter to the Bishops of the Catholic Church on the Collaboration of Men and Women in the Church and in the World." Holy See, May 31, 2004. http://www.vatican.va/roman_curia/congregations/cfaith/documents/rc_con_cfaith_doc_20040731_collaboration_en.html.

Ricoeur, Paul. *Freud and Philosophy: An Essay on Interpretation*. Yale: Yale University Press, 1979.

Roberts, Christopher Chenault. *Creation and Covenant: The Significance of Sexual Difference in the Moral Theology of Marriage*. New York: T & T Clark, 2007.

Scheeben, Matthias Joseph. *The Mysteries of Christianity*. Translated by Cyril Vollert. London: Herder, 1964.

Schillebeeckx, Edward. *Marriage: Human Reality, Saving Mystery*. New York: Sheed and Ward, 1965.

Schindler, David L. "Catholic Theology, Gender, and the Future of Western Civilization." *Communio* 20 (1993) 200–39.

———. "History, Objectivity, and Moral Conversion." *The Thomist* 37 (1973) 569–88.

———. "The Repressive Logic of Liberal Rights: Religious Freedom, Contraceptives, and the 'Phony' Argument of the *New York Times*." *Communio* 38 (2011) 523–47.

Schnackenburg, Rudolph. *Baptism in the Thought of St. Paul: A Study in Pauline Theology*. Oxford: Basil Blackwood, 1964.

Schürmann, Hans. "How Normative are the Values and Precepts of the New Testament?: A Sketch." In *Principles of Christian Morality*, edited by Hans Schürmann, et al., 18–26. San Francisco: Ignatius, 1986.

Scola, Angelo. *The Nuptial Mystery*. Translated by Michelle K. Borras. Grand Rapids: Eerdmans, 2005.

Second Vatican Council. "Dogmatic Constitution on the Church: *Lumen Gentium*." Holy See, November 21, 1964. http://www.vatican.va/archive/hist_councils/ii_vatican_council/documents/vat-ii_const_19641121_lumen-gentium_en.html

———. "Dogmatic Constitution on Divine Revelation: *Dei verbum*." Holy See, November 18, 1965. http://www.vatican.va/archive/hist_councils/ii_vatican_council/documents/vat-ii_const_19651118_dei-verbum_en.html

———. "Pastoral Constitution on the Church in the Modern World: *Gaudium et spes*." Holy See, December 7, 1965. http://www.vatican.va/archive/hist_councils/ii_vatican_council/documents/vat-ii_cons_19651207_gaudium-et-spes_en.html.

Smail, Tom. *Like Father, Like Son: The Trinity Imaged in our Humanity*. Milton Keynes: Paternoster, 2005.

Stuart, Elizabeth. "Sacramental Flesh." In *Queer Theology: Rethinking the Western Body*, edited by Gerard Loughlin, 65–75. Oxford: Blackwell, 2007.

Sweeney, Conor. *Abiding the Long Defeat: How to Evangelize Like a Hobbit in a Disenchanted Age*. New York: Angelico, 2018.

———. *Sacramental Presence After Heidegger: Onto-theology, Sacraments, and the Mother's Smile*. Eugene, OR: Cascade, 2015.

Sydney Anglican Diocesan Doctrine Commission. "The Doctrine of the Trinity and Its bearing on the Relationship of Men and Women." Yearbook of the Diocese of Sydney. Sydney: Diocesan Registry, 2000.

Talbert, Charles H. *Ephesians and Colossians*. Grand Rapids: Baker Academic, 2007.

Taylor, Jameson. "Beyond Nature: Karol Wojtyla's Development of the Traditional Definition of Personhood." *Review of Metaphysics* 63 (2009) 415–54.

Tertullian. "To His Wife." In *The Human Couple in the Fathers*, edited by Giulio Sfameni Gasparro, et al., 175–78. Boston: Pauline, 1999.

Thomas Aquinas. *Commentary on the Letters of Saint Paul to the Corinthians*. Translated by F. R. Larcher, et al. Lander: Aquinas Institute for the Study of Sacred Doctrine, 2012.

———. *Commentary on Saint Paul's Epistle to the Ephesians*. Translated by Matthew L. Lamb. Albany: Magi, 1966.

———. *Summa Contra Gentiles*. Translated by Anton C. Pegis. Notre Dame: University of Notre Dame Press, 1975.

———. *Summa Theologiae, Fathers of the Dominican Province*. Translated by E. Hill. Cambridge: Cambridge University Press, 2006.

Tolkien, J. R. R. *The Lord of the Rings*. Boston: Houghton Mifflan, 1993.

Trainor, Brian T. *Christ, Society, and the State*. Adelaide: Australian Theological Forum, 2010.

Treitler, Wolfgang. "True Foundations of Authentic Theology." In *Hans Urs von Balthasar: His Life and Work*, edited by David L. Schindler, 169–82. San Francisco: Ignatius, 1991.

Van Til, Cornelius. *The Defence of the Faith*. Philadelphia: Presbyterian and Reformed, 1955.

Voegelin, Eric. *The New Science of Politics: An Introduction*. Chicago: University of Chicago Press, 1952.

Ware, Bruce. *Father, Son, and Holy Spirit: Relationships, Roles, and Relevance*. Wheaton: Crossway, 2005.

———. "How Shall We Think About the Trinity?" In *God Under Fire: Modern Theology Reinvents God*, edited by Douglas S. Huffman and Eric L. Johnson, 253–78. Grand Rapids: Zondervan, 2002.

Ward, Graham. "There Is No Sexual Difference." In *Queer Theology: Rethinking the Western Body*, edited by Gerard Loughlin, 76–85. Oxford: Blackwell, 2007.

Westphal, Merold. *Overcoming Onto-Theology: Toward a Postmodern Christian Faith*. New York: Fordham University Press, 2001.

Wojtyla, Karol. *The Acting Person*. Translated by Andrzej Potocki. Dordrecht: D. Reidel, 1979.

———. "The Dignity of the Human Person." In *Person and Community: Selected Essays*, by Karol Wojtyla, 177–80. Translated by Theresa Sandok. New York: Peter Lang, 1993.

———. *Love and Responsibility*. Translated by H. T. Willetts. San Francisco: Ignatius, 1993.

———. "The Personal Structure of Self-Determination." In *Person and Community: Selected Essays*, by Karol Wojtyla, 187–95. Translated by Theresa Sandok. New York: Peter Lang, 1993.

Author Index

Allen, Prudence, 21n25, 24, 26n55, 26n56, 26n57, 26n58, 27, 28n71
Ambrose, 30
Aquinas, Thomas. *See* Thomas Aquinas
Aristotle, 26
Ashley, Benedict, 36, 40n122
Athanasius, 56n34, 58
Augustine, 17, 18, 20–21, 20n25, 22–23, 22n35, 24, 26, 27n60, 28, 29–30, 33n92, 33n93

Balthasar, Hans Urs von, 3, 8, 9, 21–22, 23n40, 43n123, 74–76, 81, 83–84, 87–88, 99, 102n62, 102n63, 103–6, 121n14, 127, 165–66, 168n19, 171, 178n24, 181n26
Barth, Karl, 43, 65
Barth, Marcus, 133n33, 133n36, 138
Basil, 52, 59, 61, 65
Benedict XVI, 22n31, 65
Boethius, 72n3, 85
Bonaventure, 25n51, 28
Browning, Don S., 29
Burke, Cormac, 33n93
Butler, Sara, 13

Camus, Albert, 85
Cantalamessa, Raniero, 36
Cere, Daniel Mark, 36, 39n117, 40
Chauvet, Louis-Marie, 118
Chrysostom, John, 17–19, 28, 30
Clement of Alexandria, 30–31
Cooper, Adam, 21n27, 21n28, 23n41
Cyril of Jerusalem, 6

Damascene, John, 22
Daniélou, Jean, 114n4, 114n5
Doyle, Robert, 50, 54, 55, 56n35

Erickson, Millard, 57

Fitzmyer, Joseph A., 36
Frame, John, 49, 57
Francis, 14

Gadamer, Hans-Georg, 11
Gasparro, Giulio Sfameni, 24n46
Geisler, Norman, 55, 57
Giles, Kevin, 12n4, 46, 47, 48, 49–50, 51–56, 63–64
Girard, René, 82n28, 86n33
Grenz, Stanley, 12n4
Gregory of Nyssa, 22
Grudem, Wayne, 12n3, 57–58, 58n45

Hadjadj, Fabrice, 123
Hanby, Michael, 84n32
Harper, Kyle, 26n54, 29n72, 126n23
Hart, David Bentley, 82n28
Hauke, Manfred, 13n6, 135n38
Healy, Nicholas J., 104n72
Heidegger, Martin, 43–44, 86, 87n37
Henrici, Peter, 103
Husserl, Edmund, 100

Illich, Ivan, 86n33, 82n28

Jerome, 17, 28
John Paul II, 1, 3, 4, 8, 9, 13, 14–16, 19, 24n41, 32, 36, 38n113, 61–62, 69n1, 69n2, 76–81, 83, 86, 90n45, 91–94, 97, 99, 102n60, 104, 111n1, 113, 115, 117, 120n13, 121, 124n22, 126n24, 127n25, 132n32, 146, 147, 156, 158, 159–60, 163, 169, 186–87

Käsemann, Ernst, 6n11
Knight, George, 56–57
Krell, David Farrell, 43–44

Lacoste, Jean-Yves, 87n37
Leithart, Peter J., 45n1
Letham, Robert, 46–47, 49–50, 54, 57
Leo XIII, 33n94, 96n54
Lincoln, Andrew M., 132n32, 133n34

MacDonald, Margaret Y., 132n30, 133n36
MacIntyre, Alasdair, 136n43, 149n6
Marian, Jean-Luc, 43, 100, 136n40
Mattheeuws, Alain, 106
Maximus the Confessor, 22
Mead, Margaret, 63n57
Melina, Livio, 149n5, 149n7, 150
Methodius of Olympus, 25n52, 26
Miller, Monica M., 27n59
Moltmann, Jürgen, 54

Nietzsche, Friedrich, 84, 85

Origen, 18, 22, 31
Ortland, Raymond, 46, 52n21
Ouellet, Marc, 3, 8, 9, 32, 95, 99, 102–03, 104–07, 114n5, 127, 149n5

Patterson, Colin, 73–74, 83n29, 179n25
Paul VI, 96n57
Paulinius of Nola, 31–32
Peterson, Jordan, 5n10
Pettersen, Alvyn, 58
Piper, John, 12n3

Pinckaers, Servais, 23n36, 149n5
Pius XI, 14, 96n54
Potterie, Ignace de le, 135n38
Pseudo-Jerome, 17–18

Ratzinger, Joseph, 3, 8, 9, 64, 72–74, 76, 83, 99, 135n37, 137n42
Ricoeur, Paul, 11
Roberts, Christopher C., 20n25, 29, 32n87, 129n29

Sartre, Jean-Paul, 84
Scheeben, Mathias, 114n5
Schindler, David L., 84n31, 102n63, 137n43
Schillebeeckx, Edward, 37–40, 130
Schnackenburg, Rudolph, 7n13, 39n117
Schürmann, Hans, 40n121
Scola, Angelo, 21n27, 22n33, 22n34, 22n35, 23n37, 23n38, 23n39, 32, 33n91, 95, 96n56, 102n61, 102n63, 129n28, 164n17
Smail, Tom, 57
Stuart, Elizabeth, 119n12
Sweeney, Conor, 4n9, 75n12, 103n68, 122n20

Talbert, Charles H., 132n31, 133n35
Taylor, Jameson, 76n14
Tertullian, 31, 93
Thomas, Aquinas, 18, 20–21, 22–23, 24–25, 26, 28, 33n92, 34, 72, 77, 85, 87
Tolkien, J. R. R., 154
Trainor, Brian T., xi, 1–2, 9, 13, 44, 45n1, 67–68, 162, 164, 186
Treitler, Wolfgang, 103

Van Til, Cornelius, 48
Voegelin, Eric, 118–19

Ward, Graham, 119n12, 129n29
Ware, Bruce, 9n15, 12n3, 56
Westphal, Merold, 86n34
Wojtyla, Karol, 76–77, 85, 127

Subject Index

action, 74, 77, 77n21, 80, 81, 90, 106, 147–51, 161–62
actus purus, 20, 26, 181
analogia amoris, 43n123, 103, 106
analogia baptismi, 8, 71, 100, 107, 43n123
analogia entis, 8, 42, 43, 43n123, 102–7, 104n72
analogia fides, 43, 43n123
analogia relationis, 43n123
analogia Trinitatis, 43n123, 186
anthropology
  "adequate," 69, 69n2
  baptismal, xiii, 2, 4, 8, 9, 42–44, 67–108, 109–39, 140–41, 185–86
  dramatic, 3–4, 71, 103, 106, 130, 143, 149–50, 157, 162, 185
  of Fathers and Scholastics, 17–35, 71, 72, 95–98, 110
  Pauline, xi, 94–95, 97–8, 141
  trinitarian, 5, 104–07
arche (or source) 20, 25, 27, 55, 59, 60

baptism
  as constituting the "sacramental middle," 42, 68, 71, 102, 105, 111–12, 148, 152, 185
  as filial sonship, 70–72, 89, 107, 109, 113–17, 125, 128, 141–42, 150, 151, 159–61, 186
  as fundamental ontology, xiii, 2, 71
  as immersion into salvation history, 5, 90n44, 101, 108, 115, 124–29, 131, 149
  and mission, 9–10, 71, 88, 111, 117, 127–29, 139, 140–82, 183–87
  nuptial character of, 94–101, 114–15, 114n5
  and sexual difference, 2, 9, 109–39
  as sharing in Christ's hypostatic personhood, 3–8, 44, 68–72, 98–107, 108, 110, 115, 125–26, 131, 134, 142, 178–79, 181–82, 185
baptismal relation, 8, 9, 124–25, 148–49, 152, 155, 156, 157, 166, 170, 176, 177, 179, 182, 183, 187
baptismal theology of relation, 9, 99, 102, 107, 140
body
  baptized, 99, 101, 110, 126
  of Christ, 89, 91, 98, 102, 148, 179
  and Fathers and Scholastics, 19–35
  as sacramental/signifying, 94, 112, 113, 119–21, 127, 153, 168
  Balthasar on, 21–22
  John Paul II on, 3, 92–94, 97–98, 117, 121, 147, 186
  Thomas on, 22–23, 23n36

Casti Connubii, 14, 19, 96n54, 141
celibacy/continence for the kingdom, 126–27

SUBJECT INDEX

Christ
    and Church, 6, 7, 15, 15n9, 17–18, 27, 30, 32–33, 34, 37–38, 61, 68, 70, 89, 90–91, 94–101, 108, 109, 114–15, 120, 125–26, 138–39, 141–42, 143, 148, 150, 151, 153, 161, 162, 163–64, 165, 171, 184, 185
    as concrete analogy of being, 8, 104, 105
    as head, 15n9, 17, 25, 27, 34, 37–38, 61, 150, 151, 162–64, 171, 175, 184
complementarianism, 2, 9, 12–17, 23n36, 41–44, 45–66, 67, 110, 129, 141, 150, 182
confirmation, sacrament of, 91n46, 144
conjugal politics
    according to a baptismal anthropology, 134–39, 140–87
    in complementarians and egalitarians, 12–17, 40–44, 45–66
    definitions and introduction, xi–xiii, 1–10
    in the Fathers and Scholastics, 17–32
    historical-critical approach to, 36–40, 132–34
    roles in, 8, 12–15, 17–18, 19, 29, 31, 41, 45–46, 51, 56–57, 59, 62–64, 65, 67, 129, 130, 132, 139, 149, 158, 162, 164, 171, 172, 180–81, 184
consciousness, 23n39, 77n21, 78, 80, 81, 82, 83, 92, 147, 156

death of God, 84, 86, 183, 185
Dei verbum, 136n39, 136n41
domestic church, 1, 104, 139, 152, 155, 156, 184

election, 69, 83, 88, 89, 94, 106, 113, 141, 149
egalitarianism, 2, 9, 12–17, 23n36, 41–44, 45–66, 67, 110, 129, 141, 150, 182
Ephesians, 1, 14–16, 17–18, 29, 30, 32, 34, 36, 61–62, 132–40, 158–59, 165
eternity, 19, 42, 53, 57, 90, 92, 93, 126, 128, 178, 179
eucharistic liturgy, 90–91, 94, 95, 97, 99, 107, 109, 130, 183, 186
Evangelicalism, 12–13, 41, 45, 63
exemplarism, 3, 42, 105, 106–7, 111, 149
extrinsicism, 20, 32, 33, 34, 41, 42, 70, 94, 95, 96n56, 97, 110, 112, 116, 117, 127, 128, 139, 149n7, 152

Familiaris consortio, 96n55, 104
fatherhood, 56, 112, 114, 116, 122, 127n25, 163, 172
feminist theology, 14, 112, 118–19, 141, 152
finitude, 23n39, 75, 89, 110, 126, 174, 178
freedom, 65, 77, 78, 80, 84, 85, 122, 123, 124, 127, 143, 149, 162, 174, 175, 177, 178, 179, 181, 182, 185
fruitfulness, 168–72
    and Christ and Church, 70, 89, 99, 167, 169–70
    inseparable from sexual difference and love, 129
    and the Holy Spirit, 89, 114, 115, 169–70, 171–72
    and Mary, 89, 114, 115, 166, 167, 168, 169–70, 171–72
    physical, 165, 169–70
    spiritual, 125, 126, 166, 167, 168, 169–70, 171–72, 173, 175, 177, 187

Gaudium et spes, 79n25, 96n55, 143n1

Haustafeln
    and baptismal interpretation, 130–39, 155
    hermeneutics of, 11, 130
    historical-critical exegesis of, 37–40, 132–34, 136

SUBJECT INDEX

Headship
  and authority, 12, 17–18, 17n16, 59–64, 61n52, 111, 161–64, 173–76
  as consequence of temporality and sin, 20–35, 110
  as distinct from mutual submission, 158–9
  and domination, 62, 160, 171
  as imputing responsibility to husband, 30, 61, 152, 155, 157, 165, 176
  as ingredient to the unity and stability of marriage, 13, 18–19
  in John Paul II, 14–16, 61–62, 158
  located within the return of all things to God the Father, 9, 147, 152, 165, 186–87
  as mission in love, 163–64, 178
  in the ontological difference, 174–82
  in Schillebeeckx, 37–40
  as thematizing the relation between husband and God the Father, 155–57, 160, 162, 171, 184
  as "through" rather than "over," 162
  and Trinity, xii, 45–66, 178, 185–86
  as undermining male license, 29–30
  as vocation of welcoming wife as gift from the Father, 156–58, 173
hermeneutics, xii, 1–10, 11–66, 95, 97, 96–97n57, 98, 99, 102, 104, 108, 110, 111, 113, 130–39, 140–41, 183
historical critical method, 11, 36–40, 41, 44, 68, 69, 108, 110, 130–39, 141
Humanae Vitae, 14, 96–7n57
hylomorphism, 98
hypostatic personhood, 4, 5, 7, 8, 44, 69, 71, 98–100, 102, 105, 107, 109, 110, 115, 125, 126, 131, 134, 142, 179, 181–82, 185

imago Dei
  and the body, 22–25, 23n26
  and man, 24–26, 27n61
  and rationality, 22, 22–23n35, 23n26, 24, 26

  and relationality, 4, 59–64, 70, 79, 79n25, 93–94, 102, 105, 115
  and woman, 24–27, 27n61, 28–29
imago Trinitatis, 4, 22, 22–23n36, 93, 102, 105–07, 189
imitation model, 2, 4, 24, 70–72, 95–98, 105, 106, 110, 111, 126, 134, 143, 145–46, 148–49, 178, 183, 185

Johannine and Pauline "reversal," 97–98, 100, 141, 167, 186

katology, 76, 102–04, 107
kephale, 20

maior dissimilitudo, 2, 42, 107, 151
marriage
  ends of, 33, 97, 33n93
  and the family, 1, 3, 32, 59–66, 102, 104–05, 167
  conjugal politics in; (*see* conjugal politics)
  and consecrated celibacy, 126–27, 127n25
  and imitation model, 95–98, 105
  and mission, 127–28
  natural, 32–33, 96, 97
  as primordial sacrament, 1, 91, 92–94, 95, 142
  as sacrament, 10, 32–33, 91, 94, 95, 96, 101, 106, 122–30, 142, 143, 145, 148, 168, 169, 182
  and sexual difference, 109–39
  the Spirit in, 142, 144–47
  as vision of eucharistic and baptismal existence, 90, 91–94, 99, 120
Mary/Marian, 3, 20, 27, 89, 114, 115, 129, 137, 139, 155, 166, 167, 167–73, 169, 169n20, 172, 177, 180, 183
Mulieris dignitatum, 14, 15, 36n101, 61, 62n55, 62n56, 102n60, 158n12, 169n20
mutual submission (or subordination/subjection), 14–16, 57, 61–62, 64, 132, 158–59, 163–64, 173

"mystery hidden in God . . . ," 90, 92, 93, 123, 126, 128, 156

nature and grace, 4, 6–8, 19, 21n25, 32, 34, 43, 68–69, 70–71, 95–101, 106, 118, 125
neo-platonism, 20–21
nuptial mystery, 90–101, 114, 125, 128
"nuptial trilogy," 90–94, 99, 107, 183, 186

Ordinatio Sacerdotalis, 13
ontological difference, 35, 103, 128n27, 174–82
onto-theology, 86

person
  in Balthasar, 3, 74–76, 81, 83–84, 87–88
  in the baptismal relation, 4–8, 9, 67–108, 109–39, 140–82
  in Boethius, 72, 77, 80
  and filial and nuptial character, 89–108, 109–39
  in John Paul II, 3, 76–83, 86–87, 91–94
  and nature, 5, 6, 7, 71, 75, 80, 81, 83–84, 86, 95, 98–101
  and nihilism, 84–87, 145–46
  in Ratzinger, 3, 72–4, 83
  and sexual difference, 109–39
phenomenology, 77, 79n25, 82
Paul, St., 7, 17, 25, 34, 36, 45, 58, 61–62, 64, 69, 94, 126, 130–39, 140–41
  Schillebeeckz on, 37–40

Queer theology, 112, 118, 118n10

rationality, 8, 20, 24, 43, 75, 76, 77, 80, 81, 86, 137n43
real distinction; (*see* ontological difference)
relationality, 23, 22–23n35, 60–61, 63, 65, 72, 75, 79n25, 80, 81, 94, 162, 179
Remedium concupiscentiae, 33

"sacramental middle," 42, 68, 71, 102, 107, 111–12, 148, 152, 185
sexual difference/gender, 1, 2, 9, 12–16, 20n25, 22, 40, 41, 63, 109–39, 140, 153, 164n17, 166, 180, 182, 183
submission, of wife
  because of Eve's disobedience, 17, 28
  as consequence of temporality and sin, 20–35, 110
  for the inferior/weaker sex, 26–29, 32, 33–34
  as informing and shaping male headship, 63–64, 171, 173–74, 175–76, 177–78
  as ingredient to the unity and stability of marriage, 13, 18–19
  in John Paul II, 14–16, 61–62, 158
  located within the return of all things to God the Father, 9, 147, 186–87
  and ministry, 12–14, 16
  as mission in love, 163–64, 178
  and obedience, 12, 17n16, 18, 132, 162
  in the ontological difference, 174–82
  and receptivity, 16, 31, 161, 163, 165–74
  as submission to Christ, 161, 162, 173
  and Trinity, 41–42, 45–66, 178, 185–86
subordination; (*see* submission)
substantiality, 41, 72–75, 80, 83–86, 95–100, 110, 111, 112, 115, 123, 130, 135, 148, 161, 179, 181

temporality, 19–27, 32–35, 40–44, 56, 57, 72, 75, 89, 110, 116, 126, 127, 147, 153, 174, 178–82
Theology of the Body, 3, 15–16, 23–24n41, 69n1, 77–80, 92–94, 98, 113, 117, 120n13, 121, 126n24, 127n25, 156, 159–60, 163–64, 186–87
"triple sovereignty," 9, 46, 56–58, 61–62, 64, 164

Trinity
- in complementarian theology, 13, 41–42, 45–66
- and baptism, 5, 42–44, 68, 101–02, 107–08, 115, 144–45, 149–51, 179, 182, 183, 185–86
- in egalitarian theology, 13, 41–42, 45–66
- and the family, 47, 52, 59–66, 103n67, 104–05
- and headship and submission, 8, 10, 42, 45–66
- homogenization and differentiation, 51–56
- ontological and immanent language, 47–50
- single sovereignty and triple sovereignty, 9, 46–47, 56–58, 59–64, 67

Veritatis Splendor, 146

women's ordination, 13–14, 16

www.ingramcontent.com/pod-product-compliance
Lightning Source LLC
Chambersburg PA
CBHW070257230426

43664CB00014B/2561